Using

Microsoft®
PowerPoint®
97

Using

Microsoft® PowerPoint® 97

Barbara Kasser

Using Microsoft PowerPoint 97

Copyright© 1997 by Que® Corporation

Library of Congress Catalog No.: 96-71446

ISBN: 0-7897-09341

99 98 97   6 5 4 3 2 1

Interpretation of the printing code: the rightmost double-digit number is the year of the book's printing; the rightmost single-digit number, the number of the book's printing. For example, a printing code of 97-1 shows that the first printing of the book occurred in 1997.

Composed in *ITC Century*, *ITC Highlander*, and *MCPdigital* by Que Corporation.

Credits

Publisher
Roland Elgey

Publishing Director
Lynn E. Zingraf

Editorial Services Director
Elizabeth Keaffaber

Managing Editor
Michael Cunningham

Acquisitions Editor
Martha O' Sullivan

Product Director
Melanie Palaisa

Production Editor
Linda Seifert

Editor
Mike McFeely

Product Marketing Manager
Kim Margolius

Assistant Product Marketing Manager
Christy M. Miller

Strategic Marketing Manager
Barry Pruett

Technical Editors
C. Herbert Feltner
Nanci Jacobs

Technical Support Specialist
Nadeem Muhammed

Editorial Assistant
Virginia Stoller

Book Designer
Glenn Larsen

Cover Designer
Dan Armstrong

Production Team
Heather Howell
Tony McDonald
Steph Mineart
Nicole Ruessler
Sossity Smith

Indexer
Ginny Bess

This book is dedicated to the memory of my mother—Gloria May—who was always my toughest critic and most loyal supporter. I miss you, Mom.

About the Author

Barbara Kasser is a network administrator and trainer for a Fortune 500 company. Barbara also teaches classes and writes training manuals for Computer Coach, a private training facility located in Boca Raton, Florida. She also has taught computer courses for Palm Beach County. For fun, Barbara designs Web pages.

Barbara loves spending time with her husband Bill and son Richard, and looks forward to the evenings and weekends they share together.

Acknowledgments

The process of making a collection of words and figures into a book is a long, involved process that takes a lot of people and hard work. Many of those folks at Que are people I've never met. Thank you all for your hard work.

A special note of thanks to Martha O'Sullivan, who gave me the opportunity to put my thoughts on paper. To Melanie Palaisa, who's my friend and the best-ever development editor, thanks for listening to my ideas and always being there for me with a laugh and good words. To Linda Seifert and Mike McFeely, thanks again for reading over my words and making sure they made sense.

And an extra special thank you to Herb Feltner. Herb, aside from being the world's greatest technical editor, you're my personal hero.

I consider myself lucky to be a member of the Que family.

We'd like to hear from you!

As part of our continuing effort to produce books of the highest possible quality, Que would like to hear your comments. To stay competitive, we *really* want you, as a computer book reader and user, to let us know what you like or dislike most about this book or other Que products.

You can mail comments, ideas, or suggestions for improving future editions to the address below, or send us a fax at (317) 581-4663. For the online inclined, Macmillan Computer Publishing has a forum on CompuServe (type **GO QUEBOOKS** at any prompt) through which our staff and authors are available for questions and comments. The address of our Internet site is **http://www.mcp.com/que** (World Wide Web).

In addition to exploring our forum, please feel free to contact me personally to discuss your opinions of this book: I'm **73353, 2061** on CompuServe, and I'm **mpalaisa@que.mcp.com** on the Internet.

Thanks in advance—your comments will help us to continue publishing the best books available on computer topics in today's market.

Melanie Palaisa
Product Development Specialist
Que Corporation
201 W. 103rd Street
Indianapolis, Indiana 46290
USA

Contents at a Glance

Introduction   1

I   Creating a Presentation   7

1 The Basics of PowerPoint   9
2 Creating a Presentation the Easy Way   31
3 Creating a Presentation from Scratch   47
4 Using the Slide Master to Give Your Presentation a Consistent Look   73
5 Adding Graphs and Charts   87
6 Creating Organization Charts   103
7 Creating Attractive Tables   117

II   Fine-Tuning Your Presentation   131

8 PowerPoint Writing Tools Promise a Perfect Presentation   133
9 Using Advanced Editing Techniques   147
10 Lights, Camera, Action... Add Sound and Video to a Presentation   165
11 Using Advanced Art and Graphics Techniques   179
12 Using Objects from Other Programs   191
13 Look Like a Pro: Adding Super Special Effects   205

III   On with the Show   217

14 The Final Countdown—Rehearsing Your Presentation   219
15 Creating Presentation Handouts   231
16 Preparing Your Slide Show   243

IV   PowerPoint at the Office and on the Internet/Intranet   261

17 Customizing PowerPoint   263
18 Sharing Your Presentation with Colleagues   281
19 Share Your Presentation with the World   297

V **Appendix 315**

   A Installing PowerPoint   317

Action Index 325

Index 331

Table of Contents

Introduction

What makes this book different?   1

How do I use this book?   2

How this book is put together   2

    Part I: Creating a Presentation   2

    Part II: Fine-Tuning Your Presentation   3

    Part III: On with the Show   3

    Part IV: PowerPoint at the Office and On the
Internet/Intranet   3

    Part V: Appendix and Action Index   3

Special book elements   4

New features in Microsoft PowerPoint 97   5

Part I: Creating a Presentation

1 The Basics of PowerPoint   9

How do I start PowerPoint?   11

Looking at the PowerPoint screen   13

What are toolbars?   15

How can I display other toolbars?   17

Relocating toolbars to other parts
of the screen   17

Using PowerPoint menus and dialog boxes   18

Getting the most out of Help   21

    Meet your new pal, the Office Assistant!   22

    Working with the IntelliMouse   23

    Getting Help from Microsoft on the Web   24

Views let you see your work from different angles   26

How many different views do I need?   26

Switching from view to view   27

A closer look at views   27

Outline view   28

Slide Sorter view   28

Notes Page view   29

Slide Show view   30

2 Creating a Presentation the Easy Way   31

How do I get a presentation up and running fast?   33

Working magic with the AutoContent Wizard   33

How do I add a slide to my presentation?   36

I want to delete this slide   37

Using AutoTemplate to give slides some
extra pizazz!   38

Save your presentation: make it last   40

Which should I use—my hard disk or a floppy disk?   40

Save your work for posterity   41

Opening a PowerPoint presentation   42

Can I print one slide?   43

The end of the day: shutting down PowerPoint   44

3 Creating a Presentation from Scratch   47

Placeholders let you hold that thought   48

Create your thoughts right on the slide   50

Add text on a slide   50

Deleting a placeholder   51

Make your text look attractive   51

Make your text stand out by changing the font   52

I'd like to emphasize this one word!   54

Copy fonts and attributes with a single stroke!   56

Compose your thoughts in an outline   57

Enter text in an outline list   58

Changing levels   59

The Microsoft Clip Gallery   60

    Inserting clip art from the Clip Gallery   61

    Letting PowerPoint suggest clip art   63

    Deleting clip art from a slide   64

Adding graphics images from a file   64

Adding a graphics image to the Clip Gallery   65

    Clips from the Web   67

That clip art looks lovely, but can I move it?   70

    I love the way this looks, I just wish it was smaller   71

4 Using the Slide Master to Give Your Presentation a Consistent Look   73

The Slide Master is the key to your presentation   74

    Viewing the Slide Master   75

Using the Slide Master to set the look of your presentation   77

    Modifying the default design   78

    Changing text attributes within a placeholder   78

    Moving or deleting text placeholders   79

Adding a company logo on each slide   81

Can I change the background color of my slides?   83

Adding page numbers, dates, and times to your slides   84

5 Adding Graphs and Charts   87

What types of charts are available?   88

    Getting to know chart types   88

Using Microsoft Graph to create a chart   90

    Changing data in a chart   93

    Changing the chart type   94

Give your charts pizzazz   94

    Changing chart colors and patterns   96

    Adding a legend and grid lines   97

    Adding a text box and drawing on a chart   98

I already have data in a spreadsheet—can't I use that?   100

I'd like to create an Excel worksheet in my slide   101

How can I modify or delete the worksheet?   102

6 Creating Organization Charts   103

What do I use to create an org chart?   104

Creating an org chart   106

Components of an org chart   108

Making changes to an org chart   109

Relationships in an org chart   109

Adding or deleting a relationship box in an org chart   110

Seeing the big picture   112

Changing a chart's style   113

Draw on an org chart to add emphasis   114

Can I use an existing org chart in my presentation?   115

7 Creating Attractive Tables   117

Some tips on when to use a table   118

One-button table creation   119

Modifying an existing table   122

Adding and deleting rows and columns   122

Can I change the width of a column or the height of a row?   123

Changing the alignment of text and numbers in the columns   124

Enhancing your table's appearance   125

My table looks so boring…how can I dress it up?   126

Borders make tables easier to read   126

Using the Table AutoFormat feature   128

Part II: Fine-Tuning Your Presentation

8 PowerPoint Writing Tools Promise a Perfect Presentation   133

Spell checking your presentation   134

Adding words to the dictionary   137

Can PowerPoint automatically correct my spelling? 138

Finding a word in a slide 140

Replacing text in a presentation 141
   Using the Style Checker 142

Using Microsoft Bookshelf Basics 143

9 Using Advanced Editing Techniques 147

Create your own special effects with WordArt 148
   Creating WordArt 149
   Modifying WordArt 152

Working with PowerPoint colors 154
   Applying an existing color scheme 155
   Modifying an existing color scheme 156

How can I display my text in a different color? 157

I'd like to change the look of my text 158
   Changing the alignment of text 159
   Changing the spacing between lines 159

Creating bullet lists 160
   Changing the distance between bullets and text 161
   Can I change the shape of my bullets? 162

10 Lights, Camera, Action... Add Sound and Video to a Presentation 165

Adding sound to your presentation 166

Sounds clips are great attention-getters 167
   Adding sound clips from the Clip Gallery 168
   Getting new sound clips from the Web 169
   Action settings will make people gasp "How'd you do that?" 171

I want to record a comment on my slide 172

Adding movies to your slides 174
   Adding video clips from the Clip Gallery 174

Welcome to PowerPoint Central 176
   Visiting PowerPoint Central 176

11 Using Advanced Art and Graphics Techniques   179

I only want a small portion of this image on my slide   180

Converting pictures to PowerPoint objects   182

Combining object elements into one object   182

Can I turn this object in the other direction?   184

Flipping objects   185

Nudging an object   185

I want to move several pieces of artwork at once   186

Grouping several objects into one object   186

Ungrouping multiple objects   188

Recoloring a picture   188

I'd like to change or rearrange the objects in my picture   189

12 Using Objects from Other Programs   191

Why use Microsoft Office 97?   192

Using the Clipboard   193

Updating information automatically   195

Linking documents using the Paste
Special command   195

Viewing and updating links   198

Embedding objects   199

Working with hyperlinks   201

13 Look Like a Pro: Adding Super Special Effects   205

Why should I use animation?   206

Using preset animation   207

Adding custom animation   209

Adding custom animation to a chart   211

Action buttons give you a jump on your competition   212

I want to record my narration   215

Part III: On With the Show

14 The Final Countdown—Rehearsing Your Presentation 219

Working in Slide Sorter view 220

Create a summary slide 221

Change the transition style as each slide advances 222

Changing the transition for one slide 225

What if I want to skip a slide during a presentation? 226

Rehearsing the slide show timing 227

I'd like to set the timing during the rehearsal 228

Using the Slide Meter 229

15 Creating Presentation Handouts 231

What kind of printed materials can I create? 232

An outline's always useful 232

Your audience will appreciate handouts 233

Meet the Handout Master 234

Modifying placeholders in the Handout Master 237

Printing your handouts 237

Speaker Notes keep you focused 238

16 Preparing Your Slide Show 243

Let the show begin! 244

Starting your presentation from within PowerPoint 244

The PowerPoint Viewer is a great friend 246

Downloading and installing the PowerPoint Viewer from the Web 247

Installing the Viewer from the CD-ROM 247

Starting your presentation from the PowerPoint Viewer 248

It sure would be helpful if I could write on a slide! 249

Can I see that slide again? 252

Presentation showmanship 252

Take your presentation on the road with the Pack and Go Wizard 254

Running the show in a continuous loop 257

Part IV: PowerPoint at the Office and on the Internet/Intranet

17 Customizing PowerPoint 263

Creating a shortcut on your desktop 264

I'd like to open the PowerPoint file I used yesterday 265

Change PowerPoint's printer settings 267

Change PowerPoint's behavior to suit your style! 269

Have it your way—customize the toolbars 275

Can I create my own toolbar? 276

Changing menu animations 278

18 Sharing Your Presentation with Colleagues 281

A brief introduction to networks 282

Faxing your presentation 282

Sending your presentation by fax 283

E-mail speeds your presentation to its destination 284

Sending the presentation 285

Routing the presentation 286

Saving comments from your presentation 287

Can I run my presentation over a network? 290

19 Share Your Presentation with the World 297

Exploring the Web from PowerPoint's Help menu 300

Using the Web toolbar 305

What's an intranet? 306

Designing a presentation for the Web 307

Adding a hyperlink to a slide   308

Saving your presentation for the world   311

Part V: Appendix

A Installing PowerPoint   317

Make sure this software will work on your computer   318

Before you install PowerPoint...   319

Installing the software   320

Why use the Custom installation?   321

Can I add or remove PowerPoint components?   322

Action Index   325

Creating a presentation   325

Working with the Slide Master   326

Adding clip art or imported graphics   326

Adding tables   326

Adding a chart   327

Adding an organizational chart   327

Adding information from other files   327

Using special effects   328

Running the presentation   328

Customizing PowerPoint   328

Sharing a presentation with colleagues   329

PowerPoint and the Internet   329

Index   331

Introduction

PowerPoint is the program I love most to teach! As a software instructor, I teach just about any software program you can name. But I always look forward to my PowerPoint classes.

At the beginning of the class, most people want to learn a few PowerPoint basics so that they can put together a few boring slides. But after the first hour, the students don't want to take a break. PowerPoint is so much fun to use that it doesn't seem like work to learn about it.

Most people love to use PowerPoint because they can create something fabulous with just a little time and imagination. It doesn't matter if you're planning to use PowerPoint every day or once in a while. After you've created your first slide show, complete with some exciting graphics and custom animation, you won't want to use anything else.

What makes this book different?

There are so many books on the market, why should you choose *Using Microsoft PowerPoint 97*? Well, actually, this book talks to you. I'm a real person who cares about my students. I wrote this book the same way I teach my classes—it's designed to be fun and entertaining and never make you feel silly or small. After all, I want you to love PowerPoint as much as I do. I've designed the examples to be fun and entertaining. All of the examples were created in PowerPoint, using the same tools that are available to you. And best of all, you have the staff at Que looking over my shoulder and making sure I've included all of the things you need to know.

My job is to make you feel comfortable using PowerPoint, right from page 1. I've tried to make the language simple and easy to understand. I've also included step-by-step instructions that you can easily follow. If a dialog box opens when you click a button, I let you know what it does and probably include a picture of it. After all, this book is just for you.

If you need to get your work done quickly and efficiently, *Using Microsoft PowerPoint 97* is for you. You won't waste your time learning unpronounceable terms and programming code. This book will help you get your project started, finished, and polished, and you'll learn several tricks along the way. You won't learn every method of completing every task; instead you'll learn the most efficient and quickest way to do what you need.

The best thing is, you'll really enjoy PowerPoint, and that means you'll use PowerPoint (and this book) again and again.

How do I use this book?

Start at page 1 and stop when you come to the end, or start at any page you want. Check the index to look for a task you're having trouble with, then work your way inward. Use whatever method suits you best.

Although you don't have to start at the beginning of this book, each chapter progresses logically to the next. So, if you've never ventured into the land of PowerPoint, the beginning of this book is a good place to start.

This isn't a textbook—there are no quizzes or exercises. It's more like a reference book, although compared to other reference books, you won't hurt yourself trying to lift it (and you won't need an interpreter to understand it!).

How this book is put together

When you have a big project to do, you probably break it up into smaller parts and tackle them one at a time. PowerPoint is a big program, so that's how this book is set up, too. There are five parts:

Part I: Creating a Presentation

This is the nuts and bolts section on how you create a presentation from scratch. You'll learn all of the PowerPoint basics, from opening the program and creating a presentation to printing one slide and closing the program. You'll have some fun adding pictures to your slides. You'll even have a chance to do a little Web surfing.

Part II: Fine-Tuning Your Presentation

Once you've gotten a basic understanding of PowerPoint's features, you can settle down and have some fun. You'll learn advanced graphics techniques, how to add sound and video to your slides, and how to add some fancy animation to your presentations. People who see your work after you finish this section will swear you've been using the program for years!

Part III: On with the Show

With your newfound PowerPoint expertise, each slide is a masterpiece. But now it's time to put together the slide show. After all, that's the goal, right? You'll learn some pretty impressive tricks about using slide transitions and some valuable lessons about how to be an effective presenter. You'll even produce some great handouts to distribute to the audience.

Part IV: PowerPoint at the Office and On the Internet/Intranet

In this section, you'll learn all the ways to share your presentation with your colleagues in the office—whether they're one floor below you or clear across the country. You'll also learn all about the Internet and how you can share your presentation with the universe. In this section we'll talk about intranets, too.

Part V: Appendix and Action Index

Using Microsoft PowerPoint 97 contains an appendix that tells you how to install PowerPoint on your computer. You also learn how to add or remove certain features, which will probably be of great interest when you start experimenting with more advanced PowerPoint features. This section also contains an Action Index that you'll use over and over again. The Action Index tells you what page to turn to for help in performing a particular task.

Special book elements

Throughout *Using Microsoft PowerPoint 97*, you'll find a variety of special elements and conventions to help you find information quickly.

TIP   **Tips either point out information often overlooked in the** documentation, or help you use your software more efficiently, like a shortcut. Some tips help you solve or avoid problems.

CAUTION   **Cautions alert you to potentially dangerous consequences of a** procedure or practice, especially if it could cause serious or even disastrous results (such as loss or corruption of data).

Q&A   ***What are Q&A notes?***
Cast in the form of questions and answers, these notes provide you with advice on ways to solve common problems.

❝ *Plain English, please!*
These notes explain the meanings of **computer terms** and **jargon**. ❞

If you see two keys separated by a plus sign, such as Ctrl+X, that means to press and hold the first key, press the second key, then release both keys.

Sidebars: entertainment and information

Sidebars are detours from the main text. They usually provide background or interesting information that is relevant but not essential reading.

New features in Microsoft PowerPoint 97

If you've used earlier versions of PowerPoint, you're going to love the enhancements in this new version. Now PowerPoint has more wizards than ever, making complex tasks effortless. Also new in this version:

- **PowerPoint Central**. Use this online magazine to learn new tips and download great clip art, movies, and videos to use in your slides.

- **Microsoft Clip Gallery 3.0**. This new enhanced gallery contains clip art and pictures for your slides, as well as movies and sound clips. The Clip Gallery also contains a link to Clip Gallery Live, Microsoft's spot on the World Wide Web to get additional objects for your slides.

- **Hyperlinks**. Add a jump in your slide to another slide or Office 97 document or a spot on the Web. Hyperlinks are easy to insert and easy to use.

- **Custom Animation**. Control the animation of every object on your slide. Plan the order in which objects appear, how they look, and, if you want, add a full range of sounds. Your audience will gasp in amazement.

- **Save as a Web document**. Create your presentation and then publish it directly on the Web. There's no need to learn HTML code to create a Web document—PowerPoint does the hard work for you.

Part I: Creating a Presentation

Chapter 1: **The Basics of PowerPoint**

Chapter 2: **Creating a Presentation the Easy Way**

Chapter 3: **Creating a Presentation from Scratch**

Chapter 4: **Using the Slide Master to Give Your Presentation a Consistent Look**

Chapter 5: **Adding Graphs and Charts**

Chapter 6: **Creating Organization Charts**

Chapter 7: **Creating Attractive Tables**

1

The Basics of PowerPoint

● **In this chapter:**

- **How do I start PowerPoint?**

- **When should I use a button, and when should I use the mouse?**

- **Looking at the PowerPoint screen**

- **What does this button do?**

- **Working with toolbars**

- **Getting help with Help**

Combine your ideas with beautiful artwork for a professional-looking visual feast! . . . .➤

PowerPoint is an exciting presentation graphics program that lets you create presentations that you can view on a computer screen or print out. PowerPoint is so much fun to use that you'll probably want to use it more than your regular word processing or spreadsheet software.

 Plain English, please!

> **Presentation graphics** programs, like Microsoft PowerPoint, are used to create slide shows (like the kind created with 35mm slides and a projector), visual presentations (as you may have seen in computer stores to demonstrate products), transparencies, or full-page handouts.

PowerPoint was designed by folks who know what a good presentation should contain and how it should look. Your colors, patterns, and text all look like a professional graphic artist coordinated your presentation. If you want, you can put your completed presentation on the World Wide Web for everyone to see.

Before we actually plunge into how to use PowerPoint, let's review some basic Windows 95 procedures, including how to start the PowerPoint program. (From now on, I'll refer to Windows 95 as Windows.)

Your mouse is your best friend in Windows! Some versions of Office 97 come with the IntelliMouse, Microsoft's next generation of the mouse. We'll learn more about using the IntelliMouse later in this chapter. Although you can use the keyboard, it's usually easier to use your mouse to accomplish most tasks in Windows. Some shortcuts are accessible only by using your mouse. For example, you can click the right mouse button to quickly open shortcut menus that would take several clicks to open otherwise.

Before any programs are open, the mouse pointer looks like a white arrow pointing upward to the left. Later on, you'll find that the mouse pointer changes its appearance depending on the program you're in or the task you're doing. But no matter what shape it takes or what task it's performing, it's still called the mouse pointer.

Your Windows desktop is designed to look like your desk at home or in the office, with folders and objects placed on top of it. As you move around the desktop, you'll notice that when the mouse pointer points to some buttons, a message called a **ScreenTip** appears that describes what that button does. Figure 1.1 shows the Start button.

Fig. 1.1
Using the Start button is an easy way to open PowerPoint.

Q&A

Should I use the right or left mouse button when I click?

Windows uses the right mouse button to access shortcut menus. Throughout this book, unless you're told otherwise, use the left mouse button. Windows uses the right mouse button to access shortcut menus.

How do I know whether I should click once or twice?

Buttons—either in PowerPoint or Windows—generally only need to be clicked once. The dilemma over double- or single-clicking was much greater in previous versions of Windows. If you're unsure, however, click once and if nothing happens after a second or two, try double-clicking.

Why doesn't my computer have the same pictures in the box next to the clock on the taskbar as the ones in the example?

The area next to the clock is called the system tray. Different icons, or pictures, show up in the tray based on the programs that are installed on your computer and what you are doing on the computer. For example, whenever you're connected to the Internet, an icon representing your modem appears.

How do I start PowerPoint?

Although there are lots of different ways to start any program, one of the easiest ways is to use the Start button, which you'll find at the bottom left of the taskbar. You'll find that you can open all the programs on your computer using the Start button.

The following steps show you how to start PowerPoint using the Start button on the taskbar.

1 Click the Start button on the taskbar to open the Start menu.

2 Click Programs, which contains all the programs installed on your computer. Your desktop will look similar to Figure 1.2.

3 Point to the icon called Microsoft PowerPoint to highlight it, as shown in Figure 1.3, then click.

Fig. 1.2
See all the programs on your computer from the Start menu.

Point here to see all the programs on your computer

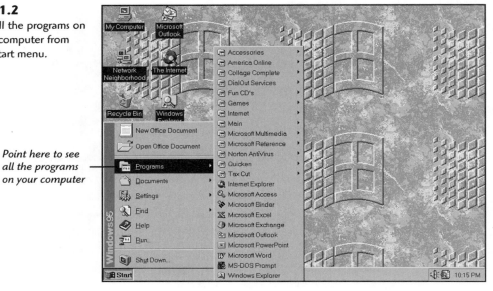

Fig. 1.3
Click the PowerPoint icon to open the program.

Click here to start PowerPoint

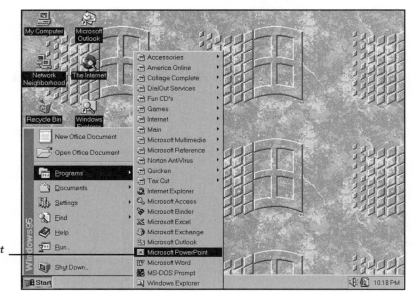

When the program opens, both the Office Assistant and the PowerPoint dialog box appear (see Figure 1.4). The PowerPoint dialog box offers you the option of creating a new presentation or opening one that already exists. You can clear this dialog box from the screen without making any selection by pressing the Esc key, clicking the Close button (that's the button with an X on it in the upper-right corner), or by clicking Cancel.

Fig. 1.4
The PowerPoint dialog box lets you create or open a presentation.

Click here to close this dialog box without creating or opening a file

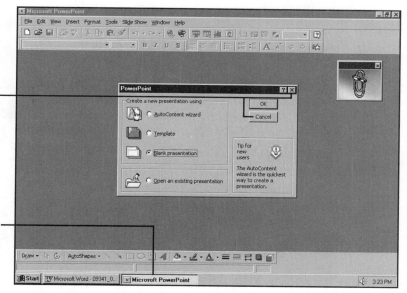

The depressed taskbar button shows that the program is open and active

Looking at the PowerPoint screen

The PowerPoint screen looks familiar because it's a Windows program and shares many common Windows elements. As with most Windows programs, the title bar, located at the top of the PowerPoint program window, shows the program title—in this case Microsoft PowerPoint. If a presentation is open and maximized (filling the full screen), the name of the presentation file is also shown on the title bar, as displayed in Figure 1.5. The menu bar sits directly below the title bar. You can access most of PowerPoint's features through the layers of menus provided in the menu bar.

Fig. 1.5
The PowerPoint 97 screen, with an active, maximized presentation file that fills the entire PowerPoint screen. Several PowerPoint toolbars are visible.

Common Tasks toolbar

Formatting toolbar

View buttons

Status bar

Standard toolbar

Reviewing toolbar

Drawing toolbar

If the active presentation isn't maximized, it has its own title bar, as shown in Figure 1.6.

Fig. 1.6
The active presentation is not maximized and has its own title bar.

The title bar moves to the top of the presentation window when it is not maximized

The PowerPoint Status bar is located at the bottom of the screen, directly above the Windows taskbar. The Status bar helps you keep track of your presentation because it shows which view is currently active, such as Slide or Slide Sorter view. If you've chosen Slide view, the active slide number is displayed. The middle box shows which PowerPoint template was used to create the active slide. The third box shows a book with a check mark over it. Whenever you misspell a word as you are typing text, the check mark changes to an X and a wavy, red line appears underneath the error. Right-click the typo and choose the correct word from the resulting list to fix the mistake. If you're a bad typist, like me, letting PowerPoint tell you about spelling errors can save you lots of embarrassment later.

Above the status bar are the PowerPoint view buttons. These buttons let you change the view of the slides. Each of these buttons displays a ScreenTip that becomes visible as you pass your mouse pointer over the button. To change your slide view, just click the button that corresponds to the view you want to see. We'll learn more about slide views later in this chapter.

TIP   **Don't waste time memorizing which button performs a particular** task—let the software work for you. If you're unsure what a button does, remember ScreenTips. Just hold the mouse pointer over the button and the ScreenTip appears.

What are toolbars?

Toolbars make your job in PowerPoint easier. If you were painting the outside of your house, you'd probably pack a box full of all the stuff you'd need—rags, brushes, maybe some extra paint—to take outside with you. Even though the same supplies could be found all through your house, having them handy when you needed them would sure speed up your work. Well, toolbars are like the supply box because they offer you the convenience of having menu commands at your fingertips. You could find all of the commands on the PowerPoint toolbars buried in the menus. But clicking one button instead of opening several menus makes your work easier and faster.

PowerPoint has many toolbars to help you. Depending on which view you choose, some toolbars may not be available. For example, the Outlining toolbar is not available in Slide view. Table 1.1 shows some of the most commonly used toolbars and a brief description of what each one does.

Table 1.1   PowerPoint toolbars

Name of toolbar	Description
Standard	Offers many standard PowerPoint program functions such as opening, saving, and closing presentations
Formatting	Provides text formatting functions like adding bold, underline, or italic attributes, changing the Font and Font Size, or changing text justification
Common Tasks	Provides quick access to three of PowerPoint's most-used features, including New Slide
Drawing	Provides basic drawing functions like drawing shapes and applying line styles
Outlining	(Available only in Outline view) Provides outlining functions to move points up or down the outline
Picture	Offers basic drawing functions such as cropping or coloring an object

Q&A   *Is there a way to add buttons to a toolbar?*

You bet there is! PowerPoint 97 lets you add buttons and even menu commands to toolbars. You can customize existing toolbars or create your own! I'll show you more about customizing PowerPoint toolbars in Chapter 17.

The buttons all start to look alike after a while!

Even though you know that you can always rely on ScreenTips to jog your memory, you may be a little overwhelmed by all the different buttons you've seen. Take all the buttons used in PowerPoint, then add the buttons used in your word processing program, spreadsheet program, and who-knows-what-else... that's a lot of buttons.

Fortunately, many of the same symbols are used from program to program. And you're really in luck if you're using a "suite" of programs, such as Microsoft Office 97.

For example, most programs use a picture of a scissors on the Cut button, a printer on the Print button, or an underlined U on the Underline button.

How can I display other toolbars?

Sometimes you don't need to do anything to see a toolbar. For example, when you create a WordArt object, the WordArt toolbar appears on the screen. It's easy to display any of PowerPoint's toolbars. Simply choose View, Toolbars. The toolbar menu, as shown in Figure 1.7, shows a check mark next to all of the currently displayed toolbars. Select the toolbar you want to display. (You can display as many toolbars as you'd like.) The menu closes and the toolbar appears on the PowerPoint screen.

To close any toolbar, repeat the procedure but, this time, click the check mark next to the toolbar you want to close. When the menu closes, the toolbar will be gone.

Fig. 1.7
The View, Toolbars menu command from Slide view. Check marks indicate which toolbars are displayed on the screen.

Relocating toolbars to other parts of the screen

PowerPoint toolbars can appear as strips of buttons across an edge of the PowerPoint screen (called docked toolbars) or they can float over the presentation. I like to use floating toolbars for tasks I don't do all of the time, like animating my presentation, because I can drag the toolbar all over the screen and I can easily close it by clicking the Close button (X) in the corner of the toolbar.

You can float or "dock" any of PowerPoint's toolbars. Click the move handle on a docked toolbar, as shown in Figure 1.8, and drag the toolbar to a new location. Or, on a floating toolbar, just click and hold the mouse button on any gray area of the toolbar that isn't covered by a button and drag it. Notice that as it's being dragged, the toolbar changes shape. When you get to the spot where you want to place the toolbar, let go of the mouse button and the toolbar appears in its new location.

Fig. 1.8
Use the move handle to drag a docked toolbar onto the PowerPoint screen as a floating palette.

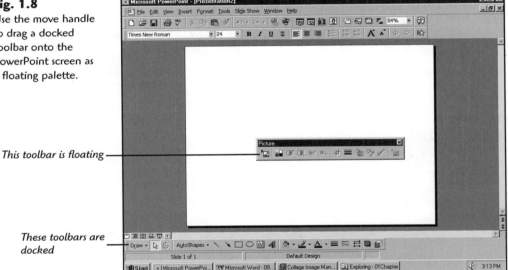

This toolbar is floating ────────

These toolbars are docked ────────

Using PowerPoint menus and dialog boxes

If you prefer using a menu rather than a button, you can still use your mouse. Sometimes, I like to use the menu if I'm unfamiliar with a program and I just want to browse. I can just click the Format menu, for example, and read what commands are there.

To make a selection from the menu, click a menu name in the menu bar, drag the mouse down the list until the command you want is highlighted, and click (see Figure 1.9).

Fig. 1.9
A dimmed menu
command means that
command is not
currently available.

This icon
appears on—
a toolbar

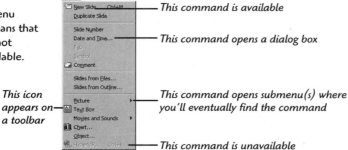

— *This command is available*

— *This command opens a dialog box*

— *This command opens submenu(s) where
you'll eventually find the command*

— *This command is unavailable*

Office 97 menus have a new flat look. Menu commands that also can be accessed from toolbars display the toolbar icon or picture next to the menu command. If a menu command has a keyboard shortcut, such as pressing Crtl+M to insert a new slide, the keystrokes are shown on the menu. You can even change the way the menu commands are displayed.

What happens after you click a menu command varies with each command. If the menu command has three dots (called an ellipsis) following it, a dialog box will appear that asks you to enter more information or choose from a list of options. If the menu command is followed by an arrow, clicking the command will open a submenu where you'll eventually find the command. Other times just clicking the command will execute it. For example, clicking File, Open opens a dialog box, while clicking File, Save saves the open file.

You probably noticed that some of the commands look dark and others look light, or dimmed. A command that is dimmed means the command isn't available at that moment. That doesn't mean that there's something wrong with the hardware or software, it just means that given what you're currently doing, that command can't be used.

TIP **Experiment with the way menu items appear. Choose Tools, Customize** and click the Options tab. Click the drop-down arrow next to Menu Animations and choose a new effect such as Random, Unfold, or Slide. Click Close to return to the PowerPoint screen. The next time you open a PowerPoint menu, you'll see the new effect!

Anytime you select a menu command that's followed by an ellipsis (…), PowerPoint provides a dialog box. Think of a dialog box as a form you need to complete and verify for PowerPoint to continue. Figure 1.10 shows a dialog box and some of its elements.

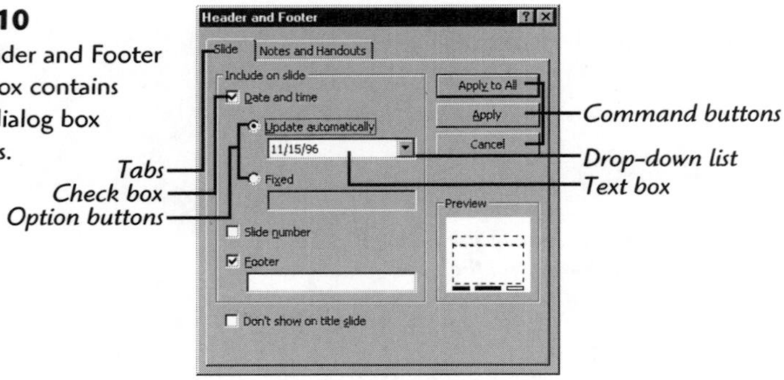

Fig. 1.10

The Header and Footer dialog box contains typical dialog box elements.

Tabs
Check box
Option buttons

Command buttons
Drop-down list
Text box

Each dialog box contains one or more of the following elements:

- **Tabs** enable you to look at different pages of options. To see a set of related options, click its tab.

- **List boxes** provide two or more available choices. You select the item you want by clicking it.

- **Drop-down lists** show only one item and hide the rest. To view all of the items in a list, click the down arrow to the right of the list box.

- **Text boxes** are "fill in the blank" boxes. Click inside the text box to activate it. If there's already text inside the box, use the Delete or Backspace keys to delete existing characters before you type.

- **Check boxes** let you turn options on or off. Click inside a check box to turn an option off if it's on (and vice versa). If there are multiple check boxes displayed together, you can select more than one option.

- **Option buttons** are a lot like check boxes, except that you can slect only one option in a group. Clicking one option deselects the option that's already selected.

- **Spin boxes** are text boxes with controls. To change a spin box's setting, type the new setting in the text box or click the up and down arrows to change the setting.

- **Command buttons** appear in every dialog box. OK, Cancel, Apply, and Apply to All are commonly used command buttons in PowerPoint.

Getting the most out of Help

Besides having this book as a ready-reference, PowerPoint provides you with several different types of on-screen Help. You can find information on many topics by using the Help menu and the Contents and Index command. To use the Contents and Index command in Help:

1 Choose Help, Contents and Index Command.

2 Click the Index tab at the top of the dialog box.

3 Type the topic you want to see in the first text box. As you type, the list scrolls to show you entries that match your typed text.

4 When the topic you want appears, click it, and then click Display.

5 A list of topics matching your text is displayed, as shown in Figure 1.11.

If your topic has a lot of information available on it, you might see an additional dialog box that has more topics from which to choose. If you see this dialog box, click the topic you want, then click Display.

Fig. 1.11
Find useful information using the Help Topics command.

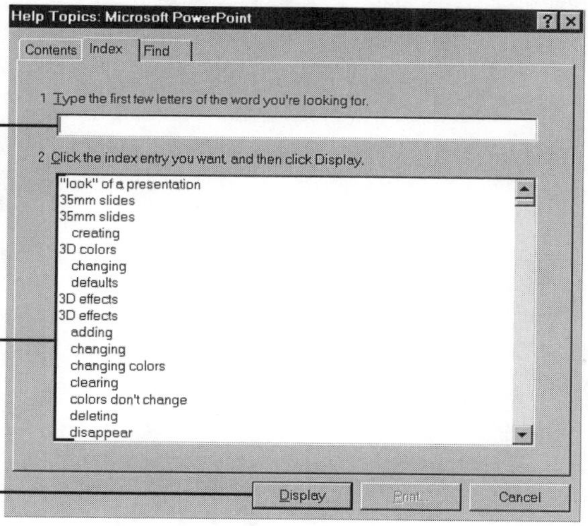

Enter the text you want to search for here

Available topics are displayed here

Click here to see information about the topic

6 Read the topic, then click the Close button (X) in the upper-left corner of the dialog box to close Help and return to the presentation.

Meet your new pal, the Office Assistant!

The easiest and most enjoyable method for getting help is to use the bouncy character called the Office Assistant that appears in its own small window when you open PowerPoint.

The Office Assistant is an amazing helper. As you work with PowerPoint, suggestions to assist you with the specific item you're working on may appear before you ask for help. Other times, the Office Assistant may suggest tips to help you with the particular feature of the program or task what you're trying to accomplish. You'll know that a tip is available when a yellow light bulb appears with the Assistant, as shown in Figure 1.12. Click the bulb to see the tip.

Even if you can't see the Office Assistant, a light bulb appears on the Office Assistant button on the Standard toolbar when a tip is available. First click the Office Assistant button and then click the light bulb to view the tip. I love knowing that there's always an extra pair of hands and eyes to help me with my presentation.

Fig. 1.12
The Office Assistant has a tip waiting for you.

Click here to see the tip

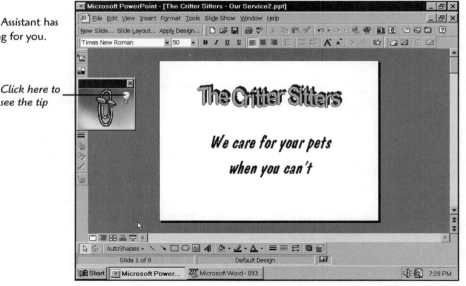

Any time you want, you can ask the Office Assistant for help. Whenever you have a question, click anywhere in the Office Assistant window. Follow the on-screen instructions and type the topic you want to know about and then click Search. The Assistant answers you by providing a list of related Help topics. Scroll the list to view all of the topics and then click the one you want to look at. After you've read the topic, return to the PowerPoint screen by clicking the Close button.

Q&A *How do I hide the Office Assistant?*

 You can hide the Office Assistant anytime. Position your mouse pointer somewhere inside the Office Assistant and click the right mouse button. Choose Hide Assistant from the menu. Bring the Office Assistant back to the screen by clicking the Office Assistant button on the toolbar or press F1. If you want to close the Office Assistant, click the Close button on the Office Assistant window.

Can I change the Office Assistant to another character?

You can change the Office Assistant to suit your mood! Click the current Office Assistant and then click Options. Choose the Gallery tab and then click Back or Next until you find the Assistant you want. I like Scribble the Cat!

The Office Assistant is great, but can I change its size?

Position the mouse pointer over any border of the Assistant until the pointer becomes a double-headed arrow and then drag the border to decrease or increase the Assistant's size.

TIP **If you'd like to see the Tip of the Day every time you open** PowerPoint, click the Office Assistant and then choose Options. Check the Show the Tip of the Day at startup box and then click OK. The next time you launch PowerPoint, the Office Assistant will provide you with the day's tip. Remember that, because PowerPoint is part of the Microsoft Office 97 suite, asking for the tip of the day will display a tip in the other suite products you've installed.

Working with the IntelliMouse

Microsoft has included a new mouse called the IntelliMouse with some versions of Office 97. Before you can use the IntelliMouse, you must install the IntelliPoint software needed to use the mouse into Windows. If your version of Office 97 came with the new IntelliMouse, follow the instructions that accompanied the IntelliMouse to set up the new mouse on your computer.

The IntelliMouse contains a wheel button located between the left and right mouse buttons. This rolling button provides a great way to move around your PowerPoint slides and other documents created with Office 97 software. With the IntelliMouse you won't need to use scroll bars to move around the PowerPoint screen.

The following table describes what the IntelliMouse does:

Function	Description
Scroll	Roll the wheel forward to scroll up, roll the wheel backward to scroll down
Pan	Press the wheel button and move the mouse pointer in the direction you want to view. The further you move the mouse pointer, the faster it scrolls
Zoom	Press Ctrl and roll the wheel button to adjust the zoom level
Data/Zoom	Press Shift and roll the wheel to expand or collapse outlines visible in Outline view

CAUTION   **The IntelliMouse wheel button works only with Office 97** product, Microsoft Internet Explorer, and Windows Explorer. You can use the IntelliMouse if you're using other software programs on your computer as a regular, two-button mouse.

Getting Help from Microsoft on the Web

One of the most exciting features about working with PowerPoint 97 is its extensive use of Internet features. (We'll learn a lot more about the Internet in Chapter 16.) When you need help, you can turn directly to the World Wide Web for your answers.

Before you can visit Microsoft on the Web, you must have a modem and an account with an Internet Service Provider. The Internet provider grants you access to the Web and stores and maintains Web sites and documents. Because Internet providers generally charge a fee, you might want to shop around a bit before you sign up with one. Your service provider will furnish you with instructions on using the Windows 95 Dial Up Networking Program to set up your account.

After your account has been set up, you can get help from Microsoft on the Web any time you are connected to your Internet service provider. From within PowerPoint, open the Help menu and choose Microsoft on the Web. Click one of the choices shown, as displayed in Figure 1.13, to view the Web site (see Figure 1.14).

Fig. 1.13
You can turn to the World Wide Web for answers.

Choose from one of these options to connect to one of Microsoft's Web pages

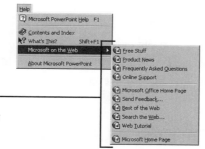

Fig. 1.14
There's lots to see and do at the Microsoft Office Web site.

Click one of these buttons to "jump" to the topic shown on the button face

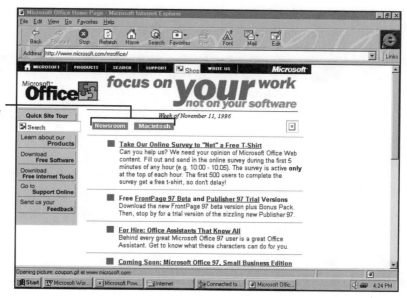

Views let you see your work from different angles

By now, you've probably figured out that PowerPoint is nothing like a word processing or spreadsheet program. Let's face it, there are only a limited number of ways you can type a document or add a group of numbers. But there are limitless ways you can create a presentation.

You and I could have the same information in mind for a presentation but design it differently. We each bring elements of our personality into creating our own presentation. To accommodate individual tastes, PowerPoint enables you to see your slides in different ways, or **views**.

66 *Plain English, please!*

A PowerPoint **view** is another way of looking at your work. When looking at a painting, sometimes you want to stand a few inches from it, other times you may want to see it from the other side of a room. Views let you see your work from different perspectives. 99

How many different views do I need?

Currently, PowerPoint gives you five different ways of viewing your information. The following table shows you each of the views, a description of it, and the button that shows you the view.

Name of view	Description	Button
Slide	See one slide taking up the full screen. You can design and modify one slide at a time.	
Outline	See the text for all slides in the presentation.	
Slide Sorter	See a miniature version of all the slides in the presentation.	
Notes Page	See one slide on a page with room beneath it where you create text you'll use when talking about this slide.	

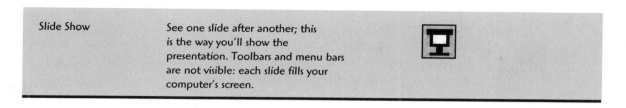

| Slide Show | See one slide after another; this is the way you'll show the presentation. Toolbars and menu bars are not visible: each slide fills your computer's screen. | |

Figure 1.15 shows you Slide view and the location of the view buttons.

Fig. 1.15
Use Slide view to create or modify one slide at a time.

Switching from view to view

You can change views at any time by clicking the button for whichever view you'd like to see. For example, to switch to Slide view from any other view, click the Slide View button.

 Q&A *How do I know which view I should look at?*

Only you know how you think and work best. I like to use the Outline view to make sure my text is logical and clear, and I use Slide view to perfect the design of individual slides. But I spend most of my time in Slide Sorter view to make sure the slides are in the right order and don't look too busy.

A closer look at views

Each view has its own advantages. Use the view that works best for you.

Outline view

Outline view, shown in Figure 1.16, displays only the text used on each slide. You can change to Outline view by clicking the Outline View button. I like Outline view because it's free of all design elements, such as background patterns or the position of the text on the slide, and it enables me to concentrate on what I'm saying. After I've got the words right, I switch to Slide view to dress up the slide.

Fig. 1.16
In Outline view you don't see colors or patterns, just text.

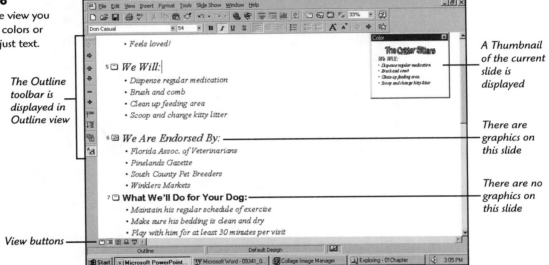

The Outline toolbar is displayed in Outline view

A Thumbnail of the current slide is displayed

There are graphics on this slide

There are no graphics on this slide

View buttons

TIP **Although Outline view only shows you slide text, it does let you** know if the slide contains any graphics. Take a close look at the slide icons for slide 5 and slide 6 in Figure 1.16. The icon for slide 5 is blank, while the icon for slide 6 has tiny designs on it. These tiny designs indicate that there's at least one graphic image on the slide.

Slide Sorter view

Slide Sorter view lets you see all your slides at once. You can switch to Slide Sorter view by clicking the Slide Sorter View button. This view is the most helpful to me because I get to see exactly how my slides will look to my audience.

In Slide Sorter view, a miniature (or **thumbnail**) of each slide is displayed on the screen (see Figure 1.17).

Fig. 1.17
Slide Sorter view lets you see how your presentation is taking shape.

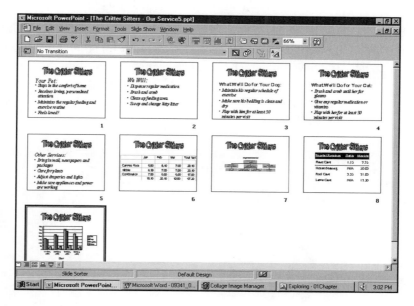

> 66 *Plain English, please!*
>
> A **thumbnail** is a small version of a slide or piece of artwork. When you're in Slide Sorter view, for example, you see each of your slides reduced to a smaller version so many slides can be viewed at once. Thumbnails are great to get an idea of what's on each slide; they're not meant to be used for detailed analysis. 99

Using Slide Sorter view is helpful to track your progress. I rely on it as I develop a presentation. After I change background colors or patterns, I switch to Slide Sorter view to see if what I've done makes logical sense and looks good with the other slides. Think of Slide Sorter view as a small art gallery in which you make sure all the artwork on exhibit works well together.

Notes Page view

Notes Page view is like having a silent assistant to help you with your presentation. Notes Page lets you add Speaker Notes (that only you will see) to your slides. You might want to add a note to emphasize a particular point or to remind yourself to speed through the slide if the audience is restless. You can also make notes on handouts you'll distribute to your audience. I like to enter the number and title of the next slide so I don't have to twist my head to see which slide is up next.

You can switch to Notes Page view by clicking the Notes Page View button. Each Notes Page has a small picture of the slide right on it, as well as any notes you've made to yourself (see Figure 1.18). If the image is too small to read, open the View menu, choose Zoom, and select a higher percentage to make it larger.

Fig. 1.18
Notes Page view lets you make notes that only you see!

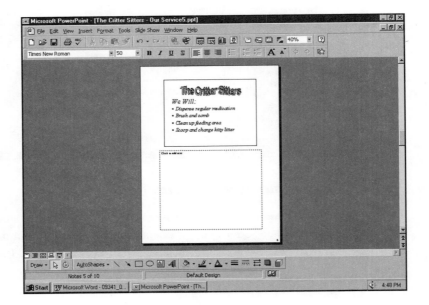

Slide Show view

After you've got the text and design elements together, you'll want to start seeing the slides as part of a show. In Slide Show view, you actually see one slide advance to the next, just as your viewers will see it. You can switch to Slide Show view by clicking the Slide Show button.

Any special effects (which are covered in Chapter 13) are seen in Slide Show view. This is the view you use to view the presentation from beginning to end. Use the opportunity to smooth out any rough edges you see as the slides go by.

2

Creating a Presentation the Easy Way

● In this chapter:

- What's the easiest way to create a presentation?

- I want to add or delete a slide

- Is there an easy way to make my presentations look great?

- How do I save and print my presentation?

- I'd like to reopen an existing presentation

Want to create a great presentation in a matter of minutes that looks like it was created by a talented team of artists, writers, and designers? Read on!. . . . . >

You're already familiar with the components of the PowerPoint screen, the types of slides available, and how the toolbar buttons and menus work. In fact, you probably can't wait to create a presentation.

You'll find that it's not only easy to create slides, but you can add and delete them easily, too! PowerPoint contains many tools that help you create text on each slide, and give your slides a dramatic look.

PowerPoint contains helpers called Wizards that make creating a presentation easy. Wizards help you through complicated tasks by first asking you questions and then using your answers.

 Plain English, please!

Wizards are helpful tools that guide you through a particular process. They generally have several consecutive dialog boxes that ask you questions about the task you want to perform. Wizards show you how your presentation is shaping up as you answer its questions, and allow you to move forward and backward in its dialog boxes. That way, if you've changed your mind, you can make changes before the Wizard is finished. Don't get the idea that Wizards are just for beginners: They're used by computer users of all abilities!

Using PowerPoint's Wizards, you can create a great presentation that looks like you hired a team of professional slide designers.

Wizards take the guesswork out of complicated tasks and allow you to concentrate on creating your presentation.

 Are Wizards included with other Microsoft programs?

Yes. Microsoft includes Wizards in many of its software programs. Each Wizard asks you questions and then uses your answers to work through a complicated process. I think of Wizards as my helpers—available to take over and automate what might take many steps. For example, the AutoContent Wizard uses my responses to create some dynamite-looking slides in a very short time. I wish I could use Wizards for other non-PowerPoint jobs, like driving to the office or working in the garden!

How do I get a presentation up and running fast?

Using the AutoContent Wizard is the fastest way to create a new presentation. All you need to know before you start is a general idea of what you want the presentation to be about.

You can use the AutoContent Wizard from the startup PowerPoint dialog box, which is shown in Figure 2.1.

Click here to create slides based on a general theme

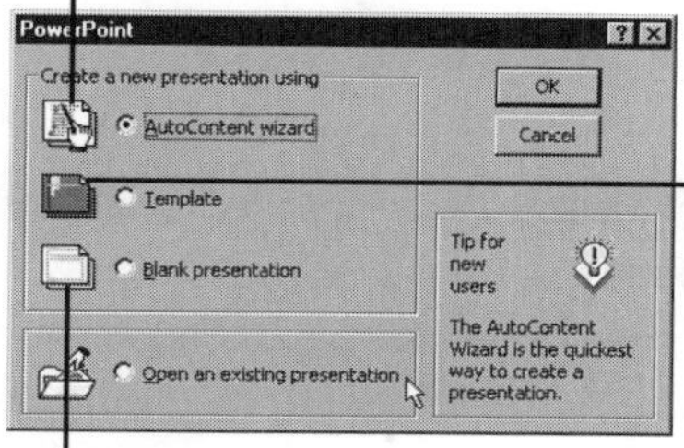

Fig. 2.1
The startup dialog box lets you create a new presentation using the AutoContent Wizard.

Click here to apply a predesigned template to your slide

Click here to open a new blank presentation

The startup PowerPoint dialog box creates all the basic slides you'll need in a presentation.

The AutoContent Wizard creates slides after you've chosen a topic and made a few selections about how you'll give your presentation. The topics are broad and the results may or may not be *exactly* what you want. If you love the slides the AutoContent Wizard created, you can accept them as is; if they're not exactly what you'd like, you can always reword text, add more slides, or delete any you don't like.

Working magic with the AutoContent Wizard

The AutoContent Wizard lets you choose a topic for your presentation based on several general themes. Each of these themes contains several slides that you'd probably want to include. Although these prepackaged presentations may not be exactly to your liking, I find they're great starting points.

From the startup PowerPoint dialog box, follow these steps to create a presentation using the AutoContent Wizard:

1 Click the <u>A</u>utoContent Wizard button from the PowerPoint dialog box, then click OK. The AutoContent Wizard dialog box appears.

2 After you've read a brief summary of what the AutoContent Wizard does, click <u>N</u>ext.

TIP **If you need Help while you're using the AutoContent Wizard, click** the Help button (the box with the question mark) located at the bottom of the each AutoContent Wizard dialog box. You'll get an explanation of the feature.

3 In the second AutoContent Wizard dialog box, you'll choose your presentation type (see Figure 2.2). From the row of buttons on the left, click the theme of your presentation, such as <u>G</u>eneral, <u>P</u>ersonal, or <u>S</u>ales/Marketing. After you've chosen the theme, select a related template from the list of template names on the right. If you want to see all of the templates, click the <u>A</u>ll presentation theme button and scroll through the list to choose a template. After you've selected a presentation theme and related template, click <u>N</u>ext.

Select one of these general topics

Fig. 2.2
Select a topic for the
AutoContent Wizard.

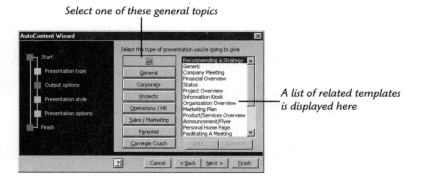

*A list of related templates
is displayed here*

4 In the third dialog box, click the option that best describes how the presentation will be used—<u>P</u>resentations, informal meetings, handouts, on the Internet, or from a kiosk. Click <u>N</u>ext.

5 In the fourth dialog box, choose the type of output you'd like for your presentation and whether you want any handouts to give your audience (see Figure 2.3), then click Next.

 TIP **Take advantage of the Back and Next dialog box buttons in the** Wizards to see the effects of your choices. This ability to go back and forth means you can change your mind as often as you like without making a commitment.

Select the style of your presentation

Fig. 2.3
Choose the type of output materials you'll need.

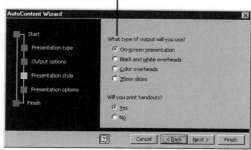

6 In the fifth dialog box, type your name, company name, and any additional information that you'd like to appear on the title slide, then click Next.

7 After you've read the sixth (and final) dialog box, click Finish.

The AutoContent Wizard takes a moment to design a presentation based on your answers. In a moment, your presentation opens in Outline view. You now have a set of slides waiting for your personal touch. Figure 2.4 shows the presentation the AutoContent Wizard designed for you.

Of course, these new slides are only suggestions. You can use them if you want, disregard any or all of them, or modify them.

 TIP **Check out Chapter 1 if you've forgotten how to change Views.** You can view your presentation in Outline view or you can look at one slide at a time from Slide view. If you wish, you can look at all of the slides from Slide Sorter view.

A thumbnail of the first slide, in color, appears in its own miniwindow

Fig. 2.4
The new presentation appears in outline view.

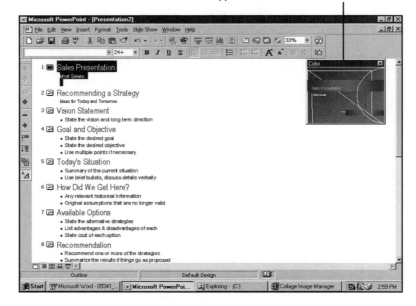

How do I add a slide to my presentation?

No matter how well you plan your presentation in advance, it always looks different when you actually sit down at the computer. I always start out thinking that I'll need just a few slides and then realize I need more slides to help make my point! It's easy to insert a new slide anywhere in your presentation.

A new slide is added in your presentation *after* whatever slide is active. (The active slide is the one that's selected.) Regardless of where the slide is added, you can always change its location.

The easiest way to add a new slide is to click the New Slide button on the Standard toolbar. (If you'd prefer, you can click the New Slide button on the Common Task box. The results are the same.) After you click the button, the New Slide dialog box opens. This dialog box lets you choose an AutoLayout.

Use SlideLayout from either Slide view or Slide Sorter view. The New Slide dialog box is shown in Figure 2.5. It opens when you're in Slide view or Slide Sorter view and you click the New Slide button.

Fig. 2.5
Choose a layout from the New Slide dialog box.

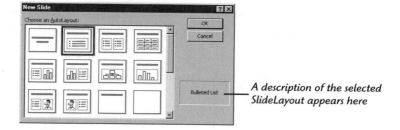

A description of the selected SlideLayout appears here

As you look at the different slide layouts, you'll see that there are many ways information on the slides can be arranged. When you've found the right one for your new slide, click it, then click OK. Remember, you can always change your mind, and you can always modify a layout, too.

After you've chosen a layout, you immediately see the results when you change to Slide view. All the elements of the AutoLayout appear on the new slide, as shown in Figure 2.6.

Fig. 2.6
The elements of the Bulleted List slide are displayed in Slide view.

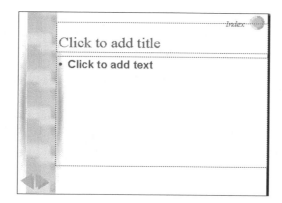

Click to add title

• Click to add text

TIP **You can also change the layout of a slide after you've** created it. From Slide Sorter view, select the slide and then click the Slide Layout button on the Standard toolbar. Select a new layout for your slide, and then click Apply.

I want to delete this slide

If you can't count on remembering to add all the slides you'll need, you *can* count on having to get rid of unnecessary slides. You can delete a slide from Outline, Slide Sorter, or Slide view.

You can delete a slide using Outline or Slide Sorter view by selecting the slide you want to delete, then pressing the Delete key.

If you're in Slide view or you prefer to use a menu, activate the slide you want to delete, then choose Edit, Delete Slide.

Using AutoTemplate to give slides some extra pizazz!

Microsoft has taken all of the hard work out of setting up the layout for your slides. Many different slide layouts that look like they were designed by a team of professional graphic artists are included with PowerPoint. The Apply Design Template allows you to apply one of these designs to your slides.

The AutoLayout feature automatically arranges individual slides, but you'll probably want to change the slide background. The Apply Design Template does this for you by applying an AutoTemplate that comes with PowerPoint directly onto your slides. Each template contains colors, boxes, and designs, and makes your slides look like you hired a graphic artist.

To apply a Design Template, click the Apply Design button from Outline, Slide, or Slide Sorter view. Click an available design template from the list on the left side of the dialog box. When you click a template, a **thumbnail** is displayed in the center of the dialog box, as shown in Figure 2.7. The sample thumbnail shows you the color and arrangement of the template, but substitutes commonly used design text for your own.

Available templates are listed here

Click here to move up one level and view additional folders that contain other template files

Fig. 2.7
A thumbnail of the selected template shows you how your template will look.

This folder contains the templates shown on the list

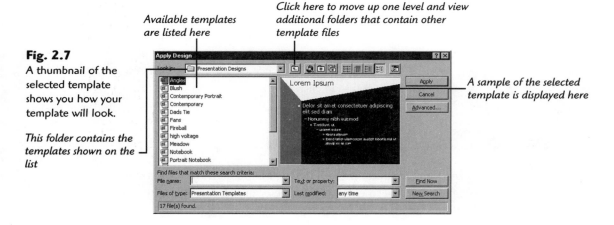

A sample of the selected template is displayed here

TIP **Don't worry that something's wrong if your screen displays the file** extensions (the three letters preceded by a dot [.] at the end of the name of each presentation). Although, by default, Windows 95 hides file extensions, you can view them. To view file extensions, go to My Computer and open the <u>V</u>iew menu and choose <u>O</u>ptions. Click the View tab and uncheck the Hide MS–Dos File Extensions box.

TIP **Microsoft has included an entire gallery of templates for** your use. If you don't find the template you're looking for from the ones shown in Figure 2.7, click the Up One Level button on the Apply Design dialog box to view additional folders which contain more templates. In the Templates folder (installed wherever Microsoft Office 97 is installed on the hard disk of your computer) you'll find many folders to pick from, including Presentations, Presentation Designs, and Web Pages.

Choosing the right AutoTemplate

When choosing which AutoTemplate to use, consider three things: your audience, your topic, and how your slides will be presented.

Obviously, you'd use a different AutoTemplate for a presentation to a group of potential corporate investors than you would to a group of camp counselors. Tailor your presentation to the people who will see it. You wouldn't want to use bright, vibrant colors for potential investors, but those same colors would probably be just right for camp counselors.

The second point, your topic, is directly related to knowing your audience. A presentation to a group of camp counselors will probably have a lighter, more humorous theme than the presentation to the corporate investors. The template you select should reflect the seriousness of your topic.

Lastly, the way you'll present your slides should influence which AutoTemplate you choose. You wouldn't want to use dark colors or patterns if you'll be photocopying the printouts; the patterns will eventually blur and the slide will look like mush. If you're planning to put the completed presentation on the World Wide Web, you might want to limit the number of graphics so the presentation will load faster on the viewer's computer screen.

Always imagine that you're sitting in the audience, as far away from the presentation as possible. Ask yourself: Can I read each slide? Do the colors blend together? Are the words visible? Am I watching the background or reading the slide?

When you apply an AutoTemplate, the design appears on every slide in your presentation.

Save your presentation: make it last

Even though you've done all this work on your presentation, it does not exist in the memory of your computer until you save it! Although you can see the entire presentation on the screen, it must be saved to use it later. If the power went out or you accidentally exited PowerPoint, the presentation on your screen would be nothing but a memory.

Saving a presentation to disk is the single most important task you'll ever do. Saving is virtually painless—you assign the presentation a unique name and, if desired, a special folder location, and the computer does the rest. Remember to save your presentation often as you work on it. Incidentally, all the work performed on slides (templates, graphics, and so on) is contained in a single presentation file, so if anything ever happened to it, *all* your work would be lost.

 CAUTION Remember to save your work frequently—any unsaved work will be lost if the power goes out.

 Q&A *How often should I save my presentation?*

It's difficult to give an exact time interval for saving your work. Every 10 or 15 minutes is a good rule of thumb, but it also depends on what you're working on. If you're trying out a new technique or something you're unsure of, it's a good idea to save your work more frequently.

Which should I use—my hard disk or a floppy disk?

In most cases, you'll save your work on your computer's hard disk or on a floppy disk. There are advantages and disadvantages to each method:

- Saving to the hard disk lets you store larger files more easily and read files quickly, but you can't take your work to another computer, and if your computer is damaged, your work is inaccessible.

- Saving to a floppy disk allows you to take your work to another computer; floppy disks are great for transporting files from one place to another, but they can only store files that are of limited size (under 1.44M), and they read all files more slowly.

TIP   **Working during an electrical storm? Better save frequently, or** better yet, save your work and shut down your computer.

Save your work for posterity

The easiest way to save a presentation is by clicking the Save button on the Standard toolbar.

When you save a presentation for the first time, the Save As dialog box opens. Figure 2.8 shows the Save As dialog box.

PowerPoint will store your presentation here unless you tell it otherwise

Fig. 2.8
The Save As dialog box is used to name a file.

Type the file name here

Save As
Save in: My Documents
Save / Cancel / Embed TrueType
File name:
Save as type: Presentation

The difference between the File, Save and File, Save As commands is confusing at first. Quite simply, when you save a file the first time, the File Save dialog box opens, even if you use the Save command (from the menu).

The Save As command is used to give an existing file a *different* name. For example, you might need to create a new presentation that will be similar to one that already exists. Rather than "reinventing the wheel," the Save As command lets you create a completely new file from an existing one. You end up with two identical files, each having a different name.

After the Save As dialog box is open, follow these steps to save an unnamed presentation:

1 Type the name you want in the File <u>N</u>ame text box. You can use upper- and lowercase letters and as many as 255 characters, including spaces.

2 Decide where you want to store the file. (Microsoft Office 97 files default to the My Documents folder.) You can change the location of the file by clicking the Save <u>I</u>n pull-down arrow. This pull-down list lets you change to a different folder or from the hard drive (normally the C drive) to a floppy drive (normally the A or B drive) or network drive.

3 Click <u>S</u>ave to save the file.

PowerPoint automatically tacks on the extension .PPT to your file. (You won't see the .PPT extension when you look at your files in the Windows Explorer, unless you've displayed the filename extensions.) This .PPT extension makes it easy for both you and PowerPoint to locate your presentations.

Opening a PowerPoint presentation

After you've saved a presentation file, you can open it any time you're working in PowerPoint. Because files are stored indefinitely, you have access to all of the presentations on your hard drive. If you want to open a presentation that's stored on a floppy disk, make sure that you have the disk handy. The procedure for opening a presentation in PowerPoint is identical to opening any other file in Windows 95.

 The easiest way to open a presentation you've already created is to click the <u>O</u>pen an Existing Presentation button on the opening PowerPoint dialog box, or click the Open button on the Standard toolbar. Choose the file name of the presentation you want to open, then click OK.

To make it really simple to open a file, PowerPoint lists the four most recently opened presentations at the bottom of the <u>F</u>ile menu, as shown in Figure 2.9. You can open one of these files by choosing <u>F</u>ile, then clicking its name in the list.

Fig. 2.9
The four most recently used files are displayed at the bottom of the File menu.

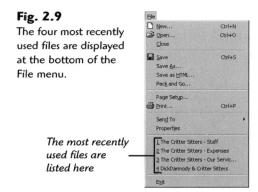

The most recently used files are listed here

Can I print one slide?

Most times, your presentations are designed to be viewed by an audience—either during a slide show or on the Web. However, not all PowerPoint presentations have such lofty goals. I use PowerPoint to create all kinds of files, like one org chart or a bulleted list to highlight important points. A few days ago, I used PowerPoint to create a Happy Birthday sign for my best friend!

You can print one slide at any time, no matter where your presentation is headed. Here's how:

1 Make sure that the slide you print is active, whether in Slide View, Slide Sorter view, or Outline view. (If you need more information about slide views, go back to Chapter 1.)

2 Choose File, Print. The Print dialog box opens, as shown in Figure 2.10.

3 In the Print Range section, click the option button next to Current slide.

4 Click OK to print the current slide.

Fig. 2.10
Print the current slide
from the Print dialog
box.

*Click here to
print the
current slide*

CAUTION **Don't click the Print button on the Standard toolbar if you only**
want to print one slide. Clicking the Print button will cause all of the slides
to print—no questions asked!

The end of the day: shutting down PowerPoint

When it's time to leave, you don't just turn off the computer in the middle of
whatever you're working on and reach for your hat and coat, right? You need
to close the program you're working in, shut down Windows, then turn off
the computer. *Then* you get your hat and coat.

You can close a presentation by choosing File, Close, or by choosing File,
Exit. The difference between the two is that closing the file removes the
presentation from memory, but PowerPoint is still open. (Remember, you
can always check the taskbar to see if a program is still running.) When you
choose Exit, the file is removed from memory, PowerPoint is closed, and the
file also is removed from memory. So, if you want to close the file but keep
using PowerPoint, use Close. To discontinue using PowerPoint altogether,
such as at the end of the day, use the Exit command.

To close a presentation without closing PowerPoint, choose File, Close. If
you've made any changes to the presentation which haven't been saved,
PowerPoint reminds you of this by showing you the dialog box shown in
Figure 2.11.

Fig. 2.11
This dialog box reminds
you that you have not
saved changes made to
the presentation.

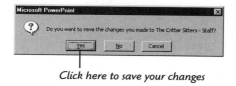

Click here to save your changes

If you want to save the changes, click Yes. If you don't want to save the
changes, click No. To evade the issue and return to the presentation, click
Cancel.

CAUTION   **Be careful not to turn off the computer while you're working in**
PowerPoint or any other Windows 95 program. A lot goes on "behind the
scenes" during a typical Windows 95 session. If you don't exit properly, files
might link together and cause your computer to run slowly the next time
you use it.

Creating a Presentation from Scratch

● In this chapter:

- How do I use placeholders to design slides?

- Add text directly on a slide

- I'd like to be able to change the appearance of text

- Can I create slides in an outline?

- I'd like to add a picture to my slide

- Can I use clip art from the Web?

Text is the meat and potatoes of your presentation. While PowerPoint can't help you think of the actual words, it makes working with the text an easy task . . . . ▶

After you've decided what to say, it's up to you to type the words onto your slides. **Placeholders make it easy to create** slide text; they determine where your text will be placed and how it will look.

If you've used a word processor to type a letter or create a flier for an upcoming event, then you'll be able to create titles and text in your PowerPoint slides with little trouble. If you've never used a word processor and your typing skills aren't the best, you'll be happy to know that there isn't that much text on a slide, and the PowerPoint tools you'll learn about in this chapter are designed to make your words look professional with fewer headaches.

Placeholders let you hold that thought

PowerPoint makes it easy to decide where your words will look best by putting **placeholders** on each slide.

66 *Plain English, please!*

A **placeholder** is a box embedded on a slide which has been designed by PowerPoint to appear a certain way and perform a specific task. For example, the Click to add title placeholder is designed to be the largest text on the slide; it's the first thing that catches the audience's eyes as they look at your slides. 99

When you create a new slide, you've probably noticed that there are place-holders on each slide that say Click to add title or Click to add text, as shown in Figure 3.1. These placeholders are automatically added to each slide by the AutoLayout you selected. (For more about AutoLayout, review Chapter 2.) Placeholders show you where PowerPoint plans to put your text on the slide.

Fig. 3.1
Placeholders show you where your text will be added.

Placeholders

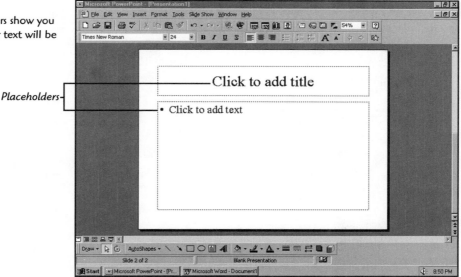

Placeholders help you add text to a slide by directing you to the right place for each type of slide text. They act like a map of the slide by determining where text will be placed and how it will look.

 Q&A *Suppose I don't want to use a placeholder? If I don't replace a placeholder with my own text, will the "Click to add..." message appear on the slide?*

No. A placeholder is just there to help you, not annoy you or force you to add text where it's not necessary. If you choose to ignore a placeholder, it won't be displayed on the slide—no questions asked.

 Placeholders automatically appear on a slide when you click the Insert New Slide button on the Standard toolbar.

 TIP **Text that replaces a placeholder appears in Outline view as well as** in Slide view.

Create your thoughts right on the slide

Take the message `Click to add title` at its word. When you click the message, it turns into an empty text box with a flashing cursor, as shown in Figure 3.2. The flashing cursor indicates that it's waiting for your input.

Fig. 3.2
An empty text box appears when you click the "Click to add ..." message.

The placeholder turns into a text box when you click it— ready for your text!

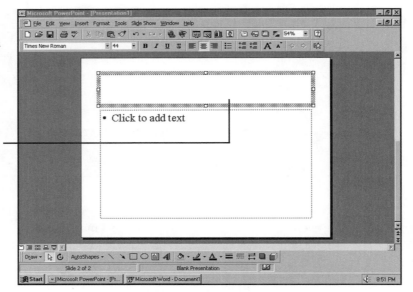

 TIP **Make each slide convey one thought. Your presentation should** move along at a regular pace. Too much text on your slides will frustrate your audience because the last few words will get lost; too little text will bore them and you'll lose their interest.

Add text on a slide

After the placeholders are visible, all you have to do to add text is click the placeholder while you're in Slide view, and type. Follow these steps to add a new slide while in Slide view and replace a placeholder with your own text:

1 Click the New Slide button on the Standard toolbar.

2 Choose an <u>A</u>utoLayout from the New Slide dialog box, then click OK.

3 Click the placeholder you want to replace.

4 Type your text in the placeholder text box.

5 Click anywhere on the slide after your text is entered. (If you press Enter, however, PowerPoint assumes you're entering multiline text and starts a new line.)

Deleting a placeholder

If you're absolutely sure that you're not going to type some text in a placeholder, it's easy to delete the placeholder. Select the empty placeholder and press the Delete key.

If you accidentally delete a placeholder, you can restore it immediately by using the Undo command. To use Undo, click the Undo button on the Standard toolbar. Like magic, the placeholder (and any text it contained) is restored to the slide.

Make your text look attractive

There are three ways to **format** your text so that it stands out. One is to change the **font**, or typeface, of the text. Another way to accent your text is by changing its size. Still another is to change the appearance of the text (by making it bold, for example).

How much text is enough?

It's your job to make the presentation as enjoyable and educational as possible for your viewers. Each slide should be easy to read and understandable so that your audience won't have to guess at the slide's subject.

A presentation is *not* a book review or detailed analysis. Each slide should be clear and concise, and contain short, catchy phrases. You don't want each slide to be covered with text; after a while, the words will all run together in the audience's minds. Remember, if in doubt, leave the extra words out!

Plain English, please!

Formatting sounds impressive, but basically all it means is changing the way characters look. A **font** is a collection of characters that have similar characteristics. For example, all the text in paragraphs in this book use the ITC Century font, while all the paragraph headings use the ITC Highlander font.

Make your text stand out by changing the font

Most of us fall into the font trap—we use too many fonts. You really should limit the number of fonts used on each slide to no more than three. The reason is simple: one font provides information, a second demands attention, and a third font gives extra emphasis. More than three fonts in a slide distracts the audience instead of impressing them.

Take a look at the slide in Figure 3.3. Each bulleted item uses a different font. This may make you feel clever when you design the slide, but it makes the text hard to read and forces the reader to notice the fonts, not the message.

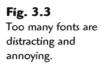

Fig. 3.3
Too many fonts are distracting and annoying.

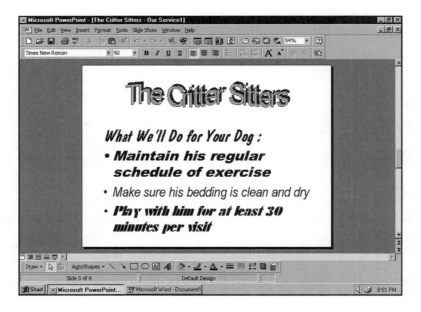

Now, look at the slide in Figure 3.4. The additional font used in the slide adds emphasis and forces you to look at the words "What We'll Do for Your Dog." It's a lot easier to read because it's not distracting. In fact, you probably didn't even notice that more than one font was used.

Fig. 3.4
An additional font used in the slide forces you to look at it.

Using an additional font draws attention to your text

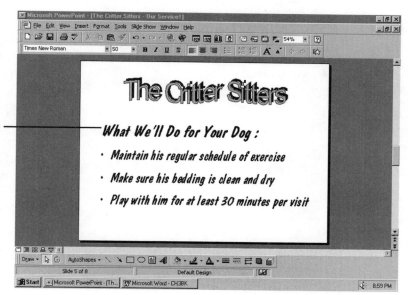

Q&A **Is there a trick to making slides look polished?**

Well, *polish* usually implies professionalism and simplicity. The trick is to use just enough information without looking busy. A polished slide is elegant: it draws your eye to no more than two areas and is easy to read.

Here's how to change the font of slide text using the Formatting toolbar:

1 Make sure the slide containing the text you want to change is in Slide view.

2 Select the text you want to change by double-clicking a single word. If you want to change the font of more than one word, select the text by dragging the mouse over all the text you want to change. (Remember, selected text is highlighted so that it appears to have a dark bar covering it.)

3 Click the arrow next to the font name on the Formatting toolbar. The list of available fonts appears in a pull-down list box as shown in Figure 3.5.

Fig. 3.5
Available fonts can be applied from the Formatting toolbar.

Available fonts vary, depending on which ones have been installed on your computer or printer

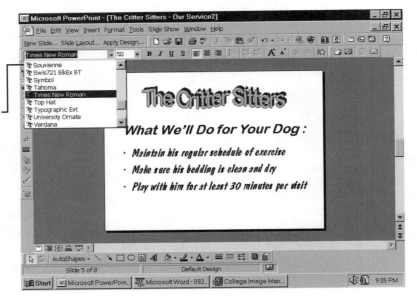

4 Click the font you want to use. The selected text now appears in the new font. You can get a better look at the new font by deselecting the text. Do this by clicking anywhere on the slide.

 **CAUTION** **You might notice that some of the fonts shown in Figure 3.5 are** not on the font list on your computer. Each font that you can use on your computer is available because its software has been installed. No software, no font. That's why a document prepared on one computer might look different when viewed or printed on another computer.

I'd like to emphasize this one word!

Sometimes changing a font might add too much emphasis or be distracting. All you might want to do is change a word's **attributes** by making it bold or underlined.

66 *Plain English, please!*

Attributes refer to cosmetic additions to text, such as making characters look **bold**, *italic*, or <u>underlined</u>. You can add all, some, or no attributes to nearly all fonts. 99

Changing attributes is similar to changing fonts, in that they are both done from the Formatting toolbar. A handy feature of using attributes is that you can always tell which attributes are applied to text by positioning your cursor in the text and looking at the Formatting toolbar.

I always have the impulse to use lots of fonts and attributes on each slide. But too many attributes on a slide just makes it look messy. When designing a slide, less is more! There's an elegance to a slide that contains the right text elements, without looking cluttered.

The following table lists the buttons on the Formatting toolbar that you'll use to apply and remove attributes.

Button	Description	ScreenTip
B	Bolds text	Bold
I	Italicizes text	Italic
U	Underlines text	Underline
S	Adds a shadow to text	Text Shadow

To apply attributes to the text, select the text, then click the button you want to apply. After you click the button, it becomes depressed and the attribute is applied to the text (see Figure 3.6).

Fig. 3.6
Attribute buttons look
like they're pushed in
when they are applied.

Depressed attribute
buttons

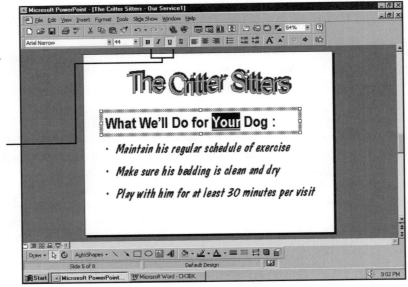

To deselect an attribute, just select the text and click the button again. The
button for an attribute that's turned off no longer looks pushed in.

Copy fonts and attributes with a single stroke!

You can put a lot of time and effort into finding just the right look for your
text. After you've found that look, PowerPoint makes it easy to apply all that
formatting to other text.

To copy fonts and attributes:

1   Make sure the slide containing the text you want to change is in Slide
view.

2   Select the text that has the attributes you want to duplicate.

3   Click the Format Painter button. The pointer changes to a paintbrush,
as shown in Figure 3.7.

Fig. 3.7
Click the Format
Painter button and
the pointer changes.

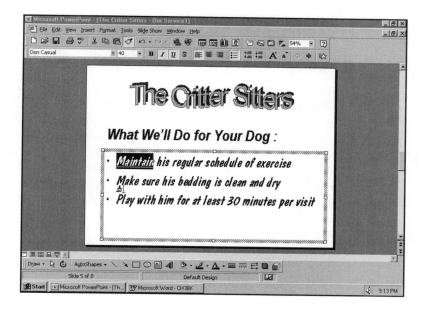

4 Select the text you want "painted" with the new attributes.

After the Format Painter has been used, the pointer returns to normal. You can turn off the Format Painter (without using it) by pressing the Esc key.

 TIP **Format Painter is a valuable PowerPoint tool. It does more than** just copy fonts and attributes—Format Painter copies the complete formatting, including tabs, margins, indents, paragraph alignment, and line spacing. Once you've set the formatting options just the way you like them, use Format Painter to copy those options quickly!

Compose your thoughts in an outline

You might prefer to type your thoughts in an outline format, rather than on the actual slides. When I'm not sure of the direction I want my presentation to take, I like to use the outline method. This lets me concentrate on my thoughts instead of what the slide will look like.

 TIP **If you work best in an orderly setting and like to see your ideas** laid out first, try creating slide text in Outline view. Then, after your outline is finished, you can design the slides in Slide view.

Enter text in an outline list

When you type directly on a slide, you click the placeholder that corresponds with the kind of text you're creating. When you create text in an outline, you don't use any placeholders at all. Rather than having placeholders, outlines have **levels**. Each indentation of text in PowerPoint represents a level, and each slide can have up to five levels.

As you can see in Figure 3.8, the outline shows all the text—including fonts and attributes—for each slide, but no graphics. Remember, even though you can't see graphics on a slide when you're in Outline view, you can tell the slide has a graphic image on it if the icon after the slide number has a small drawing on it.

In Outline view, You can move from slide to slide by clicking the mouse in any text. To edit text, point at the text you'd like to change, then click the mouse to place the I-beam where you want to start typing. (In Outline view, the mouse pointer turns into an I-beam and creates an insertion point when clicked.)

Fig. 3.8
The Outline contains
several levels.

Outline toolbar ———

No graphics are
visible in Outline ———
view

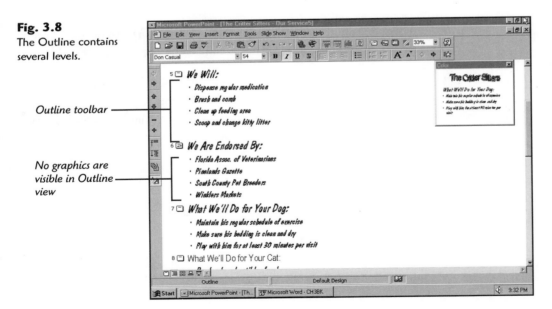

To enter text in an outline:

1 If you're not in Outline view, click the Outline View button.

2 Begin typing when you see the insertion point (the blinking vertical line).

3 To add a new slide beneath the current slide, click the New Slide button.

TIP **If you're creating a new presentation, press the Enter to create a** new slide.

To modify existing text in a slide, create an insertion point in any slide and use the Backspace or Delete keys, or double-click to select any text, then type your new text.

Changing levels

The Outline view has its own toolbar which is displayed whenever you're in that view. Slide levels can be changed using the Outline toolbar or the keyboard. Table 3.1 shows each of the buttons on the Outline toolbar.

Table 3.1 Buttons on the Outline toolbar

Button	Name	What it does
⬅	Promote	Moves selected text to a higher level
➡	Demote	Moves selected text to a lower level
⬆	Move Up	Moves selected text up through the slide sequence
⬇	Move Down	Moves selected text down through the slide sequence
−	Collapse	Hides all text except the title text on the selected slide or slides

continues

Table 3.1 Continued

Button	Name	What it does
➕	Expand	Restores text that has been hidden on the selected slide or slides
⬆≡	Collapse All	Hides all text except the title text on all slides
⬇≡	Expand All	Restores all text that has been collapsed
🗐	Summary Slide	Creates a new slide showing a bulleted list which has been made up of the titles of the selected slides. The Summary Slide is inserted as the first slide in the presentation.
ᴬ𝗔	Shows Formatting	Acts as a toggle to show the formatting of the title and body text. If the toggle is off, text formatting and attributes, like bold or different font typefaces and sizes, are not displayed.

To change the level of text while in Outline view, place the insertion point in the level of text you want to change, then click the appropriate button on the Outline toolbar to increase or decrease the level of the text. The size and placement of the text will change, based on the change you made.

The Microsoft Clip Gallery

I'm not much of an artist—in fact, I have absolutely no talent for drawing or creating artwork. Fortunately, PowerPoint comes with over 1,000 pieces of ready-to-use artwork. This artwork can be found in the Microsoft Clip Gallery, and was installed when PowerPoint was put on your computer (unless you told it not to).

❝ *Plain English, please!*

Each piece of artwork in the PowerPoint Clip Gallery is called **clip art**, and each piece of clip art has the behavior of an individual unit, or **object**. An object is a graphics image, or text, that displays handles when it's selected. While a character is any single piece of text—having the height and width of its font and size, an object can be any size, consist of any number of colors, patterns, and designs, and displays handles when selected. ❞

Inserting clip art from the Clip Gallery

Unless there's a specific piece of artwork I know I want to use—before I even begin creating the presentation—I generally add my artwork *after* the text has been written. Then I can add some visual emphasis to my words.

TIP **I like to think of artwork on a slide as "punctuation" for my words.** An exclamation point, for example, adds punch to a sentence. Greatlooking artwork does the same thing to a slide: it adds punch without distracting from the text.

To open the Microsoft Clip Gallery and insert a graphics image:

1 Make sure that the slide you want to put the clip art on is on the screen and in Slide view.

2 Click the Insert Clip Art button. The Microsoft Clip Gallery 3.0 dialog box opens, as shown in Figure 3.9.

Fig. 3.9
The Microsoft Clip Gallery lets you see a thumbnail of all the clip art in it.

Clip art categories installed on your computer

Thumbnail of artwork in selected category

Clip Art Keywords

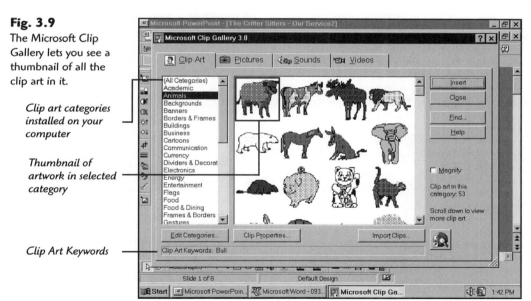

Microsoft Clip Gallery 3.0 is a miniapplication. If you look at the taskbar at the bottom of your screen, you'll see that a button on the taskbar is displayed for the Microsoft Clip Gallery 3.0.

3 The Clip Gallery contains clip art, photographs, sounds, and video. Click the Clip Art tab if it's not already on top.

4 Click a category from the categories list. The default category is All Categories, but you can see a more specific list of images by clicking any of the categories.

5 When you find a piece of artwork you want to use, click it, then click Insert.

6 The clip art is inserted on the slide (see Figure 3.10). Notice that the artwork has **handles** around the perimeter. The artwork probably won't be in the spot you want, and might not even be the right size for your purposes. You'll learn how to move and resize an image later in this chapter.

Fig. 3.10
The thumbnail you selected is placed randomly on the slide.

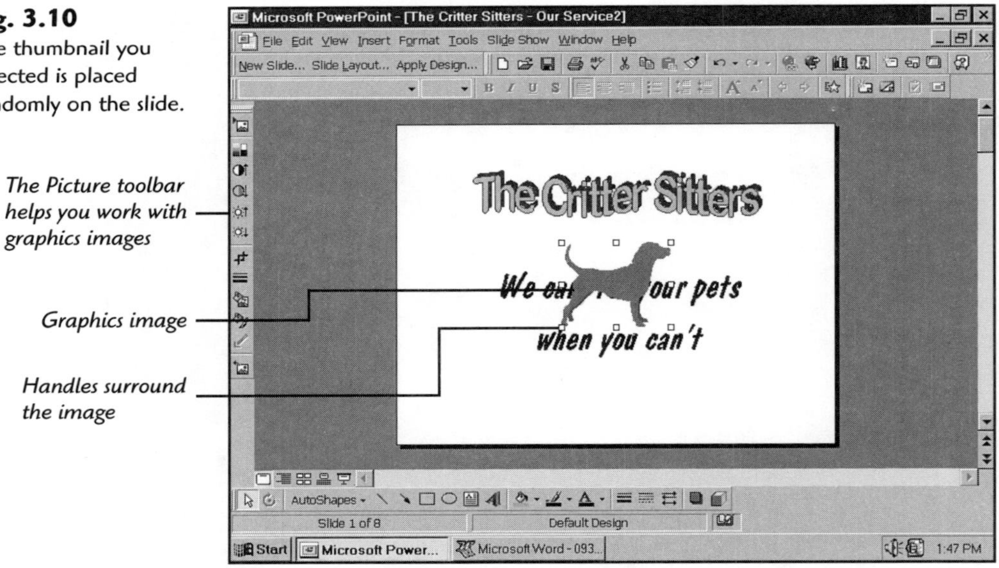

The Picture toolbar helps you work with graphics images

Graphics image

Handles surround the image

66 *Plain English, please!*

When you click a graphics box to select it, small boxes called **handles** surround it. The handles indicate that you can move, resize, or recolor the image. Incidentally, click outside the selected image to deselect it and make the handles disappear. 99

TIP **Anytime you insert clip art or work with graphics images,** PowerPoint automatically opens the Picture toolbar that has buttons just for working with pictures. When you don't need it anymore, you can close the Picture toolbar.

Letting PowerPoint suggest clip art

PowerPoint is so smart, it'll even suggest clip art for you to use. This feature is called AutoClipArt, and based on key words it finds in your slides. It can make clip art suggestions and automatically take you to them in the Clip Gallery.

You can use the AutoClipArt feature while in Slide view by clicking Tools, AutoClipArt. The AutoClipArt dialog box opens. The AutoClipArt feature is indexed to match the theme found in your slide.

Fig. 3.11
The AutoClipArt dialog box lets PowerPoint suggest clip art for your slide.

Click here to view the clip art PowerPoint suggests

Select a word from the pull-down list, then click <u>V</u>iew Clip Art. The Microsoft Clip Gallery dialog box opens and shows suggested clip art. Notice that PowerPoint created a new category of clip art called `Results of Last Find, located` (directly below the [All Categories] category).

You can insert any of these suggested clip art images by clicking the image, then clicking <u>I</u>nsert.

Deleting clip art from a slide

You always can change your mind after you've added a picture to a slide. If you thought adding clip art to a slide was easy, wait until you see how simple it is to delete. First you have to select the clip art.

Clip art, like any graphics image, is selected by clicking once anywhere within it. Regardless of how the clip art looks on the slide, its actual shape—in terms of selecting it—is probably rectangular. When the handles appear around the graphic, press the Delete key or click the Cut button, and the image is deleted.

Q&A *Is pressing the Delete key the same as clicking the Cut button?*

No. It *looks* like they do the same thing, but appearances are deceiving. The Cut button removes whatever is selected and stores it in the Clipboard. That means you can use the Paste button to insert it elsewhere. The Delete key also removes the selection, but doesn't store it anywhere. When you use the Delete key, the selection is really gone (although you could go through the Insert process if you wanted to use it later, or use the Undo feature).

Adding graphics images from a file

Graphics images other than those found in the Microsoft Clip Gallery are referred to as **pictures**. A picture, however, is still a graphics image. You work with pictures the same way you work with clip art.

Follow these steps to insert a picture onto a slide.

1 Make sure that the slide you want to put the picture on is on the screen and in Slide view.

2 Choose Insert, Picture, then choose From File from the submenu menu.

3 (Optional) If the Picture toolbar is visible on the screen, click the Insert Picture from File button.

4 Find the folder where the picture is located on your computer's hard drive. When you find the name of the picture you want to insert, click it. A thumbnail of the picture is displayed, as shown in Figure 3.12.

Fig. 3.12
Find the picture you want to insert on your slide.

The file names are located here

Preview the picture before you insert it

5 Click Insert to insert the picture onto your slide.

Because a picture is a graphics image, it can be deleted (or cut and pasted) by selecting it and then either pressing Delete, or clicking the Cut button.

Adding a graphics image to the Clip Gallery

Suppose you have a corporate logo that you use frequently, or you've had your business card scanned into a graphics image file. Wouldn't it be great if you could add this file to the Clip Gallery? Well, you can.

To add a file to the Clip Gallery, do the following:

1 Click the Insert Clip Art button. The Microsoft Clip Gallery dialog box opens.

2 Click Import Clips. The Add Clip Art to Clip Gallery dialog box opens, as shown in Figure 3.13.

Fig. 3.13
Select the image you
want to add to the
Gallery.

Selected file name

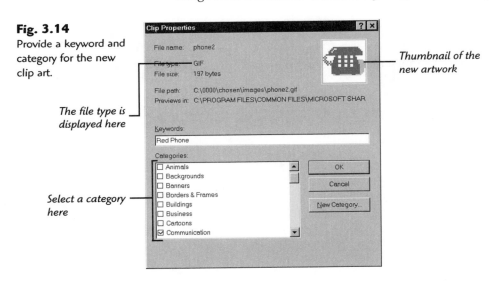

3 Locate the file containing the graphics image you want to add to the Clip Gallery, then click Open.

4 Select a category from the list in the Clip Properties dialog box, as shown in Figure 3.14. Your new clip art is added to this category. Type in a one or two word description of the clip art in the Keywords text box.

You'll see a thumbnail of your new image, as well as its file type. Click OK when you're finished to return to the Microsoft Clip Gallery. The image is now added to the existing images in the category you selected.

Fig. 3.14
Provide a keyword and
category for the new
clip art.

*The file type is
displayed here*

*Thumbnail of the
new artwork*

*Select a category
here*

5 To use the clip art once it's been added, simply select the category to which you added the clip art from the list in the Clip Art dialog box and select the graphic, just as you would any other clip art. (Since it's been added to the Gallery, you can use it immediately or in the future!)

6 To close the Clip Gallery 3.0 dialog box and return to your slide, click the Close button.

Clips from the Web

Microsoft has assembled a huge library of clip art that you can add to your personal clip art collection. The images are located on the World Wide Web on Microsoft's Clip Gallery Live site and must be **downloaded** to the Clip Gallery 3.0 on your computer before you can work with them. These dynamic, exciting images can add snap to your presentation.

66 *Plain English, please!*

Download a file means to copy a file onto your computer from a remote computer, the Internet, or a BBS. You can download all types of files from the World Wide Web. 99

When you download a clip, it's automatically added to the Clip Gallery 3.0 on your computer, along with its preview, search keywords, and browse categories. Because the clip is stored on your hard drive, you don't need to connect to the Internet the next time you want to use it.

Follow these steps to download an image to the Clip Gallery on your computer from Microsoft's Clip Gallery Live.

1 If you're not already connected, connect to your Internet Service Provider. After you're connected, switch back to PowerPoint. (You'll need to be online with PowerPoint as the active application.)

2 Click the Insert Clip Art button. The Microsoft Clip Gallery dialog box opens.

3 Click the Microsoft Internet Explorer shortcut icon. The Connect to Web for More Clip Art dialog box opens, as shown in Figure 3.15.

Fig. 3.15
The Connect to Web for More Clip Art, Photos, Sounds dialog box.

Click OK to continue

4 Click OK to continue. The Microsoft Clip Gallery Live site opens (see Figure 3.16).

 TIP **It's not necessary to have Microsoft Publisher installed on your** computer to download clips from the Web. As long as you're using PowerPoint for Microsoft Office 97, you'll be able to download all the clips without any problem!

Fig. 3.16
The Microsoft Clip Gallery Live Web site.

Click here to view all of the available categories

Click here if you're a first time visitor

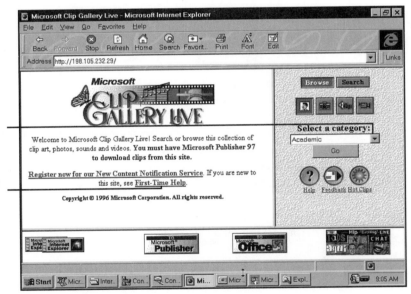

5 Click the drop-down arrow under the words `Select a category:` to view all of the available categories and click the one you'd like to see. When the list closes, click the Go button.

6 After you've chosen a category, browse through the available images until you find the one you'd like. (As it passes over the files, your mouse pointer takes the shape of a hand.)

7 Point to the file you want to add to the Clip Gallery and click the file name. (Take care not to click the preview picture above the file name.)

8 Briefly, the File Download dialog box is visible and then the Internet Explorer dialog box appears, as displayed in Figure 3.17. Choose the option Open and then click OK to continue. The image is added to the Clip Gallery on your computer.

Fig. 3.17
The Internet Explorer dialog box.

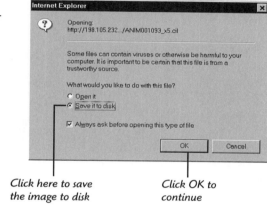

Click here to save the image to disk

Click OK to continue

9 (Optional) Repeat these steps to add additional clips to the Clip Gallery 3.0 on your computer.

10 When you're done adding clips, click the Close box to close Microsoft Internet Explorer and the Clip Gallery Live.

11 When you select the category containing the graphics image, you'll see a thumbnail of the image in the category.

That clip art looks lovely, but can I move it?

Does this remind you of the stereotypical mover saying, "Where do you want it, huh?" No matter where your furniture is placed, you probably want to move it somewhere else. Fortunately, it's a lot easier to move clip art than a couch, and you can do it yourself.

Are all graphics images the same?

All graphics images are not the same; however, they all behave similarly. All graphics images can be selected by clicking once anywhere within the image, and they all display handles once they are selected.

After selected, graphics images can be made larger or smaller and proportionately resized. They also can be cut or copied into the Clipboard for later use in PowerPoint or any other Windows application.

And yet, if you look at the Files Of Type list in the Insert Picture dialog box (refer to Figure 3.12), you'll see a dizzying array of types of graphics images. The file extension indicates the format in which the file was saved. Some of the more commonly used graphics image formats that can be used in PowerPoint are:

.BMP	Windows Bitmap
.EPS	Encapsulated Postscript
.PCT	Macintosh PICT
.PCX	PC Paintbrush

.TIF	Tagged Image Format
.WPG	WordPerfect
.WMF	Windows Metafile
.CGM	Computer Graphics Metafile
.PCD	Kodak Photo CD
.PIC	Lotus 1-2-3 graphics
.CDR	CorelDraw!
.DXT	AutoCAD 2-D files
JPG	Joint Photographic Experts Group (usually used in Internet documents)
.GIF	Graphics Interchange Format (usually used in Internet documents)

There are more graphics image file formats. It's not necessary to know what each one does, but you might want to know if that collection of images you want to purchase can be "understood" by PowerPoint.

To move artwork, just select it, click anywhere within the image, and then drag it to its new location. When you click and drag it, the artwork keeps its same dimensions.

I love the way this looks, I just wish it was smaller

That's usually what happens when I insert clip art from the Gallery: the image always comes in larger or smaller than I want it to be. Use the handles to change the size of an image. If you click and drag any one of the handles, the pointer changes to an arrow that you can drag to make the image larger or smaller.

For example, if you want to narrow an image, click the right middle handle and drag it to the left (see Figure 3.18).

Fig. 3.18
Resize an image by dragging one of its handles.

Resize pointer ——

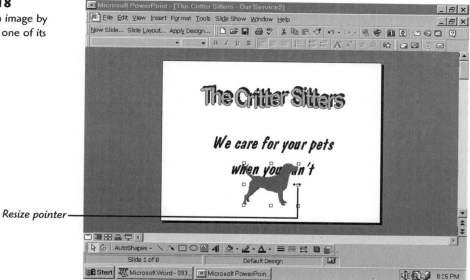

Unfortunately, you can see that our dog now appears quite starved. Dragging the handle far to the right, however, might make him look like he's had too many doggy biscuits.

If you want to change the size of your clip art but *not* the proportions, hold down the Ctrl key as your drag a corner handle. Depending on the original shape of the image, you may notice that as you drag, the outline of the image seems to have a mind of its own. PowerPoint is preventing the image from becoming disproportional. When it reaches a certain size, you might see the outline suddenly jump to a new size.

TIP **There are many other things you can do with clip art and graphics** images such as crop the picture to show only a portion of it, change its color, or rotate and flip it. For more advanced techniques for changing art in your presentation, see Chapter 11.

Using the Slide Master to Give Your Presentation a Consistent Look

● **In this chapter:**

- **What is the Slide Master and what will it do for me?**

- **Can I add my company's logo to each slide?**

- **I'd like to change the background color of my slides**

- **Can I put the date on each slide?**

Want to save time and energy while making sure that every slide in your presentation shows the same artwork, colors, and text styles? Read on . . . . ▸

If you're creating a presentation with just a few slides, you may not be overly concerned with the placement of elements common to each slide, such as your corporate logo, the date the slide was prepared, or the slide number. However, if you want to work on a presentation that contains several slides, it would be a waste of your time and energy to re-create and reposition the same items over and over again.

Fortunately, you don't need to keep repeating the same job—PowerPoint provides an assistant called the Slide Master to keep all of your slides consistent. Every time you create a new presentation, the Slide Master automatically keeps track of common elements on the slides. The Slide Master works hand-in-hand with PowerPoint's AutoLayout feature to make sure your presentation looks professionally designed.

The Slide Master controls the format and position of titles and the main text on your slides, including the font and font size, text color, and even such special effects as shadowing and embossing. You can tell the Slide Master to insert a piece of clip art or a graphics image on each slide. Any change you make to the Slide Master will be reflected on every slide. You can be assured that each slide in the presentation, no matter how few or how many, will share the same formatting.

The Slide Master is the key to your presentation

The Slide Master controls the overall look of your presentation. It holds the formatting for titles and bulleted items. The Slide Master also controls the color scheme of your slides. Using the Slide Master saves me valuable time—if I decide to change the position of the logo on one of the slides, the other slides automatically register the change. Figure 4.1 shows some of the common elements on my presentation that are controlled by the Slide Master.

 TIP There's one major difference between working with regular slides and the Slide Master. When you're working with regular slides, you're concerned about actual text. In the Slide Master, you're concerned only about the formatting of the text, not the words themselves.

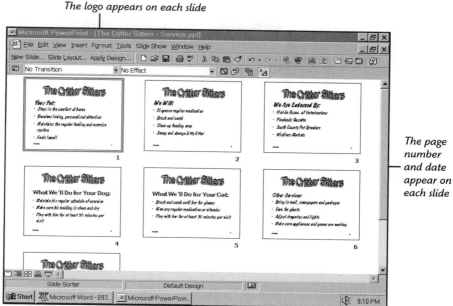

The logo appears on each slide

Fig. 4.1
Elements created in
the Slide Master
appear on every slide
in Slide Sorter view.

The page
number
and date
appear on
each slide

Viewing the Slide Master

The Slide Master looks and acts a lot like a regular slide. Objects (which are
surrounded by handles when they're selected) and placeholders (which are
formatted areas designed to hold text or objects) work the same way they do
on "regular" slides. However, there are a few terms that apply specifically to
areas on the Slide Master (see Figure 4.2), and these are described in the
following table.

Term	What does it mean?
Master title	A formatted placeholder for the slide title (this is also the title area for AutoLayouts)
Master text	A formatted placeholder for the main slide text (this is also the object area for AutoLayouts)
Background items	Any objects added to the Slide Master (other than the master title and master text), such as artwork and colors
Footer area	Formatted placeholder for the date, footer text, and Slide number

Fig. 4.2
The Slide Master contains special areas that don't appear on regular slides.

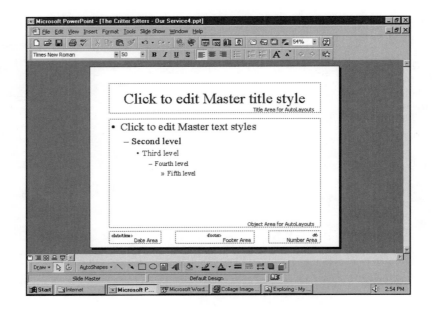

You access the Slide Master from the PowerPoint menu bar. To view the Slide Master, choose View, Master and then select Slide Master from the submenu.

TIP Want to enter the Slide Master quickly? Press and hold the Shift key and click the Slide View button located on the Slide Viewer bar. It's a great way to make a quick change to all your slides as you're designing your presentation.

The Slide Master is displayed, as shown in Figure 4.3. Notice that placeholders appear on the Slide Master just like on individual slides.

Fig. 4.3
The Slide Master contains placeholders for your data.

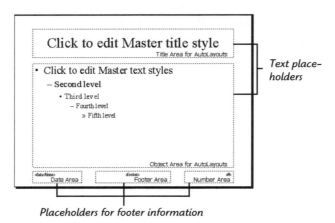

Placeholders for footer information

Think of placeholders on the Slide Master as containers that hold only formatting changes. In a regular slide, when you select a placeholder its text is replaced with any text you type. In the Slide Master, the text that appears in the placeholders when you open the Slide Master refers to styles, rather than text. In the Slide Master, only your formatting changes are recorded; any text you type is ignored.

Using the Slide Master to set the look of your presentation

You can change the look of just about everything on your presentation right from the Slide Master. Notice the different placeholders on the Slide Master screen. Within the placeholders you can change the style and appearance of text. You also can add the date, a footer, and the slide number. Want to change the default design or background color of all your slides? You're in the right place!

 Q&A   ***When is the best time to work with Slide Master?***

The best answer is whenever you want to! If you're working on a well-defined presentation, you can set up the common elements before you create your first slide. On the other hand, in a typical presentation, you'll find that you want to make changes after you've created some slides. Either time is okay...the Slide Master is always available for you. Just remember that changes you make to the Slide Master affect all of the slides in the presentation.

Using a broader perspective

Up until now, you've been working on specific areas within your presentation: a particular slide, placeholder, or word. The Slide Master encourages you to plan the overall look of your presentation.

Because the focus of the Slide Master is continuity, it forces you to think of the big picture. Instead of thinking about how slide 4 looks all by itself, for example, you need to think about how all the slides look as a unit.

You're in complete control of all the elements of the presentation. Here in the Slide Master, you can set the tone—professional, informal, or fun, for example. You also can make any other changes you'd like.

Modifying the default design

It's easy to change the default design of all your slides. Double-click the Default Design area on the PowerPoint status bar at the bottom of the Slide Master screen. The Apply Design dialog box opens, as shown in Figure 4.4.

The master slide templates that are available in the Presentations Designs folder are displayed in the Look In list. As you click each presentation name, a preview image of it appears. When you find the one you like, click the Apply button to use it for all of your slides. The Apply Design dialog box closes and the Slide Master reflects the new design. If you decide not to change the current design of your presentation, click Cancel to return to the Slide Master.

The preview of the selected design is displayed here

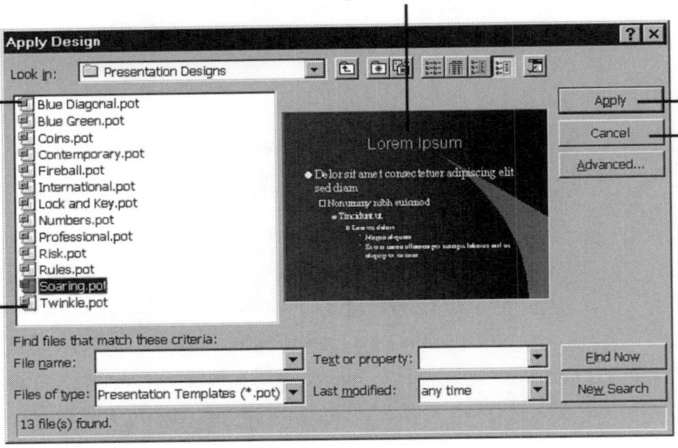

Fig. 4.4
Choose a new Default Design for all the slides from the Apply Design dialog box.

Click here to see a preview of how the design looks

Click here to apply the design

Click here to return to the Slide Master without making a change

Changing text attributes within a placeholder

Text on the Slide Master can have its attributes (such as bold, italic, or underline) changed, just like text on any other slide. The difference is that you're not working with *real* text—just placeholders. Your perspective may be a little different as well.

In a regular slide, you're probably applying attributes to make specific text stand out, such as bolding a word on a single slide. In the Slide Master, you're applying attributes to create a standard, uniform look. You might, for example, want the fifth-level bulleted text to be larger in all your slides.

To apply attributes to text in the Slide Master, click the placeholder you'd like to change. The border changes from dotted to a thick diagonal line, as shown in Figure 4.5.

Fig. 4.5
The placeholder border changes when clicked.

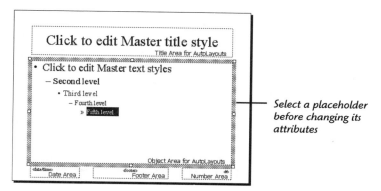

Select a placeholder before changing its attributes

 Select the placeholder text you want to change and click the appropriate text attribute buttons. Click the Slide View button on the Slide Viewer toolbar to see your changes on an actual slide.

Moving or deleting text placeholders

After you've applied text attributes, you might want to change the location or shape of the text box for either the title or text in the slides. Slide Master placeholders are manipulated like text boxes on any other slide.

 TIP **It's a good idea to apply attributes before moving Slide Master** placeholders, or even changing a placeholder's shape. In many cases, just making text bold changes the size of text, as well as the amount of space it takes up.

To move or resize Slide Master placeholders, the Slide Master must be open. Click the text placeholder box you'd like to move. The border changes to a horizontal slashed line. When the pointer is on the border, it changes from an I-beam to an four-headed arrow, as shown in Figure 4.6.

Fig. 4.6
You can move a text box when the pointer is a four-headed arrow.

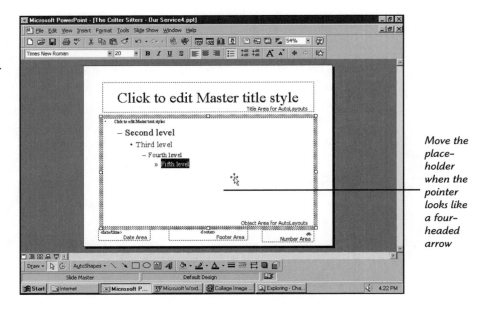

Move the place-holder when the pointer looks like a four-headed arrow

When the pointer looks like a four-headed arrow, drag the text box to its new location.

If you want to resize the box, click the text box border again so the handles are displayed. When the pointer is held over any of the handles, it changes to a double-sided arrow, as shown in Figure 4.7. To resize the box, click and drag the handle to a new location.

You can delete a text box by pressing the Delete key when handles are displayed around the box.

Fig. 4.7
The double-sided arrow means you can resize the box.

Handles

This pointer resizes the placeholder

Press the Esc key, or click anywhere outside the text box to deselect it after you've repositioned or resized the box.

TIP **When you're working with the Slide Master, keep in mind that it** doesn't matter *what* the text says, because any changes to the placeholder text (but not any text attributes) are ignored. What does matter are the placeholder's position and size, and its text box attributes, fonts, and font sizes.

CAUTION **Whenever you work in the Slide Master, always remember that** what you change here will affect all the slides in your presentation.

Adding a company logo on each slide

The Slide Master is perfect for inserting **logos** on slides. By pasting the logo on the Slide Master, you know it'll appear on every slide in exactly the same spot.

 Plain English, please!

A **logo** is artwork that you or your company uses to establish a corporate identity. Some well-known examples of logos are the Nike swoosh, the Coca-Cola script, and the Que imprint.

To add artwork to the Slide Master, you don't have to use menus or buttons. You can use clip art, which comes with PowerPoint, or your own artwork. (See Chapters 3 and 11 for more information about using clip art.) Many companies that have a logo may already have it in electronic form (a graphics file).

You can add a graphics file using the Clip Gallery, or by using the same techniques used to insert a picture. Follow these steps:

1 Open the Slide Master if it's not already open.

2 Choose Insert, Picture, From File to add an independently supplied graphics file. The Insert Picture dialog box opens.

3 Locate the folder containing the graphics file, as shown in Figure 4.8. As you select graphics files, a preview of the artwork is displayed in the preview window.

Fig. 4.8
Insert a logo using the
Insert Picture dialog
box.

*Available graphics
files are listed here*

*A preview of the
selected file appears
here*

4   Click Inse<u>r</u>t. You're returned to the Slide Master, although you may
    briefly see a dialog box telling you PowerPoint is importing a graphics
    file.

5   The graphic appears on the Slide Master with handles surrounding it, as
    shown in Figure 4.9. (The handles mean the graphic is selected.)

Fig. 4.9
A graphics image
displays on the Slide
Master and can be
moved and resized.

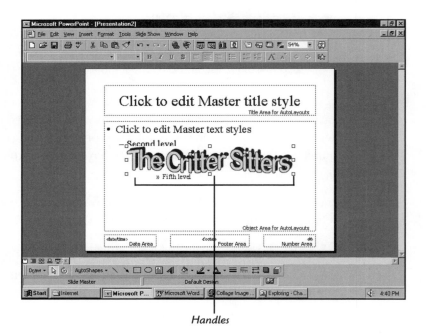

Handles

You can move or resize the image using the same techniques you use when moving or resizing any graphics image (as described in Chapter 3).

Can I change the background color of my slides?

Suppose you're really pleased with your presentation, but you'd like a different background color on your slide. Everything else about the presentation is perfect—all it needs is a different background color to make the slides stand out. That's a minor Slide Master adjustment:

1 Open the Slide Master (if it's not already open) and choose Format, Background from the PowerPoint menu bar. The Background dialog box opens (see Figure 4.10).

2 Click the pull-down arrow and then click More Colors. The Colors dialog box opens, as shown in Figure 4.11.

Fig. 4.10
Use the Background dialog box to change the background color of your slide.

Fig. 4.11
Choose a color from the palette.

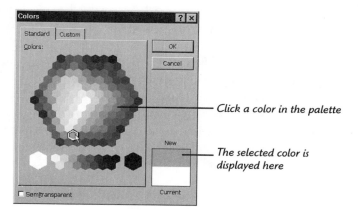

Click a color in the palette

The selected color is displayed here

3 Click a color in the palette, then click OK. Notice that the color appears in the bottom-right corner. You're returned to the Background dialog box, which displays the new color.

4 Click Apply to All or Apply to add the color to all the slides.

TIP **If you want to access the Background dialog box quickly, position** your mouse pointer outside one of the placeholders and click the right mouse button. Choose Background from the resulting shortcut menu to open the Background dialog box.

CAUTION **The Background dialog box contains both an Apply and Apply to** All button. Because you're in the Slide Master, any change you make to the background color will apply to all of the slides in your presentation, no matter which button you choose!

Adding page numbers, dates, and times to your slides

Just like word processing documents, PowerPoint slides can have **headers** and **footers**. Slide headers and footers are located on placeholders in the Slide Master and can contain information such as a page number, the date, or the time. Because this is the type of information that appears on every page, using the Slide Master is ideal.

TIP **Sometimes it's easy to lose your place during the actual presenta-** tion. Adding numbers to your slides can help you focus on your presentation dialogue if you get off-track. Seeing the slide number in the corner reminds you what to say next.

The terms header and footer have a much looser meaning in PowerPoint than in a word processing program. Generally, page numbers, dates, and times are the only uses for headers and footers in PowerPoint. That's because in PowerPoint you can create a text box and put whatever you want in it, and then put the text box wherever you want it. In a word processing program, positions of headers and footers are predetermined and can't be changed.

❝ *Plain English, please!*

A **header** is information that appears at the top of each slide; a **footer** is information that appears at the bottom of each slide. Header or footer information is added to the Slide Master, and appears on each slide. ❞

At first, you might think that numbering slides is silly. After all, it's not like having a bunch of individual 35mm slides that can be dropped on the floor and get completely disorganized. But numbering slides makes a lot of sense: this provides continuity for you and your audience, and can help you regain your focus if you find yourself straying from the subject.

Realizing that numbering slides and adding the date and time are common uses of headers and footers, PowerPoint lets you do both chores at once! The following steps show you how to number your slides and add the date and time:

1 With the Slide Master open, choose <u>V</u>iew, <u>H</u>eader and Footer. The Header and Footer dialog box appears. If it's not in front, click the Slide tab.

2 Click the <u>D</u>ate and Time check box to add the date and time, as shown in Figure 4.12.

Click the <u>U</u>pdate automatically option button if you want the date shown on the slide to always be updated to your computer's current system date. You can click the Fi<u>x</u>ed option button to enter a specific date you'd like displayed, however.

Fig. 4.12
Add page numbers and the date and time in the Header and Footer dialog box.

Click here to display a date and time you choose

Click here to have the date reflect your computer's current system date

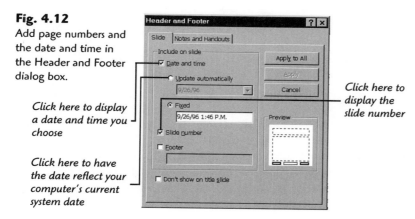

Click here to display the slide number

3 Click the check box for Slide <u>N</u>umber.

4 Click Apply to All to apply your selections to all the slides in your presentation.

When you're returned to the Slide Master, you can modify the placement of these new options by dragging the box to a new location on the Slide Master, just like a text box or graphics image.

TIP **If you're working on several variations of a presentation, placing a** fixed date on your slides is a handy reminder of which version of a presentation you're using. You can always change the date to update automatically before you run the slide show.

5

Adding Graphs and Charts

● **In this chapter:**

● **How many types of charts are there?**

● **I want to create a chart**

● **I'd like to use data that's already in a spreadsheet**

Show your audience what you're talking about! A strategically placed chart can be entertaining and informative. . . . . . ❯

Think back to a presentation you've really enjoyed. What made it worthwhile? It probably had some interesting artwork or special effects, but what really amazed you was that the numbers were presented in a way that made sense. Rather than reading boring rows and columns of numbers, the presentation contained an interesting chart or two that let you see what was being discussed.

Nobody likes to hear numbers; they just rattle around your head like loose change. You need to *show* your audience what you're talking about! A presentation should give the audience something to look at. Using a chart is a good opportunity for you to engage the audience in your topic. If your chart is successful, you should see viewers' heads nodding up and down—indicating that they understand and agree with what your chart says.

What types of charts are available?

For some people, charts are mysterious. Others see charts all the time in their everyday business activities and are used to analyzing them. Most people understand data more easily if shown a chart rather than columns and rows of numbers. Besides, if you show a group of people a chart, they'll get the message you want them to receive. An audience could draw a conclusion you hadn't intended if they're shown only raw numeric data. (Raw data also takes longer to decipher. A chart can be understood almost immediately!)

 Plain English, please!

> A **chart** is a collection of numbers that has been converted into a picture. It is just as accurate as the original numbers, but easier to understand and more fun to look at. Charts and **graphs** refer to the same thing. Microsoft products such as PowerPoint use these terms interchangeably, but prefer the term chart. **"**

PowerPoint offers a range of charts, both two- and three-dimensional. If you are unsure about charts, read on for a refresher.

Getting to know chart types

Charts are grouped into types. Each type has its own distinctive use, although there is overlap. Depending on the point you are trying to make, you'll have to decide which type of chart suits your data. You can use more than one chart type to effectively make a point.

The following table lists the most commonly used charts, whether they are available in a 2D or 3D style, and how they are best used.

Chart type	How is it best used?
Area (2D and 3D)	Illustrates a data trend over time by showing area under a curve.
Bar (2D and 3D)	Shows a relationship between data using horizontal bars.
Column (2D and 3D)	Shows a relationship between data using vertical columns.
Line (2D and 3D)	Shows trends in data over time using lines. This type works well with many series.
Pie (2D and 3D)	Shows how a single element is divided into pieces.
Doughnut (2D)	Shows how more than one element is divided into pieces by placing one doughnut shape in another.

Figure 5.1 shows some of the types of charts available in PowerPoint.

Fig. 5.1
Many 2D and 3D chart types are available.

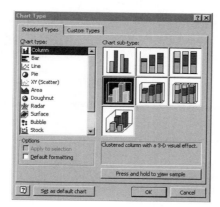

Q&A *How do I know what type of chart to use?*

Before you begin to create your chart, ask yourself what message you want to send to the audience. After your message is defined, think about what type of chart would be most effective. Business expenses, for example, can be shown in a variety of chart formats. You could use a pie chart to show each type of expense as a percentage of all expenses, or you could use a column chart to show each type of expense compared to the other expenses.

Create the chart, then stand back and examine it. Imagine you're seeing the data for the first time. Does this chart convey the message you want to send? If not, try again. It may take several attempts before your chart is just right.

TIP **As a rule, make your chart as large as possible on a slide. After all,** you've created the slide because you want people to look at it, so make it easy for them to see.

Using Microsoft Graph to create a chart

In PowerPoint, you create a chart from scratch (using raw numeric data) right on the slide. All you need are the numbers that will be used to create the chart, and a chart-building utility program called Microsoft Graph.

This powerful miniprogram is installed when you do the standard PowerPoint installation, and is available whenever you need it. In fact, Microsoft Graph is used by other Office 97 programs, not just PowerPoint. When you want to create a chart, you just click one button and enter your data.

CAUTION **Microsoft Graph is a separate program that runs from within** PowerPoint. As you create and edit charts, Microsoft Graph displays its own menus and toolbars that are slightly different from those in PowerPoint.

Charts created in PowerPoint with Microsoft Graph contain fairly simple mathematical formulas. If your chart data contains complex formulas, use a spreadsheet program, such as Microsoft Excel to create your data. However, you'll be able to create most of the charts on your slides in PowerPoint.

By default, Microsoft Graph creates charts that contain enhancements. Examples of these enhancements are **grid lines** (vertical and horizontal lines that make it easy to connect columns or bars with their axis values) and a **legend** (a box that tells you the meaning of colors or patterns used in a chart).

Follow these steps to create a chart using Microsoft Graph:

1 In Slide view, click the Insert Chart button on the Standard toolbar. This button opens the Microsoft Graph datasheet. Your screen should look like Figure 5.2.

Fig. 5.2
Default data appears in the datasheet grid.

Microsoft Graph menu bar and toolbars

Active cell

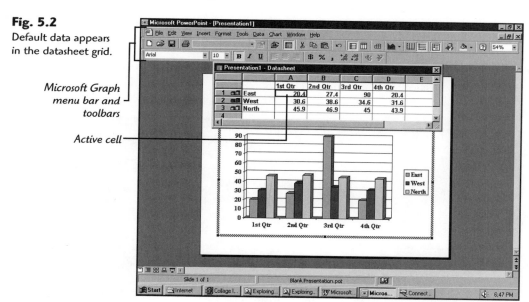

2 Notice that cell A1 has a dark outline. This is the **active cell**; the dark border surrounding the active cell is the **cell pointer**. (The active cell is always surrounded by the cell pointer.) You can move the cell pointer using the arrow keys or by clicking any cell with your mouse.

3 Type your data in the columns and rows in the datasheet. As you type data in the cell, your data replaces the default data, and the chart is created on the slide.

TIP **Want to look at samples of each chart type? From within Micro-**
soft Graph, open the Chart menu and choose Chart Type. Click on a Chart
Type and then a Chart Sub-type to view the different charts you can create.
To see your data in a sample chart, click the Press and Hold to View Sample
button.

4 When you have finished entering the data, click the View Datasheet
button to return to the slide, or click anywhere outside the datasheet
grid. A 3-D column chart with your numbers is displayed on the slide.

5 (Optional) To add a chart title, open the Chart menu and choose Chart
Options. Click the Title tab, type a title in the Chart title text box and
click OK.

6 Press Esc or click anywhere outside the chart to deselect it. Your chart
should look similar to Figure 5.3.

Fig. 5.3
Microsoft Graph
creates a 3D column
chart by default.

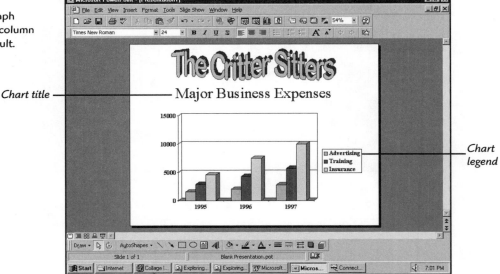

Chart title ——

Chart legend

TIP **After you've created your chart, it becomes an object on your**
slide. A Chart object, like any other graphics object, has handles around
it when it's selected and can be moved, resized, or deleted.

Changing data in a chart

You might have noticed that as you were replacing the default data in the Microsoft Graph datasheet grid with your own, the chart on the slide was being updated. Modifications in the data easily can be made, and your chart automatically reflects those changes.

If you need to change the data in the chart, follow these steps:

1 In Slide view, double-click the chart. The Microsoft Graph program opens and the Graph toolbar is displayed.

2 Click the View Datasheet button. The data you entered is displayed in the grid, as shown in Figure 5.4.

Fig. 5.4
Modify data by retyping entries in cells.

Data in the grid appears dimmed if it's not included in the chart

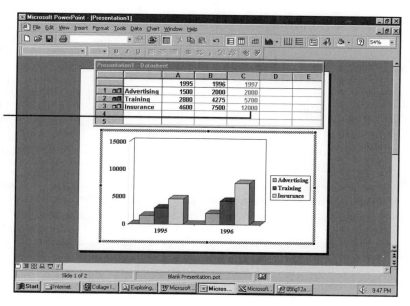

3 Click the cell that you want to modify and retype the text or number.

4 Click the View Datasheet button to see the effect of your changes.

5 Click anywhere outside the chart to return to Slide view.

TIP **You can exclude data in a datasheet for use later. Click the** column or row indicator containing the data, then click Data, Exclude Row/ Col. Data that's dimmed in a datasheet can be included by clicking the column or row indicator containing the data, then clicking Data, Include Row/Col.

Changing the chart type

Changing the chart type is so easy, you'll probably want to experiment with different types just to see how they look. Follow these steps to change the chart type:

1 In Slide view, double-click the chart. The Microsoft Graph program opens and the Graph toolbar is displayed.

2 Click the Chart Type pull-down arrow. All the available chart types are displayed, as shown in Figure 5.5.

Fig. 5.5
Click the Chart Type
button to change a
chart type.

*Select a new
chart type from
these choices*

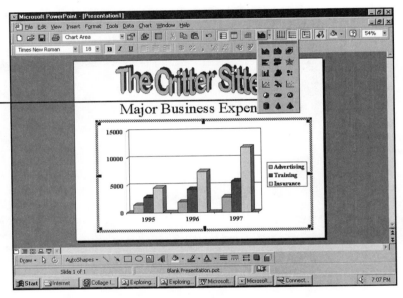

3 Click the chart type you'd like to change to.

4 Click anywhere outside the chart to return to Slide view. Your chart appears in the new format.

Give your charts pizzazz

Creating the chart is only the beginning. It's a rare day when you create a chart and it's perfect from the first moment.

After you've done the hard work of entering the numbers and creating the chart, the next steps are fun. Now you get a chance to be really creative and enhance the chart until you feel it's just right. You may want to change the type of chart; add or correct data; add grid lines, titles, or a legend; or change the colors or orientation of the data. Modifications of Microsoft Graph charts take place within Microsoft Graph.

You've probably noticed that the toolbar in Microsoft Graph is completely different from what you've seen in PowerPoint. Table 5.1 describes the Microsoft Graph buttons.

Some of the Microsoft Graph buttons are **toggles** that turn a feature on and off. (Buttons used to apply formatting attributes, such as bold, italic, and underlining, are also toggles.)

Table 5.1 The Microsoft graph buttons

Button	Description	Toggle
Chart Area	Displays selected area of chart	
	Imports an existing chart	
	Displays the datasheet grid	✓
	Changes the chart orientation to "by row"	
	Changes the chart orientation to "by column"	
	Inserts a data table	✓
	Changes the chart type	✓
	Adds or deletes vertical grid lines	
	Adds or deletes horizontal grid lines	✓
	Adds or deletes a legend	✓

Changing chart colors and patterns

Depending on how your presentation will be viewed, you may want to change some of the colors in your chart. Before changing colors, you need to consider how the charts will be seen, whether they'll be on the World Wide Web or if you'll be printing them on a color or black-and-white printer.

The default colors used in a chart might not be to your liking. Sometimes a stronger color can be an effective way of adding emphasis to a particular data series. To change the colors and patterns in your chart:

1 In Slide view, double-click the chart. The Microsoft Graph program opens and the Graph toolbar is displayed.

2 Click any data series such as a column, bar, or pie slice to select it. The selected data series displays handles.

 3 Click the down arrow next to the Fill Color button. A color palette appears, as shown in Figure 5.6.

Fig. 5.6
Choose a new data series color using the color palette.

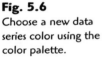

Color palette ——

These handles indicate selected data series

4 Click the color you want to change to.

5 Click F̲ill Effects on the color palette. All the available patterns are displayed.

6 Click the pattern you want to change to.

7 Click anywhere outside the chart to return to Slide view.

If your charts are printed in black and white and are going to be photocopied, consider the quality of your copier. Photocopied items usually appear much darker than the original page. Many times, the duplicating process can alter chart patterns past the point of recognition. Try choosing distinct patterns for series that are close to one another. That way, if the patterns do get blurred, your chart can still be read. Assume your chart will fall victim to a poor copier and plan ahead!

Adding a legend and grid lines

If you changed colors or patterns, you probably did so to make your chart more readable. A legend and vertical and horizontal grid lines also help viewers figure out what's going on in your chart. In chart types where a legend and grid lines are helpful, Microsoft Graph automatically adds them. You can, however, turn them off or insert them using a toggle button on the Graph toolbar.

To turn a legend and grid lines on and off:

1 In Slide view, double-click the chart. The Microsoft Graph program opens and the Graph toolbar is displayed.

 2 Click the Legend button. The legend disappears from the chart.

 3 Click the Horizontal Gridlines button. The horizontal grid lines disappear from the chart, as shown in Figure 5.7.

Click here to toggle the horizontal grid lines on and off

Click here to toggle the legend on and off

Fig. 5.7
The legend and grid lines can be turned on and off from the toolbar.

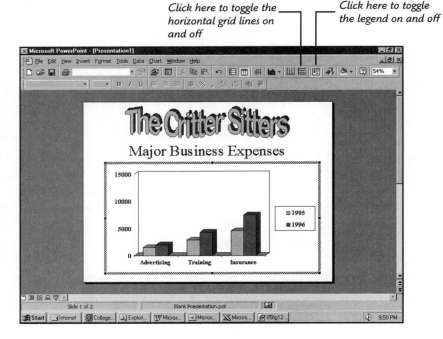

Adding a text box and drawing on a chart

Adding a chart to a presentation always gets people's attention, but if you really want to add pizzazz, try adding text and a drawing to your chart.

To add text to a chart, and then draw an arrow on the chart, follow these steps:

1 In Slide view, double-click the chart. The Microsoft Graph program opens.

2 If the Drawing toolbar is not already visible, click the Drawing button to display the Drawing toolbar.

3 Click the Text Box button. When the mouse pointer is positioned within the chart, it changes to a crosshair.

4 Drag the crosshair in the shape of a rectangle in the spot where you want the text to appear.

5 Type your text.

6 Click the Arrow button, then drag the crosshair pointer from the text to a location on the chart, as shown in Figure 5.8.

Fig. 5.8
Call attention to data in your chart by drawing an arrow on it.

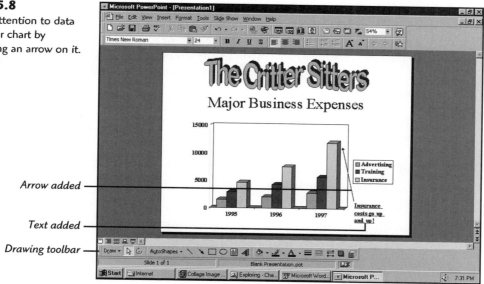

Arrow added ————

Text added ————

Drawing toolbar ————

TIP   **PowerPoint offers makes shortcut menus available when you click** the right-mouse button. Once you're comfortable with creating charts, experiment by placing the mouse pointer in a section of the chart and right-clicking. You may find that right-clicking saves you some time selecting commands available from the menu bar and toolbars.

How do I know if my chart is finished?

Creating a chart is an intangible process, just like creating a presentation! This is an art form: There is no one right answer.

I know my chart is finished when I can look at it completely objectively and draw the right conclusions from it. Learning how to look at your work (whether it's a chart or a slide) objectively is a difficult skill to learn.

If you question your own objectivity, ask a colleague or an innocent bystander for an opinion. Ask them what they think the chart is about. Their answer will tell you if your chart is finished or not.

Most confusion about charts is easy to fix. Usually, you can insert missing information such as who, what, where, or when into the chart and clear up any remaining mysteries.

I already have data in a spreadsheet—can't I use that?

It's quite likely that data you're going to include in a slide may already exist in a spreadsheet. If you already have a spreadsheet file, it would be foolish not to take advantage of it. With Microsoft Graph you can import data from an existing spreadsheet. This saves you time and the possibility of making a data entry error.

When you import data, Microsoft Graph replaces its default entries in the datasheet grid with your file. Here's how to import data into Microsoft Graph:

1 In Slide view, double-click the chart. The Microsoft Graph program opens and the Graph toolbar is displayed.

 2 Drag the mouse over all the default information in the datasheet grid, then click the Cut button. This deletes all the default data.

 3 Click the Import File button.

4 The Import File dialog box opens, as shown in Figure 5.9. If the file you want to import is not visible, change to the drive and folder where the file is located and click the file to select it, then click Open.

Fig. 5.9
Use the Import File dialog box to use an existing spreadsheet file.

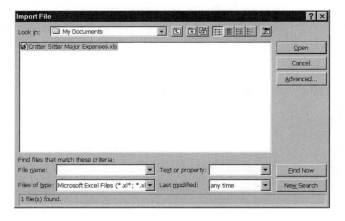

5 From the Import Data Options dialog box, click OK to confirm that the imported data will overwrite the existing data. Your data is displayed in the datasheet grid. (Don't worry if a series of pound signs (#########) is displayed in the cells. The data is there, the cells are just too narrow to show it all.)

6 Delete any nonessential imported data by clicking the column or row buttons, then choosing <u>E</u>dit, <u>D</u>elete.

 7 Click the View Datasheet button to return to the chart.

 TIP **It's easy to use your mouse to widen or narrow any column in your** datasheet. For the column you want to change, position the mouse pointer on the right side of the column heading and drag the border until the column is the width you want. When you release the mouse button, the column is resized.

I'd like to create an Excel worksheet in my slide

Microsoft Graph is a wonderful tool for creating quick and dirty spreadsheets that have no calculations. But perhaps your data will change. If so, what you really need to do is create a Microsoft Excel worksheet right in your slide.

 Add an Excel worksheet to your active slide by clicking the Insert Microsoft Excel Worksheet button on the Standard toolbar. In the grid that appears, select the approximate number of columns and rows you want in your worksheet. You can always make the worksheet larger or smaller; this initial step only effects the size of the worksheet window when it opens.

When you release the mouse button, the Excel program opens and a worksheet appears. Notice how the menu bar and toolbars have changed; this lets you know that Excel is now open. The worksheet has handles, which means it can be resized and moved just like any object. (See Chapter 3 to review how to move and resize an object.)

Figure 5.10 shows an Excel worksheet in a PowerPoint slide. The worksheet contains data and uses all of the properties and features found in Microsoft Excel. That means you can have formulas as well as charts!

When you're finished with the worksheet, click anywhere on the slide to return to PowerPoint.

Fig. 5.10
An Excel worksheet in PowerPoint uses all of Excel's features.

The formula adds numbers in a column

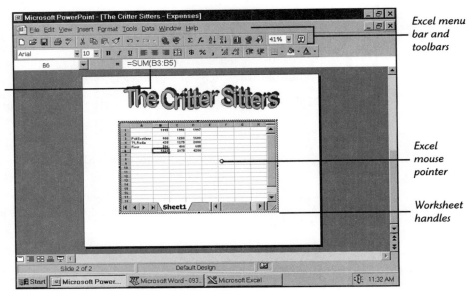

Excel menu bar and toolbars

Excel mouse pointer

Worksheet handles

TIP **You can only add or open an Excel worksheet on a slide if** Microsoft Excel has been installed on your computer.

How can I modify or delete the worksheet?

Double-click an Excel worksheet on a PowerPoint slide to open it so you can make editing changes. If you want to delete the worksheet once it's visible on the screen, select it, and then press Delete to delete the worksheet.

TIP **To learn more about Excel, Using Excel for** *Office 97,* published by Que, is an excellent reference.

6

Creating Organization Charts

● **In this chapter:**

- How do I create an org chart?

- I've got an org chart that needs a few changes

- How can I use drawing tools in my org chart?

- I'd like to use an existing org chart on a slide

PowerPoint lets you create or modify org charts with the click of a button! . . . .➤

Every organization with more than one person in it wants an organizational chart, or org chart for short. Before I used PowerPoint, the very thought of having to create or modify an org chart filled me with dread.

In a presentation, an org chart can be used to show your audience where each position fits in the corporate hierarchy. Even though your presentation may focus on a small area within a company, it can be helpful for your audience to know how a few positions relate to others in an organization.

PowerPoint makes it easy to create or modify an **org chart**. You can even put it on a slide.

66 *Plain English, please!*

An **org chart** is a map of relationships within an organization that shows how positions fit into that organization's structure. Although not every job needs to be included in an org chart, the chart generally lists an organization's key players and whom they report to. An org chart is used to define the chain of command within an organization—whether it's for a large corporation or a small group or department in a company. 99

What do I use to create an org chart?

In Chapter 5 you used Microsoft Graph to create a chart. Here you learn how to use Microsoft Organization Chart to create an org chart. This is a program that operates in PowerPoint, as well as Word and Excel, similar to Microsoft Graph. Figure 6.1 shows a sample of the type of org chart you can create.

Fig. 6.1
This org chart was
created using
PowerPoint.

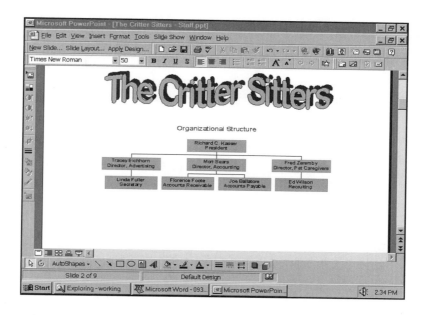

What's an org chart all about?

Any org chart illustrates the corporate structure. It displays the relationships between positions—between you and your boss, you and your coworkers, or even your boss and his boss. Although a PowerPoint org chart doesn't get highly technical in its terminology, it does use more descriptive terms than "boss" and "the person who works with me."

The **primary box**, the one with the highest position in the org chart, generally belongs to an organization's Chief Executive Officer. There can be a great deal of overlap in the types of people found beneath that most powerful person, but basically, beneath that primary box is everyone else!

"Everyone else" includes **managers**, who have employees (**subordinates**) working for them.

Subordinates also can have employees working for them, and they also can have staff who might share responsibilities and tasks, called **coworkers**. (An employee's job title and position on the corporate ladder can vary from one organization to another. One company's manager could be another company's coworker. It all depends on how positions are defined within the organization.)

Types of org chart positions also determine how much information should be added about a particular position. Manager positions include space for the manager's name and another line for the manager's official title. So, while it would be important to list titles for managers, it might not be important to include titles for all the coworkers within that department.

Creating an org chart

You can create an org chart by choosing the Organizational Chart from AutoLayout as you're inserting a new slide. When you create a PowerPoint org chart, you're the boss! PowerPoint takes direction from you and performs the most difficult of tasks—arranging the boxes.

TIP   **You might want to spend a few minutes drawing the org chart on** paper before you create it in PowerPoint. After you have the basic org chart sketched out, your drawing can serve as a map to help you get started.

To create an org chart:

1 In Slide view, click the New Slide button on the Standard toolbar. The New Slide dialog box appears, showing all of the available AutoLayouts.

2 Choose the Organization Chart AutoLayout. Figure 6.2 shows the new slide. Double-click the box to create the org chart.

Fig. 6.2
The AutoLayout
Organizational Chart.

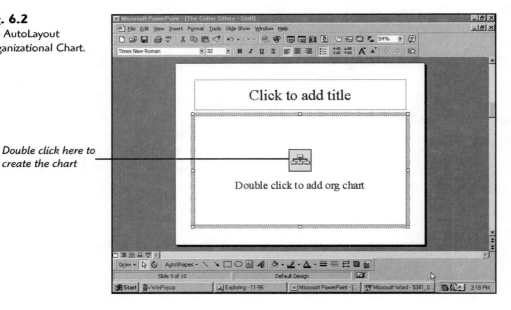

Double click here to create the chart

The Microsoft Organization Chart window opens (see the next section "Components of an org chart"). Notice that the primary box—occupied by the highest-level person in the organization—is already selected. When boxes are added to an org chart, they initially contain **placeholders**, just like the text boxes found on a new slide where you add a title or text.

TIP **The Org Chart program, unlike Microsoft Graph, opens in its own** window. That's because Org Chart is a separate application (called an applet) shared by other Office 97 programs. After the program is open, you can press the F1 key to access on-screen help on org charts. You also can use the Minimize or Maximize buttons to the right of the Microsoft Organization Chart title to resize window.

3 Type information in the selected box. With your first keystroke, the placeholder information changes, leaving room for a name, title, and two comment lines.

Press the up-or-down arrow key or the Tab key to move from entering the name to the title placeholder or comment lines.

4 When you're finished with a box, press Esc to accept it, or click another box.

5 Repeat steps 3 and 4 until all the boxes have information in them.

6 Select the words Chart Title and type the title for your chart. (As soon as you press a key, the title you type replaces the selected type.) Alternatively, if you don't want a chart title to appear on the slide, press Del after you've selected the words Chart Title.

7 Choose File, Update (the name of your presentation). For example, if your presentation is called "The Critter Sitters - Staff," you'd choose File, Update (The Critter Sitters - Staff:).

8 Return to your slide by choosing File, Close and Return to (the name of your presentation). Again, the name of your presentation appears in this command. (Using the example in step 6, this command would appear as Close and Return to (The Critter Sitters- Staff).

Components of an org chart

The Microsoft Organization Chart toolbar lets you add different types of positions to the chart. Click the type of position you're adding, then click the placeholder where you want to add the information.

The Org Chart window opens on top of the PowerPoint window.

Microsoft Organization Chart menu contains its own commands.

Replace "Chart Title" with what you want to call the chart.

The first line of the active placeholder for an employee and position is selected. When you start typing, this text box is replaced.

Here's a placeholder for information you'll add.

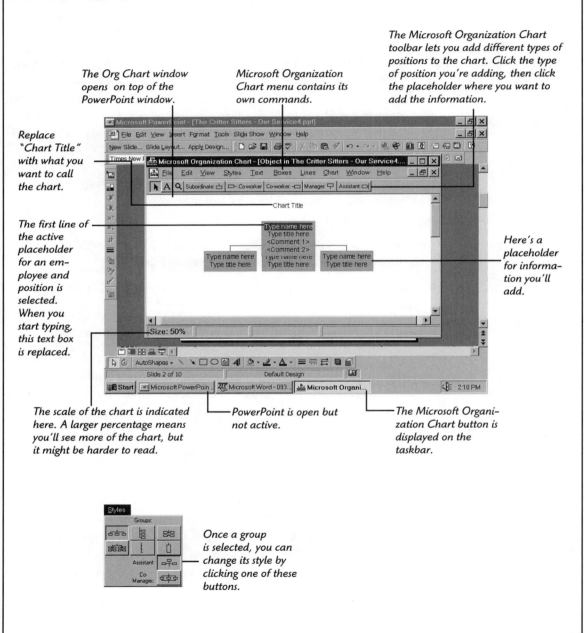

The scale of the chart is indicated here. A larger percentage means you'll see more of the chart, but it might be harder to read.

PowerPoint is open but not active.

The Microsoft Organization Chart button is displayed on the taskbar.

Once a group is selected, you can change its style by clicking one of these buttons.

Q&A ***When I double-clicked the org chart on my new slide, Microsoft Organization Chart program didn't appear. What did I do wrong?***

Well, there are probably two reasons that the Microsoft Organization Chart program didn't come up. The first one is usually the cause—the Microsoft Organization Chart program is already running. Check to see if the program is open by looking for the Microsoft Organization Chart button on the taskbar or press Alt+Tab to cycle through all of the open programs in your computer. If Microsoft Organization Chart's already open, just switch to it.

The second reason that Microsoft Organization Chart didn't open is less likely. Perhaps you performed a Custom installation of Office 97 and chose not to install Microsoft Organization Chart when you installed PowerPoint. Run the PowerPoint setup program to install Microsoft Organization Chart. You'll be on your way to creating professional org charts in minutes.

Making changes to an org chart

After you've created your org chart, you'll probably want to make changes to it. You may need to add or delete boxes. Each of the boxes in the chart represents a relationship between positions, and those relationships have a way of changing.

Relationships in an org chart

In any organization, positions are related to each other. Responsibilities and authority flow down from the top position to the lowest job. For example, in the case of The Critter Sitters, Mort Sears, the Director of Accounting, reports to Richard Kasser, the company's President. In turn, two employees report to Mr. Sears. Microsoft Organization Chart enables you to identify the **relationships** between the positions.

The following table shows the relationships that can exist in an org chart and the Microsoft Organization Chart toolbar buttons you can use to create them.

Button	Relationship
Subordinate:	Attaches to another box on the chart.
:Co-worker	Attaches to the left of another box at the same level.
Co-worker:	Attaches to the right of another box at the same level.
Manager:	Inserts a manager's box above an existing box.
Assistant:	Attaches to a manager or other existing box.

Adding or deleting a relationship box in an org chart

Microsoft never expected every organization to be exactly like the default org chart that initially opens. You can easily add or delete boxes as you see fit. The following steps show you how to add a box.

1 In Slide view, double-click the existing org chart to open Microsoft Organization Chart.

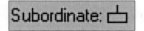

2 Add a new subordinate by clicking the Subordinate button. The Subordinate button becomes depressed and the pointer changes to the Subordinate symbol, as shown in Figure 6.3.

3 Position the mouse pointer on the box you'd like the new relationship attached to, and click. For example, if you want to add a subordinate to Ms. Foote in Figure 6.3, click the Subordinate button, then click Ms. Foote's box. Type the new information. Your results should look like Figure 6.4.

4 Type the information in the new box.

5 Choose File, Update (the name of your presentation). (Remember, the name of your presentation appears in this command.) This saves your new changes and updates the org chart already on the slide.

6 Return to your slide by clicking File, Close and Return to (the name of your presentation).

Fig. 6.3
Adding boxes to an organization chart.

Click this button to add a subordinate

The mouse pointer changes to the symbol of the new addition

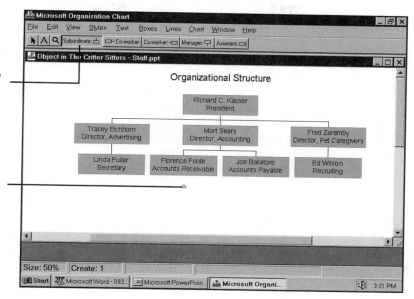

Fig. 6.4
Add a relationship box by clicking the box the addition is added to and type in the new information.

This new addition is a subordinate of Ms. Foote

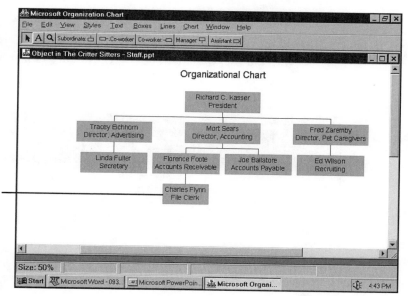

To delete a relationship while in Microsoft Organization Chart, select the relationship box and press the Del key. Choose File, Update (the name of your presentation), to save the change.

CAUTION   **If you're going to delete a box *and* its subordinates (those people** listed beneath who are directly related), delete the subordinates first. If you don't, Microsoft Organization Chart assumes the subordinates will move up in rank.

Seeing the big picture

Have you ever worked on a computer project so big that it not only didn't all fit on the screen at once, but made you feel lost and disoriented? Unless you have a monitor the size of a movie screen, this can happen when you're working on an org chart.

The following steps show you how you can reestablish your perspective and focus on individual areas in your org chart:

1 In Slide view, double-click the existing org chart to open Microsoft Organization Chart.

2 Choose View,Size To Window. The org chart appears , almost like a print preview, as shown in Figure 6.5.

3 From the View menu, Choose 200% Of Actual if you want a magnified view of part of your chart, or 50% Of Actual to see more of the chart on your screen.

Fig. 6.5
When sized to a window, a mini-version of the chart is displayed.

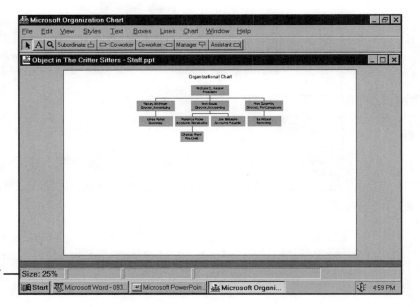

The scale automati-cally changes

TIP **To zoom in to a specific relationship in an org chart, select its box** *before* you enlarge the chart. Otherwise, you might wind up on the opposite end of the chart than what you wanted.

 Q&A *I want to keep checking my chart. Is there a quick way I can see all of it without using the menus?*

It's quicker to use the function keys to change the size of the chart on your screen. To see all of the chart, press F9 (<u>S</u>ize To Window); press F10 for <u>5</u>0% Of Actual; press F11 for <u>A</u>ctual Size; and press F12 for <u>2</u>00% Of Actual. Just remember that you may need to use your vertical and horizontal scroll bars to adjust the position of the chart.

Changing a chart's style

The style of an org chart is important. Org chart styles suggest the types of relationships that exist in a particular arrangement of boxes. You might want to change the style of a position's box that has another position reporting to it, for example.

Suppose three people work for you doing a variety of tasks, but each one of those people works independently within the group and reports directly to you. You might choose a different style for this chart than the next scenario: three people working together in a group, working with one another to get those tasks finished and reporting to you as a group. You can use different styles in the org chart to indicate the relationships within the group and their manager.

Plain English, please!

In an org chart, a **style** refers to the arrangement of boxes, or relationships.

Some companies never change their relationships, others undergo restructuring periodically. Regardless of the reasons, it's important to know how to change relationship styles.

To make changes to the relationships:

1 In Slide view, double-click the existing org chart to open Microsoft Organization Chart.

2 Hold down the Shift key and select a group of boxes whose style you want to change by clicking each one.

3 Choose the Styles menu and click the style you want to use. The new style is applied to the selected group, as shown in Figure 6.6.

Fig. 6.6
How a relationship is displayed can be changed with the click of a button.

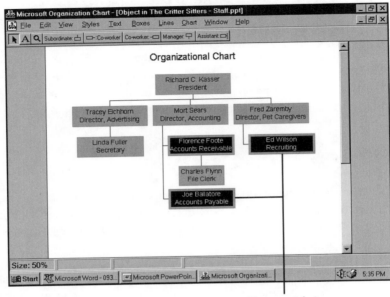

The new style is applied here

4 Click File, Update (the name of your presentation).

5 Return to your slide by clicking File, Exit and Close to (the name of your presentation).

 TIP **It's easy to move up the corporate ladder with Microsoft Organi-zation Chart!** If you need to move one box, click it and, while the mouse button is depressed, drag the box over its new manager or coworker and release the mouse button. Voila! The relationship is updated.

Draw on an org chart to add emphasis

Tools on the Drawing toolbar can be used to call attention to items on an org chart. The items you draw literally "float" on top of the org chart, because the chart is actually an object on your slide. (Information on objects is covered in Chapter 3.)

To use the Drawing toolbar, you need to be in Slide view, but the org chart *should not* be selected. (The Drawing toolbar is automatically displayed when you're in Slide view.) Choose a button from the Drawing toolbar, click the slide, and drag any shape, such as an arrow. (For more on using the Drawing toolbar, see Chapter 11.)

Add any text by clicking the Text Tool button on the Drawing toolbar. Your finished chart might look like the one shown in Figure 6.7.

Fig. 6.7
Use the tools on the Drawing toolbar to enhance an org chart.

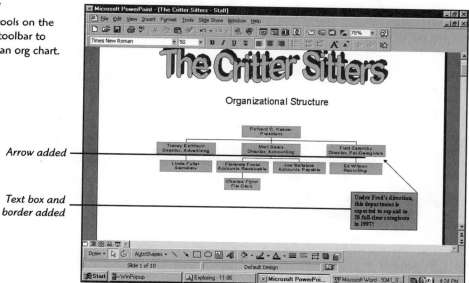
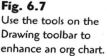

Can I use an existing org chart in my presentation?

There's never any good reason to reinvent the wheel. If you've got an existing org chart created in another program, or from a scanned image, take advantage of it!

To add an existing org chart to a slide:

1 In Slide view, choose Insert, Object.

2 Click the Create From File radio button. The Insert Object dialog box changes to allow you to define the file, as shown in Figure 6.8.

Fig. 6.8
Insert an existing org chart file using the Insert Object dialog box.

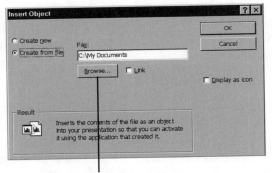

Click here to browse through the available folders and files

3 Type the file name in the File text box, then click OK.

4 Your file appears on the slide. To move or resize the object, select it and you can move it just like any other object.

TIP **If you can't remember the exact name and location of the object** you're inserting when the Insert Object dialog box is open, click the Browse button. Look through the folders and files on your computer until you find the right one, then click it to insert it.

7

Creating Attractive Tables

● In this chapter:

- When should I use a table?

- How can I create a table?

- I need to add a row to this table

- How do I add formatting and borders?

If you've ever thought it was impossible to align text using the Tab key or spacebar, you'll love PowerPoint's handy table feature!. . . . . ▶

Slides don't usually contain large amounts of text, like documents. When there is text, it's generally in the form of bulleted, indented items. Sometimes, however, you need text in a tabular form. Similar to a spreadsheet, but not quite. Similar to bulleted items, but not quite.

In this chapter, you'll learn how to create tables on slides that give you the flexibility you need to get your message across.

 TIP   **The table feature is only available in PowerPoint if Word is also** installed on your computer.

Some tips on when to use a table

I'm sure the situation seems familiar. You carefully arrange the text with tabs placed every three or four words so the words look like they're in columns. Of course, then you realize that you've forgotten a word, and when you add it, the text shifts in weird positions all over the slide.

 Plain English, please!

A **table** is an arrangement of text and/or numbers neatly arranged in columns and rows. A table is handy to use when you have text or numbers you want aligned side by side, or one above the other. Each box in the table is called a **cell**. Cells automatically grow to accommodate any information you put in them. **"**

Trying to get your text lined up properly using the Tab key or the spacebar is a thankless job. If you want text arranged in multiple columns, with neat margins in between each column, as in Figure 7.1, take the easy route and place text in a table.

Fig. 7.1
A table lets
you arrange
your information
neatly.

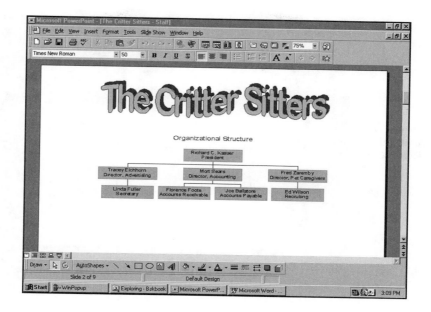

One-button table creation

Like everything else in PowerPoint, it's simple to create a table. In fact, you can create a table by clicking one button! PowerPoint's Insert Microsoft Word Table button lets you create a multi-column, multi-row table. The following steps show you how to create a table using the Insert Word Table button.

1 In Slide view, click the Insert Word Table button on the Standard toolbar. This button opens the table grid, as shown in Figure 7.2.

Each box in the table grid represents a cell in the table. As you drag your mouse over the cells in the grid, the dimensions of the table are displayed at the bottom of the grid. If you want your table to have four rows and three columns, for example, it should say 4×3 in the area below the grid.

Q&A *How come nothing happens when I try to click the Insert Word Table button?*

Even though the Insert Word Table button appears on your toolbar, this feature won't work unless Microsoft Word is also installed on your computer. The easiest fix for this problem is to install Word.

Fig. 7.2
Define the table's
dimensions using the
table grid.

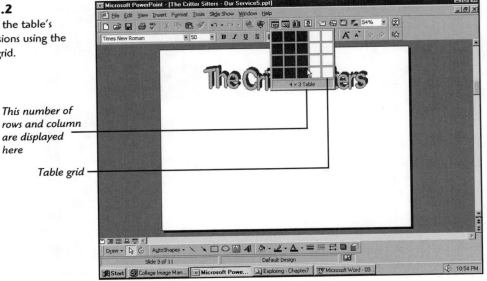

This number of
rows and column
are displayed
here

Table grid

2 Drag from the upper-left corner of the table grid until the correct number of columns and rows is selected, then release the mouse button.

3 In a moment or two, PowerPoint opens a new Microsoft Word table on the slide. Notice that the toolbars change to Microsoft Word, even though your title bar still says Microsoft PowerPoint.

4 Type your text in each cell in the table (see Figure 7.3). (Don't worry if the text in a cell doesn't fit and wraps around to the next line. We'll fix that later.)

You can move around the table by clicking in each cell, or you can press the Tab key to move from cell to cell (from left to right). Pressing the Enter key creates a hard return within a cell; it does not advance to the next cell.

5 Close the table by clicking anywhere outside the table. Notice that the PowerPoint toolbars return to the slide.

6 When handles appear around the table, click outside the table again.

TIP **Keep your table text short and clear. Remember, the text should** just give your viewers the essence of your ideas. During the presentation, you'll be able to expand on each item, if necessary.

Fig. 7.3
Microsoft Word toolbars are displayed as you're creating a new table.

Microsoft Word menu and toolbars

Word table on a PowerPoint slide

Microsoft PowerPoint title bar

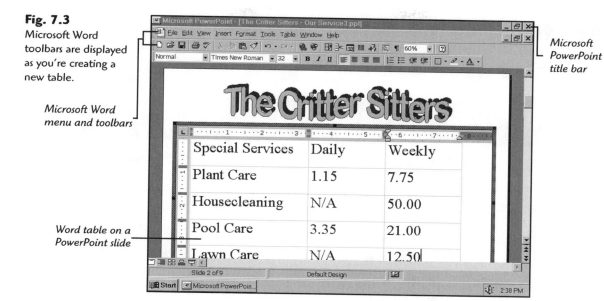

Tables are great organizers

A table can be more than just a collection of rows and columns that keep words from running into one another.

With very little effort, you can further organize the information collected in a table to make it even easier to find. For example, suppose you have a table that lists the names of the sales-people in your firm. It would be nice if those names were in alphabetical order, but you probably didn't think of that when you originally entered their names. No matter—the solution is simple. Just tell PowerPoint to **sort** the data, or arrange it in a different order. Table information can be sorted according to information in any column, and it can be sorted alphabetically or numerically in ascending or descending order. (**Ascending** order means from A to Z or 0 to 9; **descending** order means from Z to A or 9 to 0.)

This means that a table can work for you—you can input your data in any order you want because it can be organized later.

Your information can be sorted by as many as three columns, or **variables**. For example, you could sort by a salesperson's district, last name, and amount of his sales. You can change the sort order (ascending or descending) of any of the variables.

Data in a table can be sorted once it is active (meaning you've double-clicked it and the menu bar and toolbars for Word are displayed). Click Table, Sort, then choose the columns you want to sort by and whether you want them arranged in ascending or descending order. Click OK when your selections are complete, and your table will be rearranged to your specifications.

Modifying an existing table

You've created your chart, and now you'd like to add another column or row. Or maybe your table has the correct number of columns and rows, but you want the columns to have different widths.

Adding and deleting rows and columns

Adding and deleting columns and rows is a breeze! By pointing to the columns or rows you want to add or delete, and then selecting a command from the Table menu, you can change the dimensions of your table.

To add columns to a table:

1 Double-click the table. The toolbars revert to Microsoft Word, just as when you created the table.

2 Add one or more columns by positioning the mouse above a column. When the mouse pointer looks like a vertical arrow pointing down, as in Figure 7.4, click to select the column.

3 Select (highlight) the number of columns you want to add. If you want to add three columns, for example, just select three columns.

Fig. 7.4
Select a column before adding a new one.

Pointer that selects a column

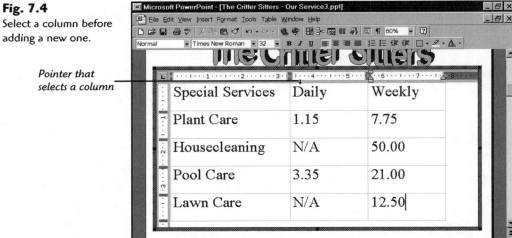

4 Choose Table, Insert Columns. The new column(s) are inserted to the left of the selected column(s).

The simplest way to add a row to the end of a table is to put the mouse in the bottom-right cell of the table, then press the Tab key. To add a row in the middle of a table, click a cell in the row below where you'd like to add a row, then choose Table, Insert Rows.

To delete rows or columns, select the unwanted rows or columns, then choose Table, Delete Cells, and then Delete Entire Row or Delete Entire Column.

When you've finished editing your rows and columns, close the table by clicking anywhere outside the table.

Can I change the width of a column or the height of a row?

It's just as easy to change a column's width or a row's height as it is to add and delete columns and rows.

- Change a column's width by dragging the mouse pointer when it's positioned on the table ruler between two columns, as shown in Figure 7.5. As you drag the column border, you'll see the table ruler and the column width change. When you release the mouse button, the change takes effect.

- Change a row's height by dragging the mouse pointer when it's positioned on the ruler between two rows.

TIP **You can automatically size a column to its widest entry by** selecting a column, then double-clicking on the column marker between two columns. Click the AutoFit button in the Cell Height and Width dialog box, then click OK.

TIP **After you've played with column widths and row heights, you** might want to make them all the same, standard size. No problem. Simply select the rows or columns you want to adjust and choose Table, Distribute Rows Evenly or Table, Distribute Columns Evenly. Like magic, the size is perfectly set for you.

Fig. 7.5
Use the mouse to change a column's width.

Pointer that changes column width

Original width

New width

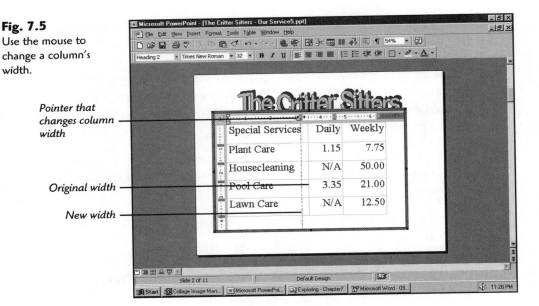

Changing the alignment of text and numbers in the columns

You may have noticed that the Microsoft Word Formatting toolbar contains alignment buttons (left, right, center, and justify).

To change the alignment of a single cell, click anywhere in that cell, then click the appropriate alignment button. To change the alignment of an entire column, select the column to be changed (the way you did when you were going to add or delete a column), then click the appropriate alignment button. Figure 7.6 shows a column's alignment being changed.

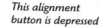

This alignment
button is depressed

Fig. 7.6
Use the buttons on
the Microsoft Word
Formatting toolbar to
change a column's
alignment.

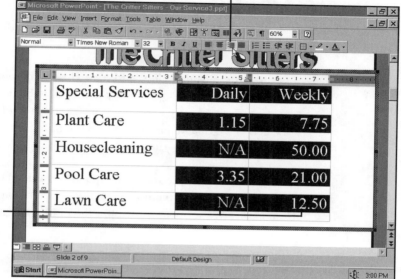

These columns
are selected

Enhancing your table's appearance

So, you've added your table, gotten your column widths and row heights just
right, but the table still doesn't generate any excitement? Read on for some
tricks you can use to make plain tables come to life!

Later in this chapter, you'll see how you can use Microsoft PowerPoint's
Table AutoFormat feature. This feature gives you "one-stop shopping" for
table formatting: Depending on which format you choose, it'll add colors,
borders, and attributes. Remember, however, that the Table AutoFormat
feature won't work unless Word is installed on your computer.

My table looks so boring...how can I dress it up?

You can use formatting attributes (like bold, italic, and underline) or insert borders to liven up your table.

TIP **Formatting a table is like adding a cherry to your hot fudge** sundae—you know, saving the "good stuff" for last. But remember, a table's content should be more important than its appearance! Leaving formatting for the end of the creative process can help you tie in all the tables in your presentation together by using the same formatting techniques in all the tables.

To add formatting attributes, open the table by double-clicking it, select any word in the table you want to emphasize, then click the appropriate formatting button. Figure 7.7 shows a table with the bold attribute added to several words.

Fig. 7.7
Add a formatting attribute to a table.

These attribute buttons are depressed

Selected table text

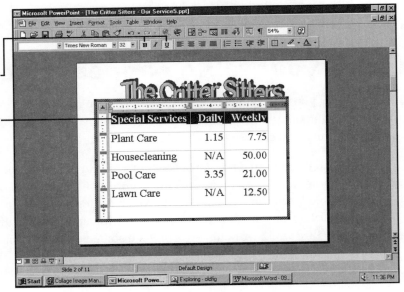

Borders make tables easier to read

You've probably noticed by now that those dotted lines, called **grid lines**, that separate your table's columns and rows don't show up on the slide. Often, a border adds impact to a table and makes it easier to read.

Here's how to add borders to your table:

1 In Slide view, double-click the table. The Microsoft Word toolbars are displayed.

2 Click anywhere within any cell in the table.

3 Choose F_ormat, _Borders and Shading. The Borders and Shading dialog box opens (see Figure 7.8).

Select your line weight for your border here

Fig. 7.8
Use the Borders and Shading dialog box to select a border.

Click here to add a grid to the table

A sample grid appears

4 Click _Grid, then click OK. (You can change the weight of the grid lines by clicking a different line style, if you choose.) When the dialog box closes, the table cells will have a border surrounding them.

5 Close the table by clicking anywhere outside the table. Notice that the PowerPoint toolbars return to the slide.

CAUTION You added a border and you hate it—it just doesn't look right! Don't fret. Click the Undo button on the Standard toolbar *immediately* after you've added the border to reverse it.

TIP When you return to the PowerPoint slide after you've been working with a table, you may notice your table has handles around it. That's because the table is an object (see Chapter 3 for more information on objects) and can be moved, resized, or even deleted.

Using the Table AutoFormat feature

Most people—me included— recognize that they need help with anything artistic. The Table AutoFormat feature is perfect for folks like us. This formatting bonanza consists of 40 different formatting arrangements. Choose one and your table is finished and your work is done!

TIP **If you plan on using the Table AutoFormat feature, don't waste** any time formatting anything in the table. Applying a Table AutoFormat to a table gets rid of any formatting attributes that were in the table.

To use the AutoFormat feature, double-click the table in Slide view. The Microsoft Word toolbars are displayed. Click anywhere in any cell in the table and choose Table, Table AutoFormat. The Table AutoFormat dialog box opens, as shown in Figure 7.9.

Fig. 7.9
Use the Table
AutoFormat dialog box
to choose an attractive
format for your table.

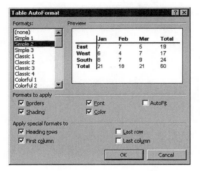

Choose one of the formats listed. You'll see a sample of the format you've selected in the Preview box, but you can change, include, or exclude any of the options listed under Formats To Apply. When the dialog box closes, the AutoFormat you've selected is applied, as shown in Figure 7.10.

Fig. 7.10
AutoFormat creates an
attractive table
instantly.

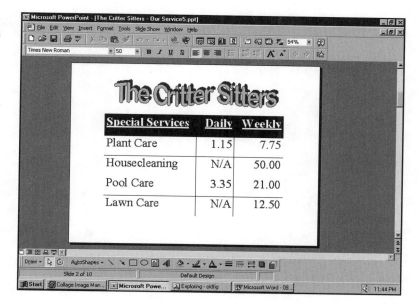

 TIP **Always remember where your table slide will be presented before** you make formatting changes. For example, if you're planning to put your presentation on the Web, go for broke with colors, borders, and attributes. On the other hand, if the slide will be printed on a black-and-white printer and passed around as hard copy, you may want to go with more subtle changes.

Part II: Fine-Tuning Your Presentation

Chapter 8: **PowerPoint Writing Tools Promise a Perfect Presentation**

Chapter 9: **Using Advanced Editing Techniques**

Chapter 10: **Lights, Camera, Action... Add Sound and Video to a Presentation**

Chapter 11: **Using Advanced Art and Graphics Techniques**

Chapter 12: **Using Objects from Other Programs**

Chapter 13: **Look Like a Pro: Adding Super Special Effects**

PowerPoint Writing Tools Promise a Perfect Presentation

● **In this chapter:**

● **How can I make sure all words in my presentation are spelled correctly?**

● **Is it possible to automatically replace one word with another word?**

● **I've heard about a feature that automatically corrects my spelling**

● **How can I do advanced research right from my computer?**

PowerPoint's writing tools make sure your audience never finds a spelling or style error in your presentation. . . . . ❯

Spelling errors in your work diminish the effectiveness of your presentation. A few years ago, one of my best friends created a spectacular presentation built around her company's new advertising slogan. But instead of the favorable response my friend expected, she heard chuckles from the audience during the entire slide show. Why? The new slogan "We're committed to exsellence" appeared on every slide—with the word "excellence" obviously misspelled! If only my poor friend had been able to use a spell checker, her presentation would have been far more successful.

Misspelled words occur for two reasons. One, because your fingers slip on the computer keys. (Errors of this nature are commonly known as "typos.") The other reason spelling errors occur is because the typist doesn't know the correct spelling of the word. But it doesn't really matter why they happen; spelling errors imply that you are hasty and unprofessional.

Fortunately, PowerPoint comes with its own spell checker program to make sure your presentation doesn't contain any spelling errors.

 Plain English, please!

> A **spell checker** is a popular feature that can be found in most programs. A spell checker compares words in your work with words in its dictionary. When a word not listed in the dictionary is found, the spell checker lets you know and gives suggested alternatives that you can either substitute for the word or ignore. Spell checkers used to be found in only the most expensive word processing programs, but now almost all types of programs include them. **"**

Spell checking your presentation

You can check spelling either as you type or after you finish creating your slides. When you check the spelling as you type, red squiggly underlines indicate possible spelling errors.

To correct the spelling errors that appear as you type, simply right-click the word with the wavy underline and choose a button. Or, if you choose, you can run the spell checker feature after you've completed your slides from Outline, Slide, Slide Sorter, or Notes Page view.

To run the spelling check, in whatever view your slides are in, click the Spelling button on the Standard toolbar. The Spelling dialog box opens, as shown in Figure 8.1. (Depending on the position of the insertion point, the spell checker looks for misspellings after that point.)

Fig. 8.1
Misspelled words are flagged in the Spelling dialog box.

The misspelled word is displayed here

Suggestions appear here

The word is misspelled here

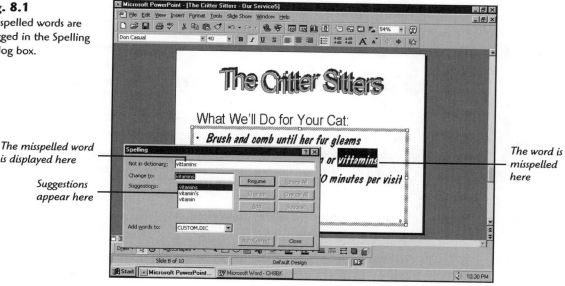

The Spelling dialog box, which is displayed when the spell checker is started, offers many options, as described in the following table.

Option	What does it do?
Ignore	Doesn't change the selected word, and resumes the spell check
Ignore All	Doesn't change any occurrences of the selected word, and resumes the spell check
Change	Replaces the selected word with the word in the text box, and resumes the spell check
Change All	Changes all occurrences of the selected word with the word in the text box, and resumes the spell check

continues

continued

Option	What does it do?
Add	Adds the selected word to the open dictionary
Suggest	Looks for optional correct spellings in the open dictionary
Close	Shuts down spell checker

 TIP **You may want to turn off the automatic spell checker** feature if your presentation contains lots of technical or scientific words, or you simply don't want to have to worry about spelling as you type. Open the Tools menu, choose Options and click the Spelling tab. Uncheck the box next to Spelling to shut off the automatic feature. Repeat the steps and re-check the box whenever you want to turn automatic spell check back on.

Click the appropriate button in the dialog box, depending on how you want PowerPoint to treat the word.

 To check the spelling of a single word, select the word by double-clicking it, then click the Spelling button on the Standard toolbar. After the word is checked, click Close in the Spelling dialog box.

TIP **It's easy to hide the wavy underlines that appear when** PowerPoint is automatically checking your spelling. To temporarily hide these lines, click Options on the Tools menu, click the Spelling tab, and then select the Hide spelling errors check box. Repeat the same steps to recheck the box when you want to see, and correct, the possible spelling errors.

 Q&A *How can I tell PowerPoint that my name isn't misspelled?*

Just add your name—or any frequently used, yet unusual word—to the dictionary, and the spell checker will skip the word each time it finds it in your presentation. You'll learn to add words to the dictionary in the next section.

 **CAUTION** **Be careful when adding words to the dictionary. If you** accidentally add a misspelled word to the dictionary, it won't be seen as misspelled in your text, and thus won't be flagged by the spell checker.

Adding words to the dictionary

Lots of names, scientific and medical words, and technical terms are not in the initial PowerPoint dictionary. In fact, the dictionary doesn't contain words that you'll probably think should be in there.

That's why PowerPoint makes it so easy to add words to the dictionary. Once you've added a word, the spell checker never bothers you again by telling you it's misspelled.

TIP **Learn to use discretion when adding to your dictionary. I avoid** adding words I know are correct if they could easily be a misspelling of another common word. For example, I haven't added the word "Starr" to the dictionary, even though I typed the phrase "Starr Market" on several slides. That's because if I add Starr to the dictionary, the spell checker won't catch legitimate misspellings of the word "star."

To add words to the dictionary, the Spelling dialog box must be open. The dictionary you want to add a word to should be displayed in the Add <u>W</u>ords To text box (refer to Figure 8.1). Simply click the <u>A</u>dd button when the word to be added is in the Not In Dictionar<u>y</u> text box.

Do you know where your words go when they're added to the dictionary? They're added to the Custom Dictionary, which is shared with other Microsoft Office programs that are installed. This means that words you add to the Custom Dictionary in Microsoft PowerPoint are available when you check spelling in Microsoft Word, Microsoft Excel, Microsoft Access, and Microsoft Outlook.

Q&A **Why didn't the spell check look for errors in my entire presentation?**

Unfortunately, you can't check the spelling in special text effects like WordArt, in inserted tables or Word documents, or in embedded objects, like charts.

When I try to check the spelling of text, a message keeps telling me that the spelling tool isn't installed.

The spelling check feature isn't installed or isn't installed properly. Run Setup and perform a custom installation. See Appendix A for installation information.

Can PowerPoint automatically correct my spelling?

AutoCorrect is so helpful that you may never know it's there! The AutoCorrect feature finds misspellings and automatically fixes them. It doesn't even let you know, it just does it. For example, if you type **teh**, PowerPoint will automatically change it to **the**. You can also add or delete words from the original list of AutoCorrect words.

Using AutoCorrect is as simple as typing your text the way you normally would. Adding or deleting words to the AutoCorrect list is also easy, but you do have to do some work. You can edit the AutoCorrect list from any view except Slide Show view.

To add words to or delete words from the AutoCorrect list, choose Tools, AutoCorrect. The AutoCorrect dialog box opens, as shown in Figure 8.2.

Checking the spelling of text in another language

PowerPoint assumes that you're using American English to create your presentation. However, if you choose to use another language, PowerPoint is so smart that it can check that language's spelling, too! Follow these steps to check spelling in another language:

1 Select the foreign text you want to check.

2 Choose Tools, Language. The Language dialog box opens.

3 In the Mark Selected Text As box, click the text's language from the 55 available

choices, and then click OK to close the Language dialog box and return to the PowerPoint screen.

4 Click the Spelling button on the Standard toolbar.

5 (Optional) To change the default language dictionary to another language, select that language in the Mark Selected Text As Box, and then click Default.

Fig. 8.2
The AutoCorrect
feature automatically
fixes spelling errors.

AutoCorrect options

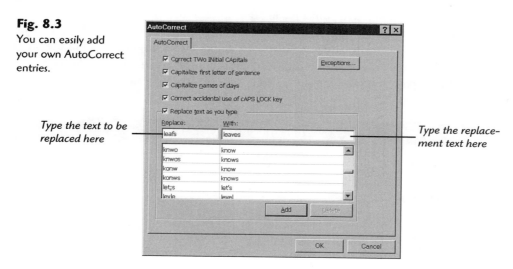

Existing AutoCorrect entries

Type the text you want replaced in the Replace text box, and the text you want to replace it with in the With text box. Figure 8.3 shows you an AutoCorrect entry.

Fig. 8.3
You can easily add
your own AutoCorrect
entries.

*Type the text to be
replaced here*

*Type the replace-
ment text here*

Click the <u>A</u>dd button. If any entry already exists, you'll see the Rep<u>l</u>ace button instead of the <u>A</u>dd button. You can use the Rep<u>l</u>ace button to modify an existing entry. If you want to delete an entry, select it from the AutoCorrect list and click <u>D</u>elete.

TIP   **In addition to correcting your spelling, you can use AutoCorrect as** a kind of personal shorthand. For example, I added "cs" (for "The Critter Sitters") to my AutoCorrect list since I use that term so much.

Finding a word in a slide

Sometimes you might want to find a particular word or **text string** in your presentation. You remember typing the word "Winkler's," for example, but now can't recall what slide it's on.

 Plain English, please!

A **text string** consists of one or more characters, such as the letters "Crit" (some of letters contained in "The Critter Sitters").

The <u>F</u>ind Next command lets you locate the next occurrence (depending on the position of the insertion point) of a word or text string in the file. The following table shows you the options available in the Find dialog box.

Option	What does it do?
Match <u>C</u>ase	Matches the text string exactly as you've entered it
Find <u>W</u>hole Words Only	Matches the text string you've entered if it occurs as an independent word (for example, it'll find "his" but not "history")
<u>F</u>ind Next	Continues the search process
<u>R</u>eplace	Changes one text string to another

To use the Find command in whatever view your slides are in, choose Edit, Find. The Find dialog box opens. When you type a text string in the Find What text box, the Find Next button becomes available, as shown in Figure 8.4.

Fig. 8.4
Use the Find Next command to locate text.

Click any options you want to use and click Find Next. PowerPoint locates the next occurrence of the text string. Click Find Next to continue, or click Close to end the search.

Replacing text in a presentation

Sometimes you might have to replace multiple occurrences of a word. Perhaps you used the word "Miami" throughout your presentation only to find out you should have used the word "Boston." It can get awfully tiresome to search through each slide for the misused word.

The Replace command is similar to the Find command, but goes one step further. Replace finds one word and replaces it with another. To use Replace in whatever view your slides are in, choose Edit, Replace. The Replace dialog box opens, as shown in Figure 8.5.

Option	What does it do?
Match Case	Matches the text string exactly as you've entered it
Find Whole Words Only	Matches the text string you've entered if it occurs as an independent word (for example, changing "his" to "hers" won't change "history" to "herstory")
Find Next	Continues the search process
Replace	Changes one text string to another
Replace All	Changes all identical text strings

Fig. 8.5
Use the Replace command to change text.

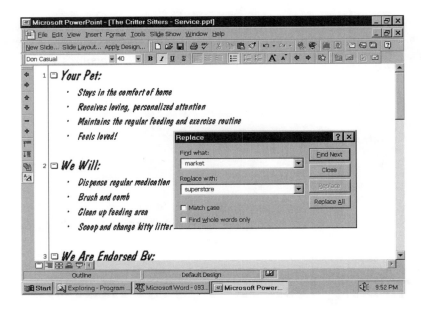

Type the text you want to locate in the Fi̲nd What text box, and type the text you want it replaced with in the Rep̲lace With text box. Select any options you want to use. Click R̲eplace or Replace A̲ll, and PowerPoint replaces either the next occurrence of the text string or all occurrences.

Using the Style Checker

In addition to the spell check feature, PowerPoint now has a Style Checker that checks your presentation for style and consistency. For example, the Style Checker can make sure that the first letter of every word in a title is capitalized.

Here's how to use the Style Checker:

1 If it's not already open, open the presentation you want to check and choose T̲ools, Style Checker. The Style Checker dialog box opens, as shown in Figure 8.6.

2 Uncheck any items you don't want to check.

Fig. 8.6
The Style Checker dialog box lets you check your presentation for style and visual clarity.

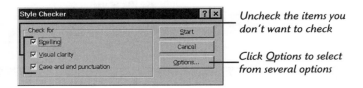

Uncheck the items you don't want to check

Click O̲ptions to select from several options

3 (Optional) Click <u>O</u>ptions to select more items from the Style Checker Options dialog box, shown in Figure 8.7. When you're done, click OK to return to the Style Checker dialog box.

4 Click <u>S</u>tart to launch the Style Checker.

Fig. 8.7
The Style Checker
Options dialog box
offers many style
choices.

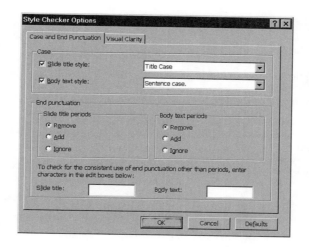

Using Microsoft Bookshelf Basics

Just as I'm settled in at my computer for a long session of using PowerPoint 97, I find that I need to get up and get a book. I might need my mega-dictionary to look up a definition, my thesaurus to help me find the right word or even a book of famous quotations to help me prepare my presentation. With Microsoft Bookshelf Basics, I have all of the tools I need, and more, to make the words in my presentation come alive!

Microsoft Bookshelf Basics is a multimedia reference collection made up of online books and materials. You can search for the information you need in a table of contents, or you can search through a particular reference book or in all reference materials at once. Bookshelf Basics is included with Microsoft Office 97, Professional Edition, and can be accessed from within any Office 97 application you've installed on your computer.

CAUTION   **Microsoft Bookshelf Basics must be installed on your computer** before you can access any of its reference materials. In addition, the Microsoft Office 97 CD must be inserted in the CD-ROM drive of your computer when you use Bookshelf Basics.

Bookshelf Basics includes the following online references:

- The Original Roget's Thesaurus

- The American Heritage® Dictionary, Third Edition

- The Columbia Dictionary of Quotations

Bookshelf automatically opens to All Books, which contains articles from all of the Bookshelf references. From there, you can open individual references and switch between them to find the information you need.

TIP   **Microsoft Bookshelf Basics is a separate program that opens from** within your installed Office 97 application. It has its own menu bar and online help system. When you open Bookshelf Basics, a new button appears on the Windows taskbar.

Take these steps to use the reference materials in Microsoft Bookshelf Basics:

1   From within either Slide View or Outline View, select the word or phrase you want to look up.

2   Choose <u>T</u>ools, Loo<u>k</u> Up Reference. The Look Up Reference dialog box opens, as shown in Figure 8.8.

Fig. 8.8
The Look Up
Reference dialog box.

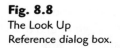

*The word or phrase
selected in the slide is
displayed here*

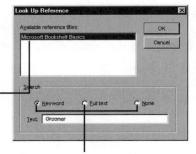

Choose a search method here

3 In the A_vailable Reference Titles box, Microsoft Bookshelf Basics is selected by default.

4 The word or phrase you selected on the slide is displayed in the T_ext box. You can replace this word or phrase with any other text, up to 255 characters, that you'd like to look up.

5 To search through the keywords of every Bookshelf article for the word or phrase you want, click K_eyword.

To search through every article for the word or phrase, click F_ull Text.

To open Microsoft Bookshelf Basics without starting a search, click N_one.

6 Click OK to open the Microsoft Bookshelf Basics. Figure 8.9 shows how the program opens in its own window, displaying the definition of the word or phrase you selected.

Fig. 8.9
Microsoft Bookshelf Basics opens in its own window.

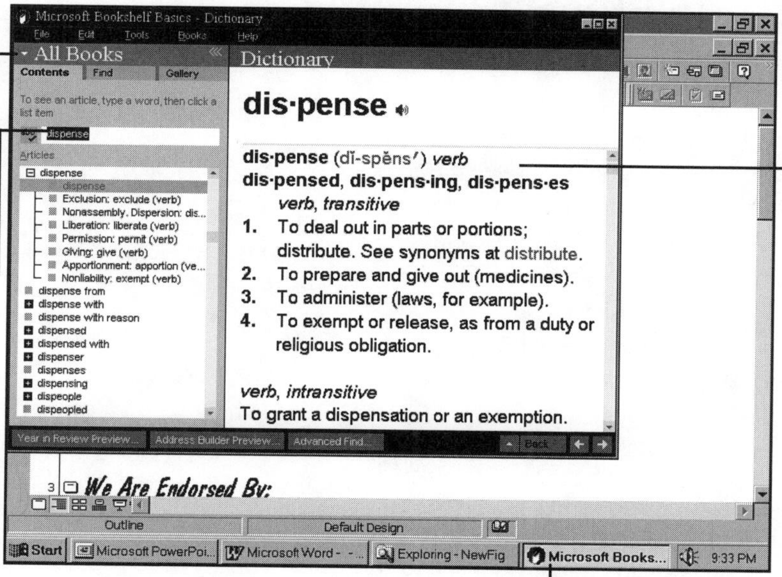

Click this arrow to view other searchable reference books

Your selection appears here

The definition appears here

The Microsoft Bookshelf Basics button is displayed on the taskbar

7   Click the drop-down arrow next to All Books to view the other searchable reference materials.

8   (Optional) To print the article, open the Bookshelf Basics <u>F</u>ile menu and choose <u>P</u>rint Article.

To copy the article, choose <u>E</u>dit, <u>C</u>opy to copy the article to the Windows clipboard (where you can paste it into any Windows application) or Copy to PowerPoint to copy the article directly into your PowerPoint slide.

9   When you're done using Microsoft Bookshelf Basics, close it by clicking its Close button.

Microsoft Bookshelf Basics

Microsoft Bookshelf Basics is a separate computer application which is included with Office 97, Professional Edition. Along with the dictionary, thesaurus, and book of quotations, are previews or abbreviated versions of widely used reference works. These include The Peoples Chronology, The Concise Columbia Encyclopedia, The Concise World Atlas, The World Almanac Book of Facts, The Year in Review, and National Five-Digit Zip Codes and Post Office Directory. The Bookshelf Internet Directory also is included.

Selected preview topics are available for you to view; simply click the red text (your mouse pointer will take the shape of a hand) to "jump" to the topic. Bookshelf entries include animation clips, musical samples, and special effects. Thousands of images are included.

The full version of Microsoft Bookshelf is available by subscription for a small fee. If you're interested in subscribing or obtaining a copy of the complete Microsoft Bookshelf CD, click Subscribe/Update from within Bookshelf Basics for more information.

Microsoft Bookshelf is an invaluable aid to research. You no longer have to go to the library and wade through volumes of material to obtain the facts you need. Instead, an entire library is available at your home, directly from your computer—whenever you want to use it. Research has never been so much fun!

9

Using Advanced Editing Techniques

● In this chapter:

● **What will WordArt do for my slides?**

● **I love color—can using colors help get my point across?**

● **I'd like to be able to control the position of text**

● **How can I use bullets to emphasize my lists?**

PowerPoint provides you with some advanced editing techniques to make your slides extraordinary. . . . .

Your presentation is really taking shape! Each of your great-looking slides tells a story and gets your message across. But why stop here? PowerPoint includes many extra tools that you certainly don't need to know to use the program, but you'll find that they make your presentation more professional. Using these tools will make your presentation stand out from the crowd and get you (and your work) noticed.

Create your own special effects with WordArt

You've probably noticed text that looks wavy, stretched, or even arched. Chances are you'd love to use an effect like that in a presentation. The feature that creates those effects is called **WordArt**, and if installed, it's available in all the Microsoft Office programs, not just PowerPoint.

 Plain English, please!

WordArt is a feature that can take ordinary text and make it look dramatic. In addition to changing fonts and adding attributes, WordArt lets you change the shape of text, change its color, and add shadows. Like clip art, WordArt changes text into an object, so when you select it later, handles appear around the box containing the text.

 TIP **If your company doesn't have a logo, WordArt can be a great** place to start. You can use WordArt to create a unique design that can become a logo! In fact, The Critter Sitter's logo used in this book was created with WordArt!

A sample of how WordArt can change the appearance of your text is shown in Figure 9.1.

In Figure 9.1, a company's name is typed into WordArt and then used as a logo. WordArt can be created on any slide in your presentation. In Figure 9.1, the logo was created on the Slide Master (covered in Chapter 4), so it appears on each slide in the presentation.

Fig. 9.1
WordArt can be created on any slide, including the Slide Master.

The company's name becomes a logo using WordArt

Creating WordArt

Like the results of Microsoft Graph and Microsoft Organization Chart, each WordArt creation is an object. That means that when selected, it's surrounded by handles. It also means that WordArt creations can be moved, resized, and deleted like any other objects you use in PowerPoint. Also, WordArt has its own toolbar buttons, described later in this chapter.

WordArt objects are not only easy to create, they're fun to make. You can create WordArt from either Slide View or the Slide Master.

The advantage of creating a WordArt object in the Slide Master is that when finished, the object will appear on every slide in the presentation. So, if you want to use a WordArt object as a logo, it's a great idea to add it to your Slide Master. Regardless of whether you create it on the Slide Master or a regular slide, the process remains the same.

Follow these steps to use WordArt:

1 Open the Slide Master if you'd like the WordArt object to be added to every slide (like a logo), or open the slide in the presentation where you'd like the WordArt to appear and switch to the Slide view.

2 Click the Insert WordArt button on the Drawing toolbar. (If the Drawing toolbar isn't visible, open the View menu, choose Toolbars and then check Drawing.) The WordArt Gallery dialog box opens, as shown in Figure 9.2.

Fig. 9.2
The WordArt Gallery dialog box shows all of the available styles.

Samples of each style appear here

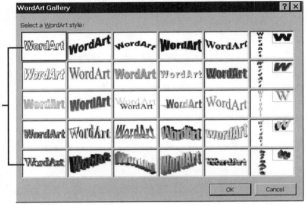

3 Select a WordArt style from the sample gallery and click OK.

4 The Edit WordArt Text dialog box opens. Replace the Your Text Here with the text you want WordArt to dramatize. (The selected text is immediately replaced with your text as you type.) Figure 9.3 shows the Edit WordArt Text dialog box.

Old WordArt versus WordArt, Office 97 style

In previous versions of Microsoft Office, you created special text effects with the WordArt program that was shipped with Office. In Office 97, you create these effects right in PowerPoint by using the new WordArt tool on the Drawing toolbar, which gives you added features, such as 3-D effects and textured fills.

If you already have a WordArt program on your computer (installed from an earlier version of Microsoft Office), it'll remain when you install Office 97. However, you'll probably want to use the new WordArt tool to create your special text effects. Text effects created with the older WordArt program won't automatically be converted to new drawing objects.

Fig. 9.3
Replace the text in the
WordArt text box.

*Change the
font here*

*Type your own
text here*

*Change the
font size here*

*Add attributes
here*

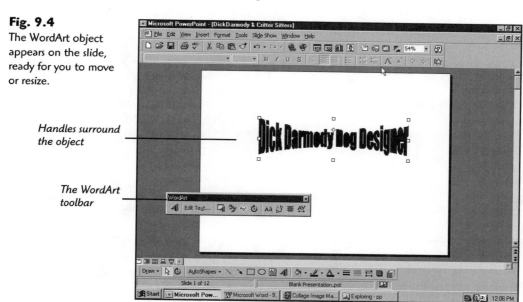

5 Change the font size by clicking the drop-down arrow next to the name of the font that's currently selected. If you want, change the font size and add attributes such as bold and italic.

6 When you've selected the font, font size and desired attributes, click OK.

7 The Edit WordArt Text dialog box closes and the object you just created is placed on the slide, along with the WordArt toolbar, as displayed in Figure 9.4.

Fig. 9.4
The WordArt object
appears on the slide,
ready for you to move
or resize.

*Handles surround
the object*

*The WordArt
toolbar*

8 Resize or move the WordArt object just as you would work with any other graphics object. (Chapter 3 contains instructions on resizing and moving graphics objects.)

Modifying WordArt

Creating the WordArt object is only the first half of the game—the real fun begins when you make those adjustments to get the WordArt object exactly right (like finding just the right clip art for your slides).

The WordArt buttons are described in Table 9.1. Once WordArt is open, you can use these buttons to change the shape, font, color, shadow, and attributes of its text.

Table 9.1 WordArt toolbar buttons

Button	Name	What does it do?
	Insert WordArt	Opens WordArt using the selected object
Edit Text...	WordArt Edit Text	Opens the Edit WordArt text dialog box and enables you to selects a font, a font size bold and italic attributes for the text
	WordArt Gallery	Opens the Edit WordArt Gallery text and enables you to select a different WordArt style
	Format WordArt	Opens the Format WordArt dialog box and enables you to change the color and lines, size and position of the object.
	WordArt Shape	Lets you change the shape of the object
	Free Rotate	Lets you rotate the the selected object
	WordArt Same Letter Heights	Makes upper- and lowercase letters the same height
	WordArt Vertical Text	Flips the object to a vertical position

Button	Name	What does it do?
	WordArt Alignment	Changes the alignment of the text
	WordArt Character Spacing	Increases or decreases the space between characters

To modify a WordArt creation, double-click the WordArt object.

CAUTION If you created your WordArt object on the Slide Master, you'll have to open the Slide Master first and then double-click the object to modify it. If you need more information about the Slide Master, please review Chapter 4.

Q&A *The WordArt button on the Drawing toolbar is always dimmed out. What's wrong?*

Chances are WordArt hasn't been installed on your computer. This is easily fixed, however, as long as you've got access to the original program disks or CD-ROM. Follow the installation instructions that came with Office 97 or the standalone version of PowerPoint, and choose the Custom installation, rather than the Typical or Compact installation. You're shown a list of options you can choose to install, and WordArt is one of them. Don't worry, there's no danger that you'll mess up your current installation.

 You can quickly change the shape of your WordArt object by clicking the WordArt Shape button on the WordArt toolbar. Forty possible shapes for your text are displayed. Click on any of them to automatically update your text.

While the WordArt object is selected, flip your text from a horizontal to a vertical position. Click the WordArt Vertical Text button and watch your text fly to its new position.

A WordArt object can be scaled and resized by pressing the Ctrl key while dragging one of its handles. Move a WordArt object to any location on the slide by clicking within the object, holding down the mouse button, and dragging it. Press Esc to deselect the object once you're satisfied with its location.

TIP **It's easy to get carried away as you modify your WordArt creation.** If you make a change and then hate it, immediately click the Undo button on the Standard toolbar to reverse the unwanted action.

Working with PowerPoint colors

In today's world, colors are everything. Colors that stand out catch your eye and grab your attention. Color plays a major role in our lives—television, movies, photos, and computer screens use color. Think about your last trip to the grocery store—you were probably attracted to a new product that was packaged in a bright, friendly color.

PowerPoint understands the importance of color in your presentation and lets you decide which colors work best.

How do I know which colors to use and which to avoid?

Any colors used in your slides should not compete with the theme of your presentation. Unless colors are the topic of your presentation, your audience should not even be aware of color on the slides, or the colors should unconsciously inspire positive emotions. Remember, colors are part of the background. And background generally implies that it is not the primary interest.

So how do you know if your colors are not quite right? Ask yourself these questions:

- Are you acutely aware of the colors while watching the presentation? Are the colors distracting you?

- Are your slides hard to read because of the color scheme?

- Would anyone think any of the colors you've used are outrageous or loud?

- Are your words hard to read because of the text color?

If you answered "Yes" to any of these questions, you may need to examine and change the color schemes in your presentation.

Applying an existing color scheme

You can apply any of the color schemes from any PowerPoint View. (Chapter 1 contains information about the PowerPoint views.) To apply color schemes to your presentation, click Format, Slide Color Scheme. The Color Scheme dialog box opens. Click the Custom tab, as shown in Figure 9.5.

Fig. 9.5
Use the Color Scheme dialog box to add colors to your slides.

Elements that can be changed

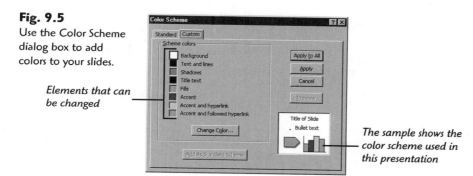

The sample shows the color scheme used in this presentation

Notice that various shades of gray (or colors) are in each of the blocks in the palette. Click the Standard tab. This tab contains the PowerPoint color schemes, as shown in Figure 9.6.

Fig. 9.6
Predefined PowerPoint color schemes.

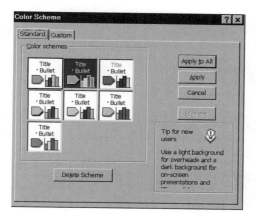

Click any of the desired color schemes, then click Apply To All (to apply the scheme to all the slides), or Apply (to apply the scheme to only the active slide). If you have any charts in your slides, they'll be updated with the new colors as well. When you look at your slides, you'll see the new color scheme has been applied as you've specified.

TIP **The number of color schemes available in the Color Scheme** dialog box varies depending on which design template you've applied to your presentation.

Modifying an existing color scheme

Perhaps you've found and applied a color scheme you like, but you'd like to change one of the colors. No problem!

You can change any or all of the colors in a color scheme. Here's how to change a color in a scheme:

1 Choose F̲ormat, Slide C̲olor Scheme. The Color Scheme dialog box opens.

2 Click the Custom tab. The colors in the scheme you selected appear in the blocks in the S̲cheme Colors list. Click one of the blocks on the list to change its color.

3 Click a color block in the palette.

4 Click Change C̲olor. The Color dialog box opens, with the color previously selected outlined in black.

5 Click a new color that appears in the lower-right corner, as shown in Figure 9.7.

Fig. 9.7
Click a color in the Color dialog box to replace one color with another.

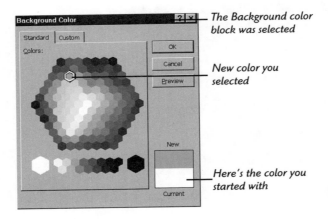

6 Click OK to return to the Color Scheme dialog box. Notice that your new color now appears in the palette in place of the previous color.

7 Click the Apply button to add the new colors to the slide that was current when you opened this dialog box, or click the Apply To All button to add the new colors to all the slides in your presentation.

How can I display my text in a different color?

PowerPoint is so versatile that it's easy to change the color of your text. You can change text color either in the Slide view or Slide Master view.

 **CAUTION** **Remember that changing text color on the Slide Master will** change that text on every slide.

 To change text color, select either the text to be changed or, to change the color of all the words in a text box, select the box. Next, click the drop-down arrow next to the Font Color button on the Drawing toolbar. The text color palette displays, as shown in Figure 9.8.

Fig. 9.8
Use the Font Color button to change the color of your text.

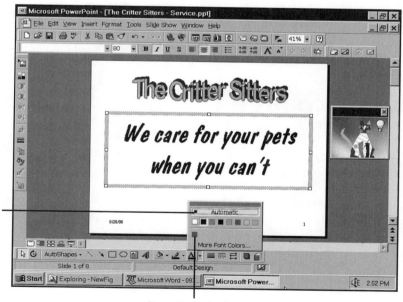

Default color of the selected text

Recently used colors

Click a color from the palette, or click <u>M</u>ore Font Colors to view additional colors. If you choose a color from the drop-down palette, it is immediately applied to the selected text. If you choose <u>M</u>ore Font Colors, the Colors dialog box opens, as shown in Figure 9.9.

Fig. 9.9
Choose a unique color for your text from the color palette.

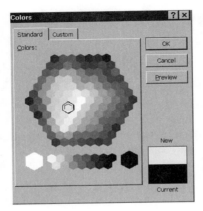

Click a color from the palette, then click OK to return to your slide. When you deselect the text, you'll see that your new color has been applied.

TIP **If you choose More Font Colors for text, the new color will** appear in the color text drop-down box. This newly added color can easily be selected again by clicking the color in the pull-down box.

I'd like to change the look of my text

Even after you've changed color schemes and the color of some selected text, you can make a few more adjustments to your slides for the maximum visual appeal.

You can change the alignment of the words, change the spacing between lines, and even add some exciting bullet characters. If you've used a word processor before, some of these options may be familiar to you. But remember, you don't have to change anything—PowerPoint provides you with many options you may not need for your presentation.

Changing the alignment of text

Alignment refers to the way that your text is lined up in its placeholder on the slide. (Chapter 3 has information about placeholders.) The text within a placeholder can be aligned to the left, the right, the left and the right (fully justified) or in the center. If a placeholder contains more than one paragraph, each paragraph can be aligned differently. However, each paragraph can only have one type of alignment.

Different kinds of text call for different alignments. For example, a bulleted list looks best when it's aligned to the left, while titles and headings usually look best if they're centered.

Perform the following steps to change the alignment of text:

1 From within Slide view, position the insertion point in the paragraph whose alignment you want to change. (It's not necessary to select the entire paragraph.)

 2 Click the Left Alignment button on the Formatting toolbar to align the text to the left.

 Click the Center Alignment button on the Formatting toolbar to align the text to the center.

 Click the Right Alignment button on the Formatting toolbar to align the text to the right.

Changing the spacing between lines

Line spacing refers to the distance between each line in a paragraph. Sometimes, changing the spacing can change the look of your text in a very subtle way. For example, a paragraph with more than three lines may look like a jumbled block of words to your audience. But when you open the amount of distance between the lines, each individual line becomes clearer.

 Changing the spacing between lines in a paragraph is a snap! Position the insertion point in the paragraph you want to change. Click the Increase Paragraph Spacing button on the Formatting toolbar to open the space between each of the paragraph's lines. Each time you click the button, the spacing increases.

Click the Decrease Paragraph Spacing button on the Formatting toolbar to decrease the amount of space between lines. Notice how the look of the paragraph changes on the slide, as shown in Figure 9.10.

Fig. 9.10
The look of the paragraph changes when you increase paragraph spacing.

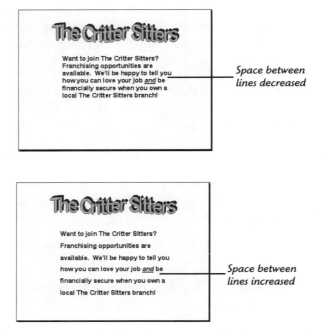

Creating bullet lists

Many presentations contain slides with listed points. A list organizes your slide and presents each point individually. As you are reviewing the slides, you may decide to add bullet characters for extra punch. If a text placeholder contains a simple list without bullets, you can easily add bullets for emphasis.

 To add bullets to a list, first select all of the items you want to be bulleted. Click the Bullet button on the Formatting toolbar. Figure 9.11 shows a list without bullets. The same list, with bullets added, appears in Figure 9.12. Notice how the bulleted items stand out.

Fig. 9.11
The points on this list don't stand out.

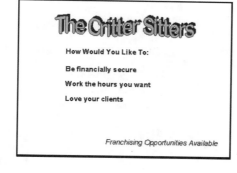

Fig. 9.12
The same points are emphasized by placing bullets in front of them.

Changing the distance between bullets and text

PowerPoint leaves the decisions up to you of how much distance should be between the bullet character and the text. If each point consists of a few words, you may want a large gap. On the other hand, if each of the points is long or contains more than one sentence, a smaller distance between the bullet and the item would be more effective.

To change the distance between the bullet and the text, you must change the paragraph indent marker on the PowerPoint ruler. Don't let the complicated-sounding words scare you; the action takes only a few clicks of the mouse.

Here's how:

1 In Slide view or Notes Page view, select the bulleted items you want to change.

2 Choose <u>V</u>iew, <u>R</u>uler. The ruler appears below the menu bar and any toolbars that are currently displayed, as shown in Figure 9.13.

Fig. 9.13
The ruler lets you
change the distance
between bullets and
text.

*Drag the paragraph indent marker
to the position where you want the
text to begin*

Horizontal ruler

Vertical ruler

*The dotted line shows
you where the text will
begin*

3 Click the paragraph indent marker and drag it to where you want the text to begin. A dotted guideline appears to show you the exact position.

4 Release the mouse button at the desired position. The selected text moves to the new position.

TIP **Change the distance between bullets and text for all the slides in** your presentation by changing the Slide Master.

Can I change the shape of my bullets?

Sure, why not? After all, each bullet is only a character stored inside your computer. However, it's important to consider who's going to view the finished product. You wouldn't want to make each bullet a smiley face character if you were presenting your slide show to a group of grief counselors.

You can change the shape, color, and size of the bullets on your bulleted lists. To change the bullet character, follow these steps:

1 From Slide view, select the items whose bullets you want to change.

2 Choose F<u>o</u>rmat, <u>B</u>ullet. The Bullet dialog box opens, as shown in Figure 9.14.

Fig. 9.14
Several formatting options are available for a bullet character.

Select a font here

Available bullet characters are shown here

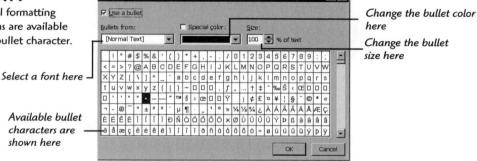

Change the bullet color here

Change the bullet size here

3 The bullet palette displays available bullet characters based on the font shown in the Bullets <u>F</u>rom text box. To view characters in different fonts, click the drop-down arrow next to the Bullets From text box and choose another font from the list of font names.

4 To view the available bullet characters, click a new character from the palette. The selected character will appear enlarged so that you can view it clearly. Click additional characters until you find the one you like.

5 To change the bullet color, open the Color drop-down list and choose from one of the listed colors on the color palette.

6 To change the bullet size, use the spin buttons to increase or decrease the percentage shown.

7 Click OK to apply the changes you made.

Q&A *Why didn't I see very many fonts when I was trying to change my bullet character?*

The fonts shown on this list are based on fonts that must already be installed on your computer. Depending on which fonts are installed, you may see a long or short list of font names.

Fig. 9.15
The bullet character is changed based on a character from the Iconic Symbols Ext font at 135% percentage of text.

10

Lights, Camera, Action... Add Sound and Video to a Presentation

● In this chapter:

- I'd like to add sound clips to my slides

- How do I associate a sound with a picture?

- Can I record a comment on a slide?

- Video clips would spice up my slides

- Tell me all about PowerPoint Central

Adding sound and video to your presentation will make your audience stand up and applaud! . . . .❯

Music, sound effects, and video clips can be included in your presentation with a little extra effort. These additions can turn your slide show into a "hit presentation."

Let's face it, sound and video constantly bombard us. Music plays in elevators and supermarkets. Visit any department store and chances are that a video presentation will be running on one of the counters. Most people are attracted to sound and video. I confess that I'm guilty of needing extra background noise—if I'm home alone, working, I turn on the television in the other room just so I'll hear voices.

 PowerPoint 97 has upgraded the way it deals with sounds and video clips. Even if you're an experienced PowerPoint user, this chapter highlights some of the new ways that PowerPoint can integrate sound and video into your presentation. Microsoft recognizes that sound and video is exciting; the new online magazine called PowerPoint Central will inform you of new ways to use the technology.

Adding sound to your presentation

Sound is a valuable tool for grabbing people's attention. In order to use sound, your computer must have a **sound card**. Use sound clips, like a ringing phone or screeching brakes, for emphasis. Or, record your own narration to a presentation. PowerPoint makes it easy to add the sounds you choose.

 Plain English, please!

A **sound card** is a special board installed in your computer that enables you to hear rich sounds. Generally, most sound-capable computers also have two stereo speakers attached. Once the sound card is properly installed, you'll be able to hear the thrilling sound effects you've assigned to your slides.

Sounds clips are great attention-getters

You can add sound clips to any slide in your presentation. Sound clips are actually stored in files on your computer's hard disk. The PowerPoint Clip Gallery contains many sounds for your use. You can also use sound clips stored in other files or that you've downloaded from the Web. You can bind sound effects to objects on your slides; when the mouse pointer clicks or passes over the objects, the sound plays.

Should I add special effects?

Music, sound effects, and video clips are powerful extras that you can add to your PowerPoint presentation. But before you pack your slides with these special effects you need to consider a few points—your target audience, the presentation topic, and where the presentation will take place.

Before you add sound or video, think of how it will affect your audience. Depending on who's viewing your presentation, sound clips may sway your audience in the opposite direction you expected. For example, even though it would be cute, a group of bank managers probably wouldn't be impressed if they saw a famous cartoon bunny say "That's all folks" on a slide that displayed financial data showing why your business needed a working capital loan.

Always consider your presentation topic and make sure that the clips you add are appropriate. Your audience will remember if the sounds and video don't compliment the topic. Unfortunately, that's all they'll remember; they won't recall the good points about your presentation.

The third point may be the most important. As you add sound and video, think of where you will present your slides. If you're going to use someone else's computer, make sure that the other computer is equipped to handle everything you've added. There's no sense in working your presentation around the William Tell Overture, only to find out that the computer that will be running the slide show is an older model and doesn't have a sound card installed.

The presentation should be complete and make a point before you add the extras. Done right, sound and video add a special touch that will make your audience remember your presentation long after it's over. However, if you overdo them, sound and video will add a major distraction to your presentation.

Adding sound clips from the Clip Gallery

The Microsoft Clip Gallery 3.0 is a great source for finding sound clips to add to your slides. Once you've added a sound clip, a sound icon is added to the slide. To play the sound during the slide show, just click the icon. Figure 10.1 shows a slide containing a sound clip.

 TIP **If you didn't install the Microsoft Clip Gallery to your computer's** hard disk when you installed PowerPoint, you can still access any of its files. Just make sure the CD-ROM that contains the PowerPoint files is inserted into your CD-ROM drive.

Fig. 10.1
This slide contains a sound clip.

Click here to play the sound

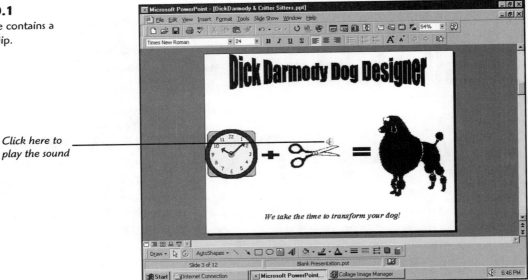

Follow these steps to add a sound clip to a slide:

1 In Slide view, display the slide you want to add the sound clip to.

2 Open the Insert menu and choose Movies and Sounds.

3 Select Sound from Gallery from the submenu. The Microsoft Clip Gallery 3.0 opens to the Sounds tab, as shown in Figure 10.2.

Fig. 10.2
The Microsoft Clip
Gallery 3.0 opens to
the Sounds tab.

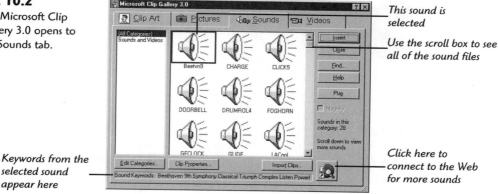

*This sound is
selected*

*Use the scroll box to see
all of the sound files*

*Keywords from the
selected sound
appear here*

*Click here to
connect to the Web
for more sounds*

3 Click the sound clip you want to add and then click Insert. The Clip
Gallery closes and the sound icon is added to your slide.

TIP **You can insert sound files that are stored in folders on your**
computer's hard disk. From Slide view, open the Insert menu and choose
Movies and Sounds and then Choose Sound from File. Locate the folder
that contains the sound. Double-click the file name of the sound and the
clip is added to the slide.

Getting new sound clips from the Web

You can add great sound clips from the Web directly to the Clip Gallery. Once
you've added the new sound clips, you can use the new files any time you
want. Remember, you must already be connected to your Internet Service
Provider or online service, like the Microsoft Network, before you can access
Microsoft's Clip Gallery Live Web site.

To connect to Clip Gallery Live, click the Microsoft Internet Explorer shortcut icon, located in the bottom-right corner of the Clip Gallery dialog box
(see Figure 10.2). A dialog box appears, as shown in Figure 10.3, that explains
that you must have access to the World Wide Web. Read the message and
then click OK.

Fig. 10.3
Read the message
before you connect
to the Web.

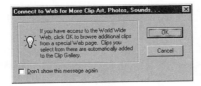

If this is your first time at the site, read the licensing agreement and accept its terms. When Microsoft Clip Gallery Live appears, click the Sounds icon. Choose a category from the Categories drop-down list. When you've chosen a category from the list, click the Go button. Figure 10.4 shows the Microsoft Clip Gallery Live Web site.

Fig. 10.4
The Microsoft Clip
Gallery Live lets you
download a sound.

*Click the Sounds
icon*

*Click here to open
the category list*

Scroll through the available sounds until you find the one you want to use. Click the file name to download it to your Clip Gallery. (If you are prompted to Open the file or Save it to Disk, choose Open.) After the sound has been added, you can add the new sound clip to a slide just as you would any other clip in the Gallery.

Action settings will make people gasp "How'd you do that?"

Have you ever heard Haydn's Surprise Symphony? For the most part, the music is pleasant but just plods along. Then, when you least expect it, the music changes from soothing to blaring and grabs your full attention. You can add the same effect to your PowerPoint presentation with a feature called Action Settings. After you've gotten the full attention of the audience, you can wow them with your facts and figures.

Think of Action Settings as surprises hidden in your presentation. You set an Action Setting to occur when the mouse clicks or passes over an object or text you've preselected. I love to include sounds that shock my audience. For example, the sound of loud clapping when the mouse pointer passes over a picture of a champion Standard Poodle wakes up the people in the back row.

The best thing about Action Settings is they're remarkably easy to set. Follow these steps to add an Action Setting sound to your slide:

1   From Slide view, select the object you want to associate with an Action Setting. (Handles will appear around it.)

2   Open the Slide Show menu and Choose Action Settings. The Action Settings dialog box appears, as shown in Figure 10.5.

Fig. 10.5
The Action Settings dialog box lets you add a surprise sound to your presentation.

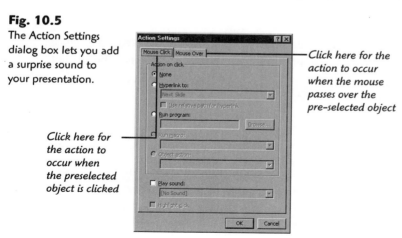

Click here for the action to occur when the mouse passes over the pre-selected object

Click here for the action to occur when the preselected object is clicked

3 Depending on when you want the action to occur, click the Mouse Click or Mouse Over tab.

4 To add a sound, check the Play Sound box. Click the down arrow next to No Sound and choose a sound from the drop-down list (see Figure 10.6) and click OK.

Fig. 10.6
The sound will play when the mouse pointer passes over the preselected object.

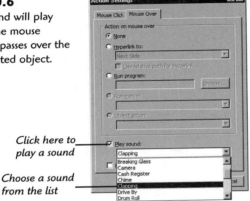

Click here to play a sound

Choose a sound from the list

I want to record a comment on my slide

It's simple to record a comment on a slide—if your computer has a microphone. Comments can be serious or funny. They can remind you to do something or they can add emphasis to one of your points. For example, I had my boss record a brief comment stating his approval to the budget requests I was making to the executive committee. The committee members all chuckled when they heard Ed's voice seconding my recommendations!

Once you've recorded the comment, you'll only be able to listen to it during the Slide Show.

Make sure that your microphone is working before you begin recording the comment. Here's how to record a comment on a slide:

TIP   **The "sound byte" you record should be short and to the point.**
Remember, you're recording a comment, not a long narrative. In Chapter 13 you'll learn how to record a narration to go along with your presentation.

1 Display the slide in Slide view that you want to record the comment to.

2 Open the Insert menu, and choose Movies and Sounds, then select Record Sound. The Record Sound dialog box, shown in Figure 10.7 appears.

Fig. 10.7
The Record Sound dialog box lets you record a brief comment on your slide.

When you're done recording, type a name for your comment here

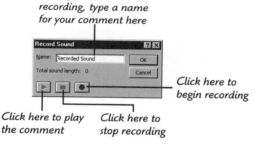

Click here to begin recording

Click here to play the comment   *Click here to stop recording*

3 To begin recording, click the box with the red ball (the third box to the right).

4 When you've finished recording your comment, click the middle button with the square on it to stop recording. The total time length of your comment is displayed.

5 Type a name for your comment in the Name box.

6 If you want to hear the comment, click the Play button (the first button on the left).

7 Click OK to close the Record Sound dialog box and insert the comment into your slide. A sound icon, as shown in Figure 10.8, is added to your slide.

Fig. 10.8
Click the sound icon
during the Slide Show
to hear the comment.

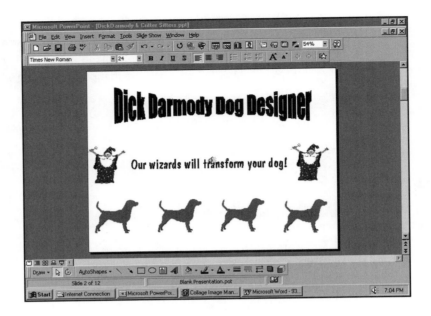

Fig. 10.8
Click the sound icon
during the Slide Show
to hear the comment.

Adding movies to your slides

Video clips work very similarly to sounds that you add to your slides. The major difference is in the medium itself—while sound can be heard across a crowded room, the audience must watch the slides to see the video clip play. Most video clips include sound effects.

TIP **The terms movie and video clips mean the same thing in** PowerPoint. The terms are used interchangeably.

Adding video clips from the Clip Gallery

The Microsoft Clip Gallery 3.0 is not only a great place for clip art and sounds, but an excellent place to find video clips. When you add a movie to your slide, a still picture is inserted directly into the slide. For example, if you insert a movie clip of an arrow missing a target, the picture of the target is inserted into your slide.

Follow these steps to add a movie clip to a slide:

1 In Slide view, display the slide you want to add the movie clip to.

2 Open the Insert menu and choose Movies and Sounds.

3 Select Movies from Gallery from the submenu. The Microsoft Clip Gallery 3.0 opens to the Videos tab, as shown in Figure 10.9.

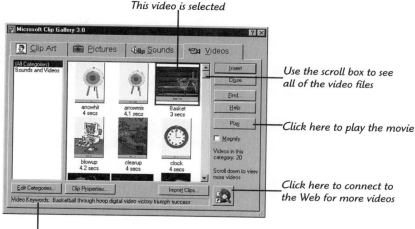

Fig. 10.9
The Microsoft Clip Gallery 3.0 opens to the Videos tab.

This video is selected

Use the scroll box to see all of the video files

Click here to play the movie

Click here to connect to the Web for more videos

Keywords from the video appear here

4 Click the video clip you want to add and then click Insert. The Clip Gallery closes and the video still picture is added to your slide, as shown in Figure 10.10.

5 To play the video, double-click the still picture. In a few seconds, the movie will play, complete with sound effects.

CAUTION **Because inserting a video clip to a slide adds a still picture, you** should build the slide around the picture. The clip needs to be the focal point of the slide, not an afterthought. If the slide looks cluttered, the effect of the movie will be lost.

Fig. 10.10
The video clip is added to the slide.

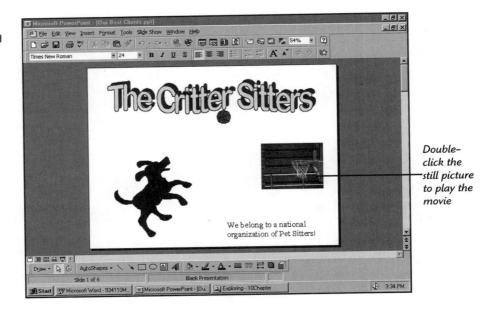

Double-click the still picture to play the movie

Welcome to PowerPoint Central

PowerPoint Central is a new feature that launches an online magazine for PowerPoint users that contains articles and tips on how to create better presentations. PowerPoint Central also includes hyperlinks that jump to Internet sites or to the Office 97 ValuPack folder on the CD-ROM for additional clip art, videos, sound clips, graphic effects, templates, and presentation tips. The PowerPoint Central site is updated every three months so there's always something to see and do.

TIP **The PowerPoint Central feature is installed during setup when** you select the Typical installation. If you didn't install it, follow the PowerPoint installation instructions in Appendix A of this book to install new program components.

Visiting PowerPoint Central

You must have a modem attached to your computer to visit PowerPoint Central. The modem must be connected to your Internet Service Provider or online service before you can access the site. Once you've connected, open the Tools menu and choose PowerPoint Central. After a few seconds, PowerPoint Central will appear on your screen.

PowerPoint Central is designed as several different slide shows. Many of the slides contain hyperlinks, or jumps, to other Web sites or to folders on the Office 97 CD-ROM. Figure 10.11 shows you the opening PowerPoint Central slide. When your mouse passes over a hyperlink the pointer will turn into the shape of a hand. Click any of the hyperlinks to jump to a new site or slide show.

When you're through with PowerPoint Central, close it as you would any other Windows 95 program. You can revisit PowerPoint Central any time.

Fig. 10.11
PowerPoint Central has lots to see and do for novice and experienced PowerPoint users.

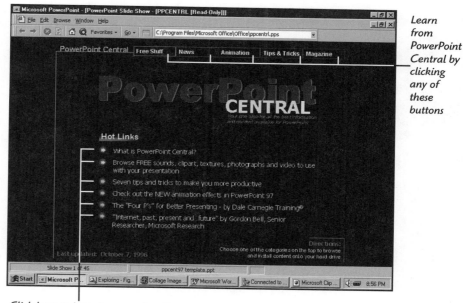

Learn from PowerPoint Central by clicking any of these buttons

Click here to jump to a new location

11

Using Advanced Art and Graphics Techniques

● In this chapter:

- How can I get a small portion of a picture on my slide?

- I'd like to recolor a picture

- Can I move several pieces of art work at the same time?

PowerPoint makes your slides look like a group of famous artists worked on them! . . . .

If you're like me, you see the most beautiful pictures in your head. Colors, placement, details—each picture is perfectly designed. However, when you try to transfer your dream to paper, it never comes out looking quite like you imagined. Let's face it, most of us are short on artistic ability.

Fortunately, you don't need years of art training to create sophisticated pictures for your PowerPoint slides. In Chapter 3, we learned how to add clip art to a slide and how to perform some basic functions with graphics objects. But that was only the beginning. PowerPoint lets you work all kinds of magic with clip art objects. You can rotate and recolor a picture or even group several pictures together to create one object. You're limited only by your imagination.

 TIP **Give yourself a lot of time whenever you work with clip art and** graphics objects. You'll find that working with pictures is so much fun, the time will speed by!

I only want a small portion of this image on my slide

Sometimes, you find the ideal piece of artwork for your slide. Unfortunately, the "perfect" image is included in a clip art picture that contains other images as well. PowerPoint lets you crop a clip art image to the size you want it. Cropping an image is a great way of getting exactly the material you want, without the other stuff.

 Plain English, please!

Cropping an image means you can "cut away" the unnecessary information that surrounds what you really want to use. For example, if you wanted an image of a tropical bird on a perch, you could cut away the tree trunk that appeared in the original picture.

 TIP **When you use the cropping tool, the portion of the picture you no** longer see is still there—it's just not visible. Think of a cropped image as one in which you glued blank paper on top of parts of an image you wanted to hide. The covered information is still available, even though you can't see it.

In PowerPoint, you can crop both vertically and horizontally. Artwork is cropped after it's placed on the slide. To crop an image on a slide:

1 Make sure the slide containing the image to be cropped is active and in Slide view.

2 Select the image by clicking it so that handles appear.

3 From the Picture toolbar, select the Crop tool. The pointer changes to the cropping tool.

4 Position the pointer over one of the handles you want to crop from.

5 Drag the handle. Figure 11.1 shows an image in the process of being cropped. Notice that even though the handles of the original artwork are shown, a dotted line shows you the part of the image that will be displayed on the slide when you're finished cropping.

6 When you're satisfied with the image, release the mouse button, then press Esc to turn off cropping. The handles disappear from the image, and the pointer returns to an arrow.

Fig. 11.1
Crop an image to use only what you want.

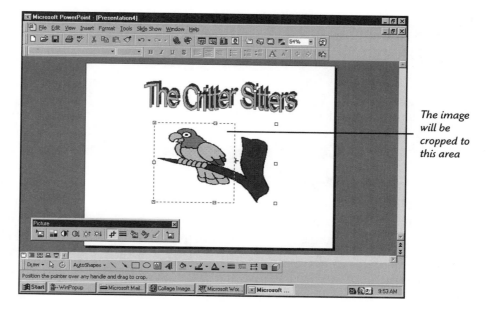

The image will be cropped to this area

Converting pictures to PowerPoint objects

You can change most graphic objects to fit your particular slide. However, before you can change them, you may have to convert clip art items from the Microsoft Gallery or pictures from files to **PowerPoint objects** before you can work on them.

66 *Plain English, please!*

If you want to rotate or flip clip art or a picture you've drawn on your slide, it must be converted from its original format to a **PowerPoint object**. This special PowerPoint format then lets you make any number of changes to the basic picture. 99

It's simple to convert a picture to a PowerPoint object. In Slide view, select the object you want to convert. (Handles will surround it.) Click the down arrow on the Draw button of the Drawing toolbar to open the drop-down menu. Choose Ungroup. The dialog box shown in Figure 11.2 opens, asking if you want to convert the object to a PowerPoint object.

Fig. 11.2
Convert a picture to
a PowerPoint object.

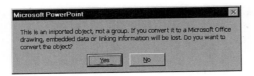

Click Yes to convert the object. Your picture is now a PowerPoint object.

Combining object elements into one object

Converting a picture or piece of clip art into a PowerPoint object means that you'll be able to work with it in PowerPoint. But, there's a potential problem waiting for you when you try to resize or move the new PowerPoint object. Based on the content of each picture it converts, PowerPoint looks at each element that makes up the picture and, accordingly, converts the picture into many separate objects.

For example, when a clip art picture of a door from the Microsoft Clip Gallery is converted to a PowerPoint object, different parts of the door become separate objects. The door itself is converted to one object, while the door frame is converted to another object, as shown in Figure 11.3. That's great news if you want to color or work with different sections of the door, but not so great if you simply want to rotate or flip the total image of door within the frame.

Fig. 11.3
A clip art picture is converted into several PowerPoint objects.

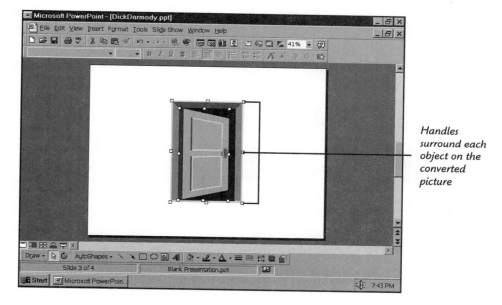

Handles surround each object on the converted picture

If you want to work with the total image, (for example, the door and the door frame) instead of several different pieces of the image, you'll need to **group** each of the separate objects into one.

Follow the steps shown next to group several objects into one object.

1 From Slide view, hold down the Shift key and click on the converted object. The mouse pointer becomes an arrow with a four-pointed star attached. When you click, handles surround a portion of the image.

2 Continue to hold down the Shift key and click the additional objects that make up the picture until handles surround all of the objects that make up the picture.

3 When all of the individual objects are selected, click the Draw button on the Drawing toolbar and choose Group. The objects are combined into one PowerPoint object.

4 Press Esc or click outside the object to deselect it.

The picture is now a single PowerPoint object, ready for your creative handiwork.

TIP   **If PowerPoint breaks a clip art picture into so many separate** components that selecting each element would be too time-consuming, you can easily select all of the components with a few simple steps. First, click anywhere on the item. Next, open the Edit menu and choose Select All. Handles surround each of the picture's components. Click the Draw button on the Drawing toolbar and choose Group to combine the objects into one PowerPoint object.

Can I turn this object in the other direction?

Isn't it always this way—you find the absolute, perfect picture for your slide, but it's facing in the wrong direction? PowerPoint lets you flip or rotate just about any object you've inserted onto your slide. Follow these steps to change the direction or rotate an object:

1 Select the object you want to rotate. Handles appear around it. (Remember, you must have already converted it to a PowerPoint object.)

2 Click the Free Rotate tool on the Drawing toolbar. The mouse pointer changes to the Free Rotate tool.

3 Position the Free Rotate tool over one of the object's handles and then drag the mouse in the direction you want to turn the object (see Figure 11.4). When you release the mouse button, you'll see that the object has rotated.

Alternatively, you can click the Draw button on the Drawing toolbar, choose Rotate or Flip and then choose Rotate Left or Rotate Right to rotate the item 90 degrees.

Fig. 11.4
Rotate a PowerPoint
object.

*The Free Rotate
tool pointer shows
that the object is
being rotated*

Flipping objects

Flipping an object turns it over. It's easy to flip any picture, as long as you've converted it to a PowerPoint object first. Select the object and click the Draw button on the Drawing toolbar. Choose Rotate or Flip and then select Flip Horizontal or Flip Vertical. The object appears flipped on the slide (see Figure 11.5).

CAUTION **Be careful if you flip or rotate an object that contains text. The** text may be backward or unreadable when the object changes direction.

Nudging an object

As you learned in Chapter 3, you can move artwork on your slide by dragging one of its handles. Sometimes though, it's impossible to move it a teensy bit. No matter how hard you try, you can't get it in the exact spot. Instead of dragging, you can nudge an object to move it in very small increments.

Fig. 11.5
The dog was flipped horizontally on the slide.

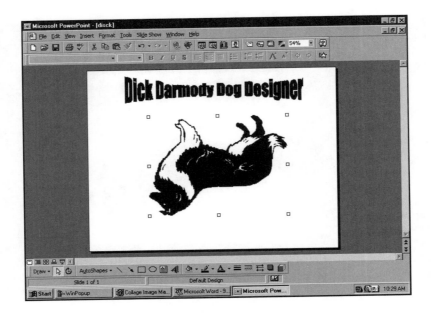

To use Nudge, first select the object you want to move. Click the down arrow on the Draw button of the Drawing toolbar to open the drop-down menu. Choose Nudge and click the direction you want to nudge the object.

I want to move several pieces of artwork at once

You have some powerful tools at your disposal when you're using PowerPoint. Not only can you add professionally created clip art, but you can also resize or crop out parts of that artwork that you don't want.

PowerPoint lets you work with multiple images by combining them into one easy-to-manage object.

Grouping several objects into one object

If you've arranged several pieces of artwork to form a design, you can group them into one object.

❝❝ *Plain English, please!*

Grouping two or more graphics images means that where you once had several objects, you now have one. That object can be flipped or rotated, resized, deleted, or copied like any other single object. When you're done manipulating the grouped object to fit on your slide, you can **ungroup** the object into separate pieces. **❞❞**

Figure 11.6 shows two sets of images on a single slide. The images were taken from the Microsoft Clip Gallery, then resized and arranged. The images on the left are ungrouped, while those on the right have been grouped. You can see that the grouped image has only one set of handles, while the ungrouped image has many.

Fig. 11.6
Grouping artwork lets you create a single object.

Ungrouped objects (handles appear around each object)

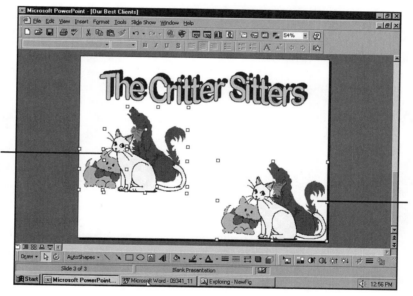

Grouped objects (handles appear around the combined object)

To group objects while in Slide view, select all the objects you want to group by holding down the Shift key as you click each object. (You'll see handles for each of the objects you've selected.) After all of the objects are selected, release the Shift key and right-click the mouse pointer in one of the selected images. Choose Group from the resulting menu. (You'll now see only one set of handles around the perimeter of all of the objects.) To deselect the grouped object, press Esc.

TIP   **Grouping several pieces of clip art into one object makes it easy** to move that object around on the slide. No matter where you move the grouped object, it always looks right.

Ungrouping multiple objects

Any time you want to, you can ungroup objects. For example, I may decide that the kitty in the center of the grouped object in Figure 11.7 is just a shade too large. That's just the nature of getting your work just right!

Objects can be ungrouped as easily as they are grouped. Select the object you want to ungroup by clicking it, then right-click the mouse pointer inside the handles and choose Ungroup. Each object now has its own set of handles. Press Esc to deselect each selected object.

Recoloring a picture

Your presentation is really coming together. You can devote your attention to small details, like the color of some clip art in one of your slides. Not only can you use any clip art you want, move it, resize it, and crop it, but you can also change the colors in it.

 TIP   **You can recolor any clip art—even images you've added to the** Clip Gallery. The only condition is that any grouped images must be ungrouped first.

The capability to change the colors in any of the Clip Gallery images means you have incredible control over your slides. To recolor an object:

1 In Slide view, select the object you want to recolor.

 2 Click the Recolor Picture button on the Picture toolbar. The Recolor Picture dialog box button opens, as shown in Figure 11.7.

3 Select the color in the Original column that you would like to change, then click the pull-down arrow in the New column and choose a new color. You can change as many of the original colors as you like.

4 Click Preview to see the effect of your changes.

5 When you're done, click OK.

Fig. 11.7
Change any of the
colors in an object.

*Original colors are
displayed here*

TIP **Choose your artwork based on its content, not its color.**
Remember, you can always change the colors to make the art work look
right.

I'd like to change or rearrange the objects in my picture

As you add art work to your slide, PowerPoint automatically stacks the
objects. The stacking order is especially visible when one of the objects
overlaps another, because the top object covers a portion of the of objects
beneath it (see Figure 11.8). It's easy to stack so many objects that the
bottom ones become almost invisible.

Fig. 11.8
The order of the
stacked objects has
been rearranged on
the slide.

*This object
is in the
back*

*This object is
in the front*

CAUTION **If you "lose" an object in a stack, press Tab to move forward or** press Shift+Tab to move backward through the stacked objects until the object is selected.

 After you've arranged several objects on a slide, experiment to determine the best order for the objects. Select the stacked object and then click the Draw button on the Drawing toolbar. Choose Order and then select one of the options. Table 11.1 describes each of the menu selections and its effect on your picture.

Table 11.1 **Menu selections**

Object order	Description	Button
Bring Forward	Places selected object at top of the stack	
Send to Back	Places selected object at bottom of the stack	
Bring Forward	Moves the selected object one layer closer to the top of the stack of objects	
Send Backward	Moves the selected object one layer closer to the bottom of the stack of objects	

12

Using Objects from Other Programs

● In this chapter:

- How can I get data from one program into another?

- I'd like to link data so changes are updated automatically

- What's the difference between linking and embedding?

- Can I use a hyperlink in my presentation?

Other programs on your computer can share data with PowerPoint through some Windows magic! . . . . ◗

Microsoft Office 97 makes your workload easier to manage. Using a program from the Office 97 collection of software means that data you create in one Office 97 program, like PowerPoint, can be shared with the other programs in the suite. If you change or edit the original data, it's automatically updated in the other applications that share the information. Just think, you would never have to type information into one program and then retype that same information into another program.

PowerPoint gives you several ways to get your data from one program to another, and several options of maintaining it as well. And you'll be pleased to know that retyping the data is *not* one of those options!

Why use Microsoft Office 97?

Microsoft Office 97 is the best **software suite** in the world. Microsoft Office 97 provides all of the software you'll need to create presentations, documents, spreadsheets, and databases. Additionally, Office 97 gives you an electronic messaging package (including the capability to send and receive electronic mail and faxes), a scheduling program, and an Internet browser. When you use an Office 97 product, you know that you're using software created and tested by the top designers and system engineers at Microsoft.

❝ *Plain English, please!*

> A **software suite** is a collection of different computer applications, such as Word, Excel, and PowerPoint, that are designed by one company and share a common look and commands. Suite programs are tightly integrated so that data from one program easily can be shared with the others. Each program hooks into the other programs in the collection. **❞**

There are many benefits to using Microsoft Office 97 programs. All the programs are designed to work in the Windows operating environment and take full advantage of all Windows features. You can choose to install all of the programs in the suite or pick only the ones you need. You always can add or delete one of the programs later. Because most companies and offices use Microsoft software, the files you create in one location can be used just about anywhere.

Microsoft Office 97 programs all share a common interface—the design of the screens, toolbar buttons, and menus are remarkably similar. You only need to learn one set of basic commands in an Office 97 program to be able to use the other programs. For example, you can add a hyperlink in Microsoft Office 97 programs by using the Insert, Hyperlink menu command.

Using the Clipboard

The easiest way to exchange data between PowerPoint and other programs is through the Windows Clipboard. Any text or object that is selected can be copied and then pasted anywhere else on your computer. The selected text or object can be pasted within PowerPoint or to another program, like Word or Excel. It can also be pasted from another program to PowerPoint. When data is cut or copied, it is temporarily stored in an area called the **Clipboard**.

❝ *Plain English, please!*

The **Clipboard** is a Windows feature that spans all Windows programs and provides temporary storage for text or objects you've copied or cut. You can paste the contents of the Clipboard once or over and over. The Clipboard holds one selection at a time. Whenever you use the Copy or Cut command in a Windows program, the current contents of the Clipboard are replaced by the new selection. When you turn off your computer, the Clipboard is automatically emptied. **❞**

  Add selected text or graphics to the Clipboard by first selecting the information and then clicking either the Cut or Copy button on the Standard toolbar. When you use Cut, an imaginary scissors "cuts" the selected information and removes it from its original location. When you use Copy, a carbon copy of the information is sent to the Clipboard, while the information in the original location is preserved. The next time you click the Cut or Copy button, the current contents of the Clipboard will be replaced with the new selection.

 Click on the location where you want the Clipboard information to be pasted. This location can be another slide, or a document in another program. Click the Paste button on the Standard toolbar, and the contents of the Clipboard is added to your current location (see Figure 12.1). This is a great way to get information from one file or program to another.

Fig. 12.1
Data from Excel can
be copied into
PowerPoint.

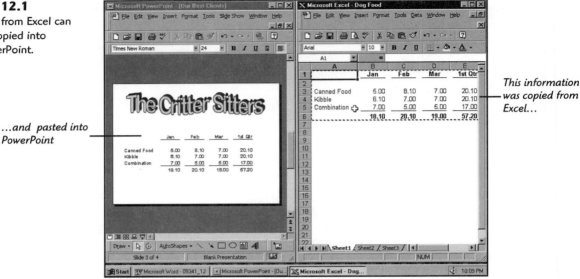

This information
was copied from
Excel...

...and pasted into
PowerPoint

TIP **All of the Office 97 programs are designed to share information**
with one another. A spreadsheet created in Excel can be added to your
slide or text from your presentation can be copied into Word. The cut-and-
paste method always works: it's a sure-fire way of moving data from one
program to another.

Q&A ***Can I cut or copy text, such as a point on a bulleted
list, from one position in a placeholder to another
position without using the Cut, Copy, and Paste
buttons?***

Yes. You can move or copy text using the drag-and-drop method. First,
select the text you want to move or copy. When it is highlighted, place the
mouse pointer over the selection. To move the selected text, press and hold
the mouse button. To copy the text, press and hold the mouse button and
the Ctrl key. A box which represents the selected text appears below the
mouse pointer. Drag (move) the box to the new location you want the text
to appear. Release the mouse button (and the Ctrl key) at the new location
to drop (insert) the text.

Updating information automatically

Using the Paste command to place an item from the Clipboard is fast and easy, but it has one limitation. If you make modifications to the original data, the pasted data does not change. For example, say you've pasted a column containing monthly sales figures from an Excel spreadsheet into a PowerPoint presentation. If you change the sales data in Excel, the PowerPoint slide does not change and therefore, displays the incorrect information. To make the PowerPoint information match the current Excel data, you'd need to retype the figures onto the slide.

Instead of pasting the information, you can link data between two documents. **Linking** documents means that when information in one document changes, the other document is automatically updated. Whenever you link objects, you create a live connection back to the original data.

When linking documents, it's important that you identify the **source** document, where the original information is stored, and the **destination** document, which contains the copied information. Data that has been copied from one source document can be pasted into more than one destination document.

66 *Plain English, please!*

The **source** document is the original file containing the information you put in the Clipboard. This is the data that, when modified, is updated in all the destination documents. The **destination** document receives the information from the source document. 99

Linking documents using the Paste Special command

Use the Paste Special command on the Edit menu to link information that may require further updating. The Paste Special command creates a link between two or more files—whether they were created in PowerPoint or not.

To create a link:

1 Open the source document and select the data that you want to link, then choose <u>E</u>dit, <u>C</u>opy or click the Copy button on the Standard toolbar. You can leave the source document open, or close it if you'd like; it has no effect on the linking process.

Figure 12.2 shows data that has been selected in Microsoft Excel.

Fig. 12.2
Data from Excel is ready to be copied.

Click here to copy the selected information

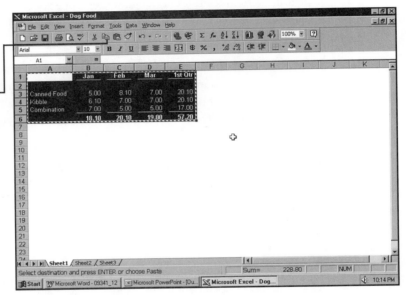

2 Click the location in the destination document where you want the linked data to appear. The destination document can be another document in the same application—for example, Excel to Excel or a different application—Excel to PowerPoint.

3 Choose <u>E</u>dit, Paste <u>S</u>pecial. The Paste Special dialog box opens. The PowerPoint Paste Special dialog box is displayed in Figure 12.3.

4 Make sure the correct type of source document is identified. You might be linking a Microsoft Excel Worksheet Object or a Microsoft Word Document Object. (You also can use the Paste Special dialog box to place the contents of the Clipboard in a document, without creating a link.) To display the linked data as an icon, click the <u>D</u>isplay As Icon check box.

5 Click the Paste Link option, then click OK. The link is created and the Excel data appears on the PowerPoint slide.

The source data and
location appear here

Fig. 12.3
Use Paste Link to link
two documents.

Click here to
create a link

Click here if you want to display
the pasted information as an icon

The result of the Paste Link
command is displayed here

TIP **If your computer's processor is slow, or if your linked data is very** large or contains many graphics, it's a good idea to display the linked data as an icon. That way the information is in your document and prints just fine, but won't slow down your system because of its size.

Q&A *I know I copied the information correctly from the source document but the Paste Link option is dimmed. Why?*

Some programs are designed to be "server" programs, which means they can only send data, not receive it. Applets like Notepad or Paint, as well as Microsoft Graph, are examples of server applications.

I'd like to link data from Excel and PowerPoint. How can I set my screen up so that both programs are side by side?

Windows magic makes this easy! First, make sure that both programs are open. Move your mouse arrow to a blank spot on the Windows 95 taskbar and click the right-mouse button. Choose Tile Vertically from the resulting shortcut menu. The programs are displayed side by side.

Viewing and updating links

You can see what links are in a file, or make sure your links are updated, by clicking <u>E</u>dit, Lin<u>k</u>s. The Links dialog box opens, as shown in Figure 12.4.

Fig. 12.4
Verify links with the
Links command.

*Links in the destination
document appear here*

Click here to break a link

The Links dialog box lets you update an existing link, change the link's source or the way in which the data is updated, or break a link entirely.

There are many reasons why you might want to break a link. I've broken links when I decided that now I want information to reflect a specific time, rather than being current (showing sales as of a specific date, as opposed to a year-to-date figure). Or, I've decided that the linked information is no longer necessary in my presentation.

Options available in the Links dialog box include:

- **<u>U</u>pdate Now.** Click this button to make sure all the links information is identical to the current version in the source document.

- **<u>O</u>pen Source.** Click this button to open the selected source document.

- **<u>C</u>hange Source.** Click this button to modify the source document used by a link.

- **<u>B</u>reak Link.** Click this button to sever the link.

It's standard for links to be automatically updated whenever a destination document is opened. If you want the links to be manually updated, click the <u>M</u>anual option located at the bottom of the Links dialog box.

 **CAUTION** **Be very careful not to move the source file to another folder on your computer or give it another name. If the source document's file name or location is changed, your computer will not be able to maintain the original link.**

Embedding objects

An alternative method of getting information from one location to another is to **embed** it. Embedding uses a process called Object Linking and Embedding, or OLE for short. When you use OLE, PowerPoint's toolbars and menus are temporarily replaced with those of the application that originally created the object. You were introduced to OLE when you created charts in Chapter 5, PowerPoint's menu and toolbars were replaced by those of Microsoft Graph.

 Plain English, please!

An **embedded** document looks like any object in a document, but when the object is double-clicked, the program that created it opens. Where a linked document looks at another file and updates information, an embedded document actually opens another application so you can make changes to the linked document—without leaving the active application that's on the screen.

For example, a Word document can be embedded in a PowerPoint slide. (The Microsoft Word menu, ruler, and toolbars appear on the PowerPoint slide.) The Word document can be opened and edited from within PowerPoint by double-clicking the document object. Figure 12.5 shows an embedded Word document open in PowerPoint.

 TIP **Embedding a document creates a larger file than when files are** linked. But if you have the disk space and you don't want to risk breaking a link, try embedding.

The advantages of linking

The biggest advantage to linking documents is the capability to have multiple copies of the same object in different files. For example, The Critter Sitter's logo file (originally created in WordArt) appears on slides in PowerPoint, the company's letterhead template file in Word and in the monthly invoices that are maintained in Excel. At some point, if the management of The Critter Sitters decides to update the corporate logo, changing it in the source document will automatically update the logo it in all of the files it's been linked to.

Fig. 12.5
An embedded Word document is open in PowerPoint.

Word ruler

PowerPoint slide

Word document

Word menu and toolbars

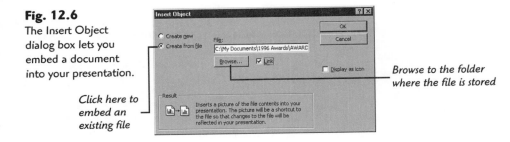

The technique for embedding a file is different than linking a file. Here's how to embed a document:

1 Open the destination document. If you want, open the source document. (It's not necessary for the source document to be open.)

2 Click in the location in the destination document where you want to insert the embedded data.

3 Choose Insert, Object. The Insert Object dialog box appears as shown in Figure 12.6.

Fig. 12.6
The Insert Object dialog box lets you embed a document into your presentation.

Click here to embed an existing file

Browse to the folder where the file is stored

4 Click Create From File.

5 Click the Browse button to view the folder where the source file is stored. Click the file name and then click OK to close Browse and return to the Insert Object dialog box.

6 Make sure the Link box is checked and then click OK. The selected document is embedded into the slide.

Embedded documents take up considerably more disk space than linked documents, but offer you the flexibility of modifying the original document on the spot. You never have to worry if the links have been updated, because you can open another program from within PowerPoint.

 TIP **Linking and embedding work very differently. When you link** documents, the link enables the data in the destination to update if it's changed in the source document. When you embed an object from one document into another, the embedded object must be double-clicked to first open the program it was created in and then you can update the data.

Working with hyperlinks

 Because most presentations are created from a group of related files, Microsoft has added the capability to create **hyperlinks** from your presentation directly to a specific file, or even to a specific location in a specific file. During the slide show, the hyperlink can jump to a location in your current presentation, to a different presentation, or to a file that was created in a different program such as Word or Excel.

 *Plain English, please!*

Hyperlinks are jumps that whisk you to another location when you click them during the presentation.

You can even use hyperlinks to jump to multimedia files, such as sounds and videos. In fact, you can add a hyperlink to jump directly to a page on the World Wide Web. (See Chapter 19 for more information about adding a hyperlink to the Web.)

Adding a hyperlink to any Office 97 program is easy—Microsoft has designed a common Insert Hyperlink dialog box that covers all Office 97 programs.

1 If it's not already open, activate the PowerPoint presentation in which you want to insert the hyperlink.

2 Select the word or object to which you want to attach the hyperlink.

3 Click the Insert Hyperlink button on the Standard toolbar. The Insert Hyperlink dialog box opens, as shown in Figure 12.7.

Fig. 12.7
The Insert Hyperlink dialog box is the same for all Office 97 applications.

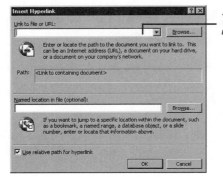

Type the path and file name or URL of the link

4 In the Link to File or URL text box, type the folder path and the name of the file you want the presentation to jump to. If you're not sure of the file name, click the Browse button and locate the file on the hard drive of your computer.

5 It's not necessary to click in the Path text box as it displays the folder and file name of the link automatically.

6 (Optional) Click in the Named Location in File if you want to jump to a Word bookmark, a named range in Excel, a database object in Access, or a specific slide number in another PowerPoint presentation.

7 When all of the information in the Insert Hyperlink dialog box is correct, click OK.

8 The Hyperlink is inserted into your slide, as shown in Figure 12.8.

Fig. 12.8
The slide contains a
hyperlink.

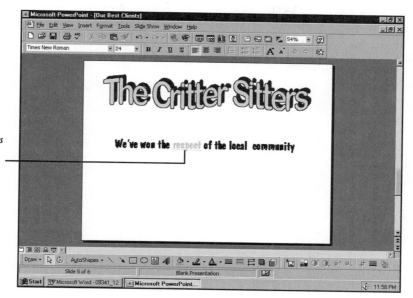

The hyperlink appears
underlined and in a
color different than
the rest of the text

 Q&A ***Why doesn't anything happen when I click a hyperlink
in my slide?***

Hyperlinks work only while a slide show is running. They don't work while
you're working on your presentation in Slide view, Slide Sorter view, or
Outline view.

13

Look Like a Pro: Adding Super Special Effects

● In this chapter:

- I want to add animation to my slides

- I'd like to give my charts some special effects

- Can I record my own narration for the slide show?

Become a special effects expert and give your presentations pizzazz using PowerPoint's bag of tricks. . . . .➤

When you think of special effects, you probably think of Hollywood blockbusters involving the likes of Steven Spielberg, *Star Trek*, or the special effects folks from the Industrial Light and Magic company. Well, your presentation probably won't have any exploding spaceships in it (although it could!) but you can use some awesome special effects.

Special effects hold the audience's interest and force them to pay attention. Have you ever seen a weather report on the news where one graphic fades into another? If so, you've seen one of the special effects you'll be able to put into your presentation using PowerPoint. You can add this special effect, and more, into your slide show.

Why should I use animation?

Animation is one of PowerPoint's most improved features. Animation settings let you control how objects and text appear on the slide during the presentation. You can set up the order that bullet points appear on a list or how a graphic object is displayed. Animation effects add real punch to the slide.

If you want, you can even set up the animation to occur automatically during the presentation. You can preview the animation you've set at any time.

The evolution of PowerPoint

I don't think of myself as old, but when it comes to PowerPoint, I've been around since the program was an infant. Just a few short years ago, I remember being amazed that I could create a slide show on my computer! Now, I can add all kinds of Hollywood special effects.

With the help of PowerPoint's army of design and automation tools, my presentation can rival anything produced by a professional graphic artist. After it's finished, I can share my presentation with my colleagues at work or the world through the Internet. Pretty amazing when you realize that a few years ago, none of this was possible.

One thing hasn't changed over time, though. No matter how many extras—sound, video, color, animation—a presentation contains, it must start with good, sound information to be effective. Flying text bars and the sound of clattering typewriter keys will never disguise figures that don't make sense.

Animating objects can be a complicated process. In this chapter, I'll try to walk you through the easiest ways to use animation.

 **Plain English, please!**

> **Animation** refers to the way you add special visual or sound effects to a graphical object or text. For example, you can add an animation effect that causes the text in a bulleted list to fly in from the left. You can animate objects on the slide or even some elements from a chart. **99**

Using preset animation

Using PowerPoint's preset animation controls make animating any object a breeze. To animate an object such as a picture or a placeholder, make sure you're in Slide view and the object you want to animate is visible. Select the picture or text placeholder you want to animate (handles will surround it). If you need to learn more about working with text placeholders and graphics objects, refresh your knowledge by reviewing Chapter 3.

After the object you want to animate is selected, choose Slide Show, Preset Animation. A list of animation effects appears, as shown in Figure 13.1.

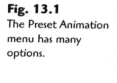

Fig. 13.1
The Preset Animation menu has many options.

Click an effect to add it to the graphic

Handles surround the selected object

To preview the animation effect you've just added, choose Sli<u>d</u>e Show, Animation Pre<u>v</u>iew. The animation plays in the slide miniature that appears. To replay the animation, click the miniature. Continue adding preset effects to each item you want to animate, previewing the effect each time you add a new one.

TIP **Remember that you're not stuck with an animation** effect that you've just added. Immediately after you add the effect, preview it. If it doesn't add the punch you wanted, click the Undo button on the Standard toolbar.

CAUTION **Working with any kind of animation is very memory-intensive and** can tax the resources of even the most powerful computer. To prevent your computer from locking up whenever you work with Animation, close all but the applications you're using. You can close an open application by right-clicking its icon on the Windows 95 taskbar and choosing C<u>l</u>ose from the resulting shortcut menu.

The simple slide shown in Figure 13.2 actually has three animation effects when it appears during the presentation. The title flies from the top, the door appears, and the text has a drive-in effect.

Fig. 13.2
Each element of this slide has a preset animation effect during the slide show.

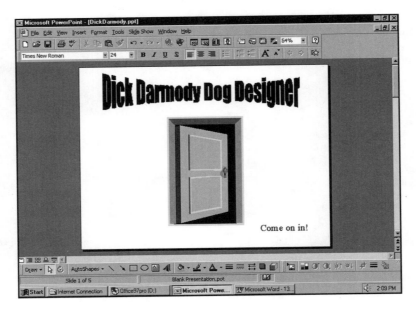

Adding custom animation

Custom animation is difficult to work with, but gives you greater control over the special effects you add to the slide. You can add a different custom animation effect to each element of the slide.

Follow these steps to add custom animation to a slide:

1 Make sure that the slide to which you want to add the custom animation is displayed in Slide view.

2 Choose Slide Show, Custom Animation. The Custom Animation dialog box appears, as shown in Figure 13.3.

Fig. 13.3
The Custom Animation dialog box lets you control the animation effects on your slide.

Animation tabs

Slide objects are listed here

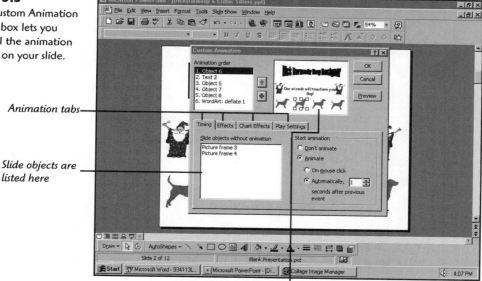

A thumbnail of the slide with the object to animate selected appears here

3 In the Slide Objects without Animation box, select the item you want to animate. (If you're not sure which item is which, watch as handles in the thumbnail surround the different items as you click each item's name.)

4 Click the Animate option. To start the animation by clicking the text or object, click the On Mouse Click option. To start the animation automatically, click the option next to Automatically and then type in the number of seconds to pass between the previous animation and this one. (If this is the first item to animate on the slide, you don't need to set up a time limit.)

5 Click the Effects tab. As shown in Figure 13.4, the item title you chose appears selected in the Animation order box. Handles surround it in the thumbnail of the slide.

6 From the Entry Animation and Sound boxes, use the down arrows to open the drop-down lists and choose how the text will appear and what, if any, sound will be played.

7 Choose what you want to happen after the animation from the After Animation list.

Fig. 13.4
The Effects tab on the Custom Animation dialog box.

Choose how the item will appear here

Choose what sound will be played here

Choose what will happen after animation occurs

The Effects tab

Choose how the text will be introduced here

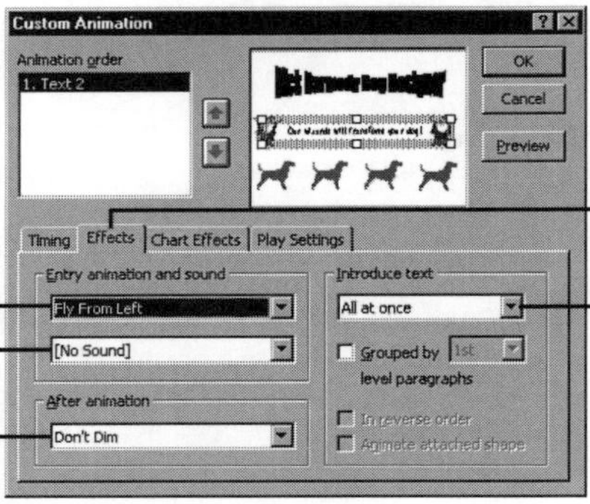

8 Click the Preview button to preview the animation you've just set.

9 Repeat steps 3 through 8 for each item on the slide you want to animate. Each item that you animate is added to the Animation Order list.

10 If you want to change the order in which each item appears, select the item on the Animation Order list and then click the up or down arrow to move the item up or down on the list (see Figure 13.5).

11 When you've added all the animation you want to the slide, click OK to close the Custom Animation dialog box and return to the slide.

Fig. 13.5
Move an item up
or down on the
Animation Order list.

Selected item —

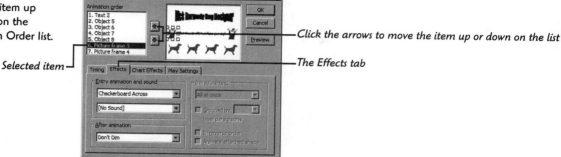

Click the arrows to move the item up or down on the list

The Effects tab

Q&A *No sounds come out of my computer, or the Sound pull-down option is dimmed. What's wrong?*

Sound effects are only available on computers that have an installed sound card, such as a Sound Blaster. Your computer may not be equipped with a sound card, or it may be malfunctioning. Check to see if other sounds work, such as when Windows 95 starts up. If other sounds are still working, there may be a hardware problem. If there are no other sounds, there may be nothing wrong at all—your computer may not produce sounds.

Adding custom animation to a chart

Generally speaking, charts provide the most information in your presentation but are the hardest to understand. Most people are uncomfortable with looking at numerical data—even in chart form—and tend not to understand it. I've seen people turn away from a presentation when a chart appears, even if it contains important data.

PowerPoint 97 allows you to animate several different chart elements. Looking at charts can be so entertaining that your audience will forget how much they hate numbers!

To add animation to a chart, make sure that it's visible on your screen in Slide view. Choose <u>S</u>lide Show, Custo<u>m</u> Animation. Click the Chart Effects tab (see Figure 13.6).

Fig. 13.6
Animating elements on a chart generates real visual interest.

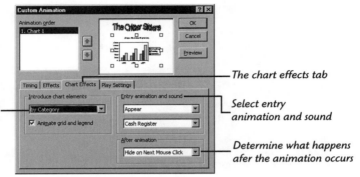

Choose how different elements will be introduced here

The chart effects tab

Select entry animation and sound

Determine what happens afer the animation occurs

Just as you did in the Effects tab, set the Animation entry and sound and what will happen after the animation takes place. From the Introduce Chart Elements drop-down list, choose how different chart elements will appear. Click the Preview button to see the results of your handiwork and then click OK to return to the slide. The animation effects you've added are waiting to enthrall your audience!

TIP **There are so many different ways you can add animation to your** slides. The timing, order, and effect are an individual choice—you and I might each look at a slide and animate it differently. Take the time to experiment with what you like and what you think your audience will like. And always remember not to add so many effects that your audience forgets the purpose of your presentation!

Action buttons give you a jump on your competition

Action buttons give you some extra control over your presentation. When you add an action button to your slide, you define what action you want to associate with the button. For example, you might add an action button that jumps to another slide or starts a movie. It's up to you whether to use the button during the course of the presentation. For example, if you unexpectedly spend some extra time answering an important question or mention some additional, nonscripted points, you're not locked in to the action button's movement.

PowerPoint makes it easy to add an action button. The following table describes the function of each action button.

Button	What does it do?
	User defined action
	Home
	Opens Help
	Displays information
	Returns to previous location
	Moves forward or next
	Moves to the beginning
	Moves to the end
	Return
	Opens a document
	Plays a sound
	Plays a movie

Make sure the slide that you want to add the button to is displayed in Slide view. Click AutoShapes on the Drawing toolbar and choose Action Buttons. Click the button you want to add to the slide, (your mouse pointer will take the shape of a cross) and then click the slide where you want the button to appear.

The Actions Setting dialog box automatically appears with the option checked that corresponds to the button's action (see Figure 13.7). For example, if you've added the Document button, the Run Program option is checked, waiting for you to fill in the drive, folder name, and the file that launches the program that the document was created in, along with the folder path and name of the document.

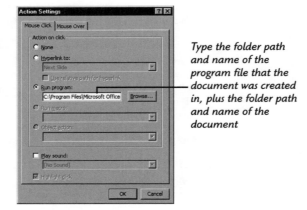

Fig. 13.7
The Action Settings dialog box lets you set actions that will occur when the action button is clicked.

Type the folder path and name of the program file that the document was created in, plus the folder path and name of the document

After the button is placed on the slide, you can drag the button to move it or resize it.

CAUTION **Before you set an action button, you need to do a little homework.** Be sure you know what you want the button to do. For example, if you're setting an action to open a document, write down the folder and file location of the program that was used to create the document, as well as the folder and file name of the document. If the button will play a sound or a movie, make sure you know the exact location of the sound or movie file.

Q&A *I know I set up the button correctly but when I click it nothing happens. Why?*

You need to be running the Slide Show for the action you assigned the action button to occur. Nothing will happen if you're in Slide, or Slide Sorter view.

I want to record my narration

As long as your computer is equipped with a sound card and a microphone, you can record the narrative you'll give during the presentation.

You might want to include a recorded narration if you know that you won't be present when the slide show is run. Or, you might plan to make multiple copies of your original presentation and send them to many different locations. By recording your own narration, you're assured that the presenter (you) will cover the important points in the correct order.

CAUTION **While recording a narration is convenient, make sure that you** have lots of free space on your computer before you begin. Sound files consume incredible amounts of disk space.

When the presentation runs, your recorded narration will automatically play with the show. If you want to run the slide show without narration, choose Slide Show, Set Up Show menu, and then select the Show without Narrations check box.

TIP **While you're recording your narration, you won't be able to hear** any of the other sounds you've inserted in your slides. That's because you can't play and record sounds at the same time. Don't worry, both your narration and any other sounds you've inserted in the slides will be audible during the Slide Show.

Make sure that your microphone is functioning properly before you begin recording the narration. If you're not very familiar with the microphone, take a few minutes and review the documentation that came with it. Once you're ready, open the presentation and perform the following steps:

1 Choose Slide Show, Record Narration. The Record Narration dialog box shown in Figure 13.8 appears.

2 To begin recording and to insert the narration on your slides as an embedded object, click OK. The slide show begins on your screen.

3 As you advance through the slide show, record the narration.

4 At the end of the show, the message shown in Figure 13.9 appears.

*Current recording
quality is shown here*

Fig. 13.8
The Record Narration
dialog box lets you
make changes to the
recording settings.

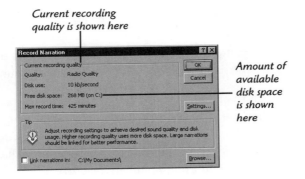

*Amount of
available
disk space
is shown
here*

Fig. 13.9
Click <u>Y</u>es to save the
slide timings or <u>N</u>o to
save only the narration.

The narration you recorded is added to each slide. A sound icon appears in
the lower-right corner of each slide that has recorded narration. Your spoken
words are now part of the slide show.

CAUTION **Before you record your narration, plan what you're going to say**
and then rehearse it several times. Hearing a number of "umms" or pauses
between words will make your audience think you were unprepared and
make the presentation seem unprofessional.

Part III: On with the Show

Chapter 14: **The Final Countdown—Rehearsing Your Presentation**

Chapter 15: **Creating Presentation Handouts**

Chapter 16: **Preparing Your Slide Show**

14

The Final Count-down—Rehearsing Your Presentation

● **In this chapter:**

- Can I create a summary slide?

- I want to add some special effects as my slides advance

- How do I skip a slide during the presentation?

- Can I time my delivery?

The big day's almost here—rehearse your presentation to make it perfect! . . . . **>**

You've put a lot of effort into your presentation. Every slide tells a story. You've gotten the exact mix of graphics and text necessary to make each of the slides picture-perfect. You're ready to wow the audience with the facts and figures you've carefully researched. What's left to do? Why, rehearse the slide show, of course!

PowerPoint has many tools for you to get your presentation ready for the "big day." There's no need to be nervous. You and PowerPoint will make a great team.

Working in Slide Sorter view

The best place to handle most of the rehearsal is from Slide Sorter view. (Views were covered in Chapter 1.) In Slide Sorter view, you have the opportunity to look at all of the slides in the presentation and work with them as a group. When you switch to Slide Sorter view, the Slide Sorter toolbar appears. Table 14.1 describes what each button does.

Table 14.1   The Slide Sorter toolbar

Button	Name	What does it do?
	Slide Transition	Sets slide transitions for the selected slide or all of the slides
No Transition	Slide Transition Effects	Displays the transition effects set for the selected slide
No Effect	Text Preset Animation	Displays type of preset animation for text in the selected slide
	Hide Slide	Hides the current slide
	Rehearse Timing	Starts the slide rehearsal

Button	Name	What does it do?
	Summary Slide	Creates a Summary slide from the slides you've selected
	Show Formatting	Shows the formatting of the selected slide

Create a summary slide

Before you begin the "fun stuff," it might be a good idea to create a summary slide. This slide contains the titles from other slides that you've selected for your presentation. After you've created the summary slide, you can use it to keep on track as you set up the presentation.

Follow these steps to create a summary slide:

1 Open the completed presentation you want to create the summary slide for in Slide Sorter view. The Slide Sorter toolbar appears on the screen.

2 Click the first slide whose title you want to include on the summary slide.

3 Hold down the Shift key and click each additional slide whose title you want to include. If you want to select all of the slides, choose Edit, Select All.

4 When you've clicked all of the slides you want to include, click the summary slide button on the Slide Show toolbar.

5 The summary slide, as shown in Figure 14.1, is inserted in front of the first slide you selected.

6 If you want to change the position of the summary slide (I like my summary slide to be the last slide), select it and drag it to its new position in the slide order.

After you've created the summary slide, you can use it to keep yourself on track as you rehearse the presentation. If you don't want to include the slide in the actual presentation, you can hide it. (We'll learn more about hiding slides later in this chapter.)

Fig. 14.1
The summary slide contains the headings from slides you've selected.

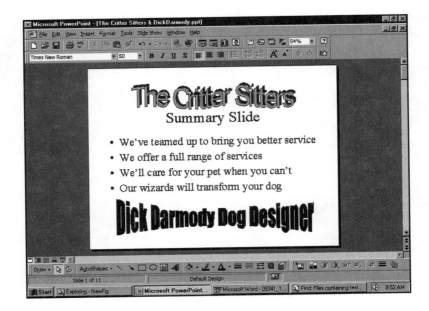

Change the transition style as each slide advances

Delivering a presentation involves a lot of thought. You need to know how to hold your audience's attention by giving them information in small doses—not all at once. That's why it's important to control the **transition style** of your slides.

 *Plain English, please!*

> A **transition style** is the style you set that controls how a slide appears and then disappears during your presentation. PowerPoint offers over 40 different transition styles for your slide show.

You can assign one style for the entire presentation or you can apply different transition styles to individual slides. Although it's tempting to include several different transition styles, it's best if you stick to only one. However, changing the style for one or two important slides that you want the audience to notice can be an effective tool.

CAUTION **Before you get busy adding slide transitions, consider the work** you've already done on the presentation. If you've added a lot of animation and sound, a flashy transition will be a distraction. If you've used minimal animation, transitions can add some needed excitement to your presentation. To be on the safe side, keep repeating to yourself, "Less is more!"

Take a good look at your slides before you add transition effects. To a certain extent, the overall style of your slides should dictate the transition style that presents them. For example, slides that contain lots of text and few pictures could be combined with snappy transitions for a memorable presentation. Another important consideration is who's going to see the slide show. A presentation that's aimed at business executives might need more subtle transitions between slides than a presentation set up for a gathering of dog groomers.

 TIP **The default slide transition style in PowerPoint is "No Transition."** If you don't choose a transition style, the only way each slide will advance is when you click the mouse or press a key on the keyboard.

The following steps show you how to assign a transition style to all of the slides in your presentation:

1 Open the presentation on your screen in Slide Sorter view.

2 The Slide Sorter toolbar appears.

3 Select the first slide in the presentation so that a dark border surrounds it.

 4 Click the Slide Transition button on the Slide Sorter toolbar. The Slide Transition dialog box appears, as shown in Figure 14.2.

Fig. 14.2
The Slide Transition dialog box lets you choose how your slides advance.

Thumbnail

Choose a transition effect from the list

Set how the slides advance here

Add a sound here

5 Click the down arrow in the <u>E</u>ffect text box and choose an effect from the list. As you click different transition effects, the effect will preview in the thumbnail and the sample picture will change. Figure 14.3 shows some of the available transition effects.

Fig. 14.3
Experiment with different transition effects from the drop-down list.

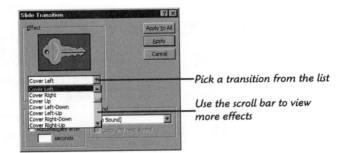

Pick a transition from the list

Use the scroll bar to view more effects

6 After you've chosen a transition effect, choose <u>S</u>low, <u>M</u>edium, or <u>F</u>ast to set the speed of the transition.

7 Set the slide Advance option. To have the slide advance when it's clicked by the mouse, choose the option next to <u>O</u>n Mouse Click. To set the slide to advance automatically, click the option next to Automati-<u>c</u>ally After and type in the desired number of seconds in the box.

8 If you want a sound to accompany the transition, choose a sound from the So<u>u</u>nd drop-down list.

9 When you've made all of the choices, click the Apply <u>t</u>o All button to apply the transistion effects to the presentation. (In the next section, you'll learn how to apply a transition effect to one slide.) The dialog box closes and you're returned to your slides in Slide Sorter view.

Now that you've added transition effects to the entire presentation, this would be a great time to run through the slides and see what you think. Click the Slide Show button for a preview of what your audience will see. You can cancel the show at any time by pressing Esc. Pretty neat, eh?

Changing the transition for one slide

Sometimes, you can add something extra to the presentation by changing the transition effect for a particular slide. Maybe that slide contains some bullet points that are important or the slide makes an important announcement. Changing transition effects for one slide takes just a few mouse clicks.

From Slide Sorter view, click the slide in which you want to change the transition effects. Right-click the slide and then choose Slide <u>T</u>ransition from the resulting shortcut menu, as shown in Figure 14.4. Choose whatever options you want from the Slide Transition dialog box and then click OK. The new effects are added to only the selected slide.

Fig. 14.4
Right-click to bring up the shortcut menu for the selected slide.

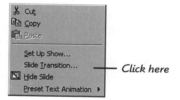

— *Click here*

 CAUTION **Be aware that your computer's processor speed can influence how** your build effects look during a slide show. For example, if you use a Pentium to create your presentation and apply your build effects, then show the slides on a slower computer, your effects might not look so great. (I've seen an effect like the Checkerboard Across look downright silly, because the computer the show was running on was so slow that the "checkers" appeared to "stall" on the screen. The effect looked jerky, not fluid like it would look with a faster computer processor.) Knowing the processor speed of the computer you'll be using for your slide show means you can plan which features you should use or avoid. It can save you time before your presentation because you won't have to make last-minute adjustments.

What if I want to skip a slide during a presentation?

No matter how much you plan, you always can count on the unexpected. Suppose you anticipate that one of your slides may not be relevant by the time you give your presentation. PowerPoint gives you the option of hiding that slide. You can decide whether to show the slide on-the-fly during your presentation.

You can hide a slide in Slide, Outline, Notes Page, or Slide Sorter view. If you use Slide Sorter view, the international No symbol appears, indicating that you've hidden the slide. (The international No symbol is a circle or square with a diagonal slash through it.)

 After you've selected the slide to hide, click the Hide Slide button on the Slide Sorter toolbar if you're in Slide Sorter view, or Slide Show, Hide Slide. The international No sign appears next to the Hide Slide command to remind you that the slide is hidden.

 TIP **The Hide Slide command, accessed either from the Slide Show** menu or by clicking the button on the Slide Sorter toolbar is a toggle command. That means that one mouse click turns it on, while another mouse click turns it off. Windows toggle commands work just like the light switches in your house.

During the presentation, you'll know that the next slide is hidden by the hidden slide icon that is displayed in the lower-left corner of the current slide.

 Click the Slide Show button. Figure 14.5 shows the Slide Show menu icon you can use to reveal a hidden slide during a show. (You might have to move the mouse to see the icon on-screen.)

Press H on the keyboard to display the hidden slide, or click the Slide Show menu icon to display a pop-up menu. Choose Go, Hidden Slide. Skip the hidden slide by clicking the mouse button to advance to the next (non-hidden) slide. Click Esc to end the slide show and return to the current slide.

Fig. 14.5
Display a hidden slide
using the Slide Show
menu icon.

The Critter Sitters
Summary Slide

- We've teamed up to bring you better service
- We offer a full range of services
- We'll care for your pet when you can't
- Our wizards will transform your dog

Dick Darmody Dog Designer

*Click here to display
the hidden slide*

Rehearsing the slide show timing

Planning your presentation is important. You've applied lots of animation and transition effects, and probably included a few sound and movie clips, too. You need to be able to keep control of the timing of all the various elements you've added to the presentation. You and your slides need to be in "synch."

If you speak too slowly, the next slide might appear before you're done talking about the current one. Talk too fast and you'll be left with dead air. (Even a few seconds of empty silence is uncomfortable for you and the audience.) Fortunately, PowerPoint provides some sophisticated rehearsal aids.

 The easiest way to set the time that each slide will appear on the screen is already familiar to you. From Slide Sorter view, select the slide whose timing you want to set. Click the Slide Transition button on the Slide Sorter toolbar. When the Slide Transition dialog box appears, set the time that the slide will remain on the screen, as shown in Figure 14.6.

Fig. 14.6
Set the time that the
slide will remain on the
screen.

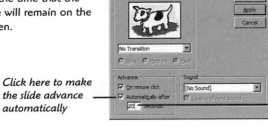

*Click here to make
the slide advance
automatically*

*Type the number of
seconds here*

Review the contents of each slide and set the timing accordingly. Some slides
might require a long period on-screen, while a few seconds may be sufficient
for others.

I'd like to set the timing during the rehearsal

The rehearsal for the presentation is important. It gives you the opportunity
to get the kinks out of the presentation and keeps you from having the jitters
the on "P" (Presentation) day. What you'll wear, where you'll stand, what
you'll say—now's the time to work out all these details.

Fortunately, you can let PowerPoint work with you to set the slide timings
during the rehearsal. The Rehearsal dialog box is a valuable tool used to get
your timing just right. The Rehearsal dialog box contains the following
elements:

Button	Name	What does it do?
▷	Record	Records the elapsed time for the current slide. Click to advance to the next slide.
❚❚	Pause	Click once to pause timer, click again to resume
Repeat	Repeat	Resets timer to zero for the current slide so you can rehearse it again

Button	Name	What does it do?
00:00:53	Presentation Elapsed Time	Shows the elapsed time for the presentation
00:00:53	Slide Elapsed Time	Shows the elapsed time for the current slide

Here's how:

1 Choose Slide Show, Rehearse Timings.

2 In a few seconds, the slide show rehearsal starts and the Rehearsal dialog box appears, as shown in Figure 14.7.

3 Rehearse your delivery for each slide, clicking the Record, Pause, and Repeat buttons as you need to.

4 When you're finished, click the Close button (X) to return to end the rehearsal.

5 If you want to use the timings you just recorded, click Yes. If you want to discard the timings you just recorded and start over, click No.

You can rehearse the slide show as many times as you need to to feel comfortable with the presentation material.

Fig. 14.7
The Rehearsal dialog box records the elapsed time.

Using the Slide Meter

Sometimes setting the timing for a presentation is the hardest part! For example, if you're presenting your slides to a group of people you don't know, it's hard to predict whether you'll be able to go smoothly from slide to slide or stop in between slides to answer questions. The PowerPoint Slide Meter, as shown in Figure 14.8, is the ideal tool for exactly such situations. The Slide Meter monitors the time you're spending against the time you've allotted and keeps you on track. To start the Slide Meter, right-click during the slide show and choose Slide Meter from the shortcut menu.

Fig. 14.8
The Slide Meter
measures your progress
against the rehearsed
times.

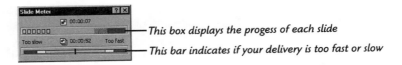

— *This box displays the progess of each slide*
— *This bar indicates if your delivery is too fast or slow*

The Slide Meter measures your progress against the times you've set during rehearsal. Numbers at the top of the meter display the elapsed time for the current slide. Numbers at the bottom display the elapsed time for the total slide show. The progress bar in the middle measures the time you're taking now against the rehearsed time you set previously.

If you're within the time you set in the Rehearsal dialog box, green boxes appear. If you start to go beyond the rehearsed time, yellow caution boxes appear. Red boxes mean that you've gone way past the time you set during rehearsal. The bar at the bottom of the Slide Meter indicates whether your delivery is to fast or too slow, based on the rehearsed time you've already set.

Q&A   *How do I stop the slide show?*

You can stop the slide show any time during the presentation. Just press the Esc key or right-click and then choose End <u>S</u>how from the shortcut menu.

Can I black the screen for a few moments while I collect my thoughts?

Sure. During the slide show, right-click to bring up the shortcut menu and choose S<u>c</u>reen. Next, select <u>B</u>lack Screen. When you're ready, just click anywhere on the blackened screen to get the show going again.

15

Creating Presentation Handouts

● **In this chapter:**

- **I want to print my outline and slides**

- **I'd like to create a handout**

- **Can I make Speaker Notes on my slides?**

Distributing presentation handouts is like passing out party favors—your audience loves to get something to take with them after the event . . . .

People love paper! No matter how many visual aids you provide, most people want something on paper they can refer to long after the presentation's done. PowerPoint makes it easy to create all sorts of handouts, enabling everyone to follow along during your presentation and serving as reference points afterward. So much for the paperless society!

What kind of printed materials can I create?

Printing the results of all your hard work can be helpful not only for your audience, but for colleagues and yourself as well. That's because we all like to follow along on a hard copy agenda—and because we all love to know what's coming up next!

An audience that can make notes during a presentation is also able to ask you more meaningful questions and give you better feedback.

An outline's always useful

The simplest item to print is an outline of your presentation. An outline lets you know, at a glance, if your slides follow a logical progression. Your outline not only guides you as you create the presentation, but can serve as an agenda for your audience when it's printed. Why waste time re-typing a program when you already have an outline? You can print an outline by clicking the Outline View button on the toolbar above the status bar, then clicking the Print button.

You can also print an outline from any view by clicking File, Print, then clicking Outline View from the Print What pull-down menu, as shown in Figure 15.1. (Notice that when you click File, Print, the Print What options vary depending on which view is active at the time.)

Fig. 15.1
Slides can be printed
in a variety of ways,
including as an outline.

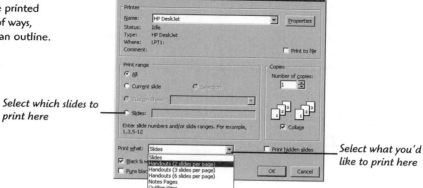

Select which slides to
print here

Select what you'd
like to print here

Your audience will appreciate handouts

Even though you've provided a spectacular slide show for your audience,
they may still want something they can refer to later, especially if the presentation contains a lot of financial data or training materials. Put yourself in the
shoes of your audience—imagine you're attending your presentation, not
giving it. What would you like to have (or hold on to) that might help you
follow the discussion better? Wouldn't you like to have sheets with miniature
slides on them, perhaps with a place for you to write your own comments?
That way, you could write down questions to ask the presenter, and have
information to share with your colleagues later.

 Plain English, please!

A **handout** is a printed reproduction of the slides you create in Power-
Point. A **slide** is a single slide per page, while a handout can display two,
three, or six slides on each page.

When you distribute handouts, your audience can focus on what you have to
say without taking copious notes. Since they have a copy of the slide, it's not
necessary to write down everything. Handouts also provide a reference point
for question-and-answer sessions. You can add additional text or graphics to
your handouts.

Each presenter has a different opinion about handouts. Personally, I find that people tend to focus on the handout and not the computer when I present a slide show. I get flustered when I hear sheets of paper rustling! However, if not everyone in the audience has a clear view of the computer, or the lighting or acoustics in the room are less than great, handouts are an indispensable tool.

 TIP **To maximize the effectiveness of your on-screen slide show and** your handouts, you might want to mention at the beginning of the presentation that all of the relevant points are contained in the handout.

Handouts can be created from any slide view by clicking File, Print. In the Print dialog box, click the Print What pull-down arrow to see the different formats in which you can print your slides. Choose the way you want your slides to print, specifying the range of slides and quantity, then click OK when you're done.

 **CAUTION** **The Print button on the Standard toolbar automatically prints all** the slides, one to a page, of your entire presentation. It only prints slides, not handouts or notes. It doesn't give you any options, and it doesn't ask you which pages you want printed. So if you want anything other than one printed page of each slide, use the Print command on the menu bar.

 Q&A *Will the colors in my slides look OK if my printer only prints in black and white?*

Some colors don't print very well. For example, you'd think that red would print out dark in black and white, and yellow would be so light it would be unreadable. In fact, the opposite is true. Red prints out light and grainy, and yellow looks almost black when printed using a black-and-white printer. To ensure that your colors don't translate poorly, make sure you've checked the Black & White check box on the Print dialog box (refer to Figure 15.1). Printing in black and white eliminates the guesswork: You know your handouts will be readable and not too light or too dark.

Meet the Handout Master

If you'd like to add a little flash to your handouts, The Handout Master is available to help you. Use the Handout Master to add text or graphics, such as the presentation date and the company logo, to every page of your handouts.

Follow these steps to add text or graphics to the Handout Master:

1 Open the presentation you want to use.

2 Choose <u>V</u>iew, and then <u>M</u>aster. The Master submenu appears.

3 Select Handout Master. The Handout Master and Handout Master floating toolbar appear, as displayed in Figure 15.2.

 TIP **Text or graphic images you include on the Handout Master will** not be visible during the slide show. They will appear only on the handouts that accompany the presentation.

Fig. 15.2
The Handout Master has placeholders for as many as six slides.

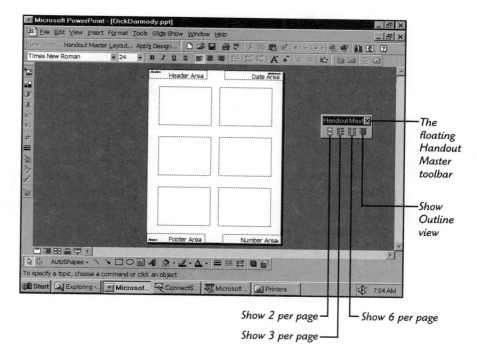

The floating Handout Master toolbar

Show Outline view

Show 2 per page
Show 3 per page
Show 6 per page

 4 The Handout Master toolbar displays views for two, three, or six slides per page, plus an Outline view. Click the view that will work best for your handouts.

 5 To add text to the Handout Master, click the Text Box button on the Drawing toolbar and create a text box (placeholder) where you want the text to appear. Click inside the text box and type your text, then format it as you would any other text on your slides. You can move the text boxes around on the Handout Master. (See Chapter 3 if you need help moving a text placeholder.)

6 If you want to include a header, footer date or number on the handout, click inside the corresponding placeholder and type the information.

7 If desired, you can add a piece of clip art or graphic to the Handout Master. Figure 15.3 shows a completed Handout Master.

Fig. 15.3
The Handout Master contains a footer, date, and a picture.

9/21/96

Modifying placeholders in the Handout Master

You can move, resize, or delete the four placeholders in the Handout Master for the date, header, footer, and number anywhere on the page. You can also move a text box or graphic object you added to the Handout Master. Just keep in mind that like the Slide Master, any changes you make in the Handout Master will affect every page of the handout.

To move a placeholder, the Handout Master must be displayed. Click the dashed line that surrounds the placeholder you want to move. A gray border appears. Click anywhere on the gray border, taking care not to click on any of the handles. Drag the placeholder to its new location and release the mouse button.

To resize a placeholder, click the dashed line that surrounds it and then click a sizing handle and drag the handle in the direction you want to enlarge or shrink the box.

 To delete a placeholder, click it and then press Delete or click the Cut button from the Standard toolbar. If you decide later that you'd like the placeholder back, choose Format, Handout Master Layout to open the Handout Master Layout dialog box, as shown in Figure 15.4.

Fig. 15.4
Click any of the options to restore a missing item.

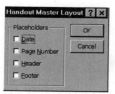

Printing your handouts

Printing your handouts is the easiest part of the operation. Here's how:

1 Open the File menu and choose Print. The Print dialog box appears, as shown in Figure 15.5.

Fig 15.5
Decide how you
want your handouts
to print from the
Print dialog box.

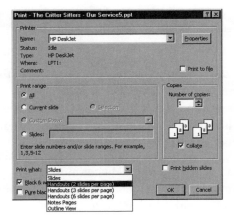

2 From the Print <u>W</u>hat drop down box, select:

> Handouts (2 slides per page)

> Handouts (3 slides per page)

> Handouts (6 slides per page)

3 Click OK to close the Print dialog box and print the handouts.

TIP **Handouts are easier to read if each slide appears in a separate** frame. Select Fra<u>m</u>e Slides in the Print dialog box to place a frame around each slide on the handouts.

Speaker Notes keep you focused

I consider myself a pretty good public speaker. Anytime I know I'm going to speak in front of a group, I rehearse my presentation and try to memorize as much as I can. A few weeks ago, though, all my careful preparations literally flew out the window. Just as I was about to begin, I noticed a big wasp buzzing around the mouse of the computer. Instead of focusing on my presentation, all I could think of was the wasp! Fortunately, I had Speaker Notes to get me back on track.

The people who designed PowerPoint understand that it's easy to lose your place during your presentation—maybe because of nerves, questions you're asked from the audience, or even a buzzy wasp. That's why Speaker Notes are so handy.

 Plain English, please!

Speaker Notes are pages that display a single slide and any notes you've made for that slide. You can include any kind of information you want in your Speaker Notes. ""

You can create Speaker Notes for any slide in a presentation—you don't need to create them for every slide.

 1 From any active slide, click the Notes Page View button.

The Notes Page screen for the active slide appears, as shown in Figure 15.6.

Be prepared—bring handouts!

You never can predict what's going to happen during a presentation. Although you expect the best conditions, you might be unpleasantly surprised if you're not prepared.

Over the years, I've heard thousands of horror stories from presenters. Stories about power failures, about how people packed the wrong presentation, or nightmarish stories about computers that just weren't available or crashed during the presentation. The only thing that saved the unfortunate presenters from humiliation was the fact that they'd brought handouts!

During a presentation when everything goes right, handouts are an excellent vehicle for note taking and future reference. During a presentation when everything goes wrong, handouts can be the only tool that ties your audience to you.

Let's face it—you've done a lot of hard work to design your presentation. Take one more step and bring handouts of your slides. If all else fails, you can use them as overheads and visual aids. It's maybe not as high-tech as you'd like, but in a pinch, you'll be able to salvage something of your presentation (not to mention your dignity).

Be prepared. Expect the unexpected!

Fig. 15.6
Make notes to help
you with the presenta-
tion using the Notes
Pages View button.

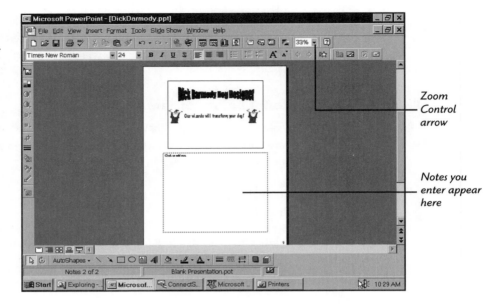

Zoom
Control
arrow

Notes you
enter appear
here

2 Click the notes box. The notes box is a placeholder.

3 Because you probably can't read what's in the box, click the Zoom
Control pull-down arrow and select a larger view to make the characters visible. (I like to use the 66% view, but the size of your monitor—
and the strength of your eyes—will determine what zoom works best
for you.)

4 Type your text. You can use most word-processing techniques you
already know, including cut, copy, and paste. Figure 15.7 shows text
that is entered in Notes Page view and zoomed for easier reading.

5 Click anywhere outside the text box when you're finished. Your text
will be saved when you save your slides.

TIP **If you have information you'd like to have in your Speaker Notes**
in an existing word-processing document, you can copy that text into the
Clipboard and paste it into Notes Page view.

Fig. 15.7
Notes can be zoomed
for easier reading.

*Notes entered in
Notes Page view*

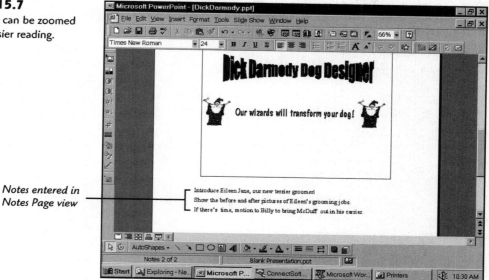

Once you've created your notes, you'll want to print them. PowerPoint lets you print Speaker Notes from either the File menu or Tools menu.

In an earlier section in this chapter, you learned how you can select the way your slides print out. You can also print Speaker Notes by selecting Notes Page from the Print What pull-down arrow in the Print dialog box.

16

Preparing Your Slide Show

● **In this chapter:**

● I'm ready to start my slide show

● What if I want to back up to the previous slide?

● I want to run my slide show in a continuous loop

● Can I run my presentation on a computer that doesn't have PowerPoint installed?

PowerPoint has many helpers to get your slide show ready—wherever you're planning to make the presentation . . . .

You've gotten the nuts-and-bolts work done on your presentation, but you're not finished quite yet. There's still some tweaking left to do. I enjoy all the different phases of putting together a presentation, but this is the part I really love—not only in terms of its message, but how your audience receives it. This is the time you really have to see your presentation through your audience's eyes, because it's now or never.

Let the show begin!

You've probably thought about when and how you'll actually give the presentation. Presumably, you've even made arrangements for the equipment you'll be using to run the show. If you're lucky, you'll have access to some sort of projection equipment, but even if you have to make do with an ordinary 15-inch monitor, you can still have a dynamic presentation.

Regardless of the size of the monitor, slide text must be large, clear, and legible. You can probably have larger clip art on slides that will be projected, but you don't want your viewers to have to strain to read the information on the slides.

You can run your presentation from within PowerPoint or by using the PowerPoint Viewer—as usual with PowerPoint, the choice is yours! The method you use to start your presentation makes no difference to your audience; the show they see will look the same.

Starting your presentation from within PowerPoint

 Once you're in PowerPoint, you can start your presentation from any view by clicking the Slide Show button on the toolbar above the status bar. The slide show starts, beginning with the active slide (see Figure 16.1).

While starting a slide show using the Slide Show button starts the show from whatever slide is active, you can have more control over the starting slide using the Slide Show menu. To use this method, open the Slide Show menu and choose Set Up Show. The Slide Show dialog box opens, as shown in Figure 16.2. To see all the slides starting with Slide 1, click the All option. To see selected slides, type the beginning and ending slide numbers in the From and To text boxes. The Manual Advance option means that each slide—and each animation (or appearance of individual text lines or graphic images)—will advance each time you click the mouse button. When you're done making your selections, click OK.

Fig. 16.1
Neither the menu nor toolbars are displayed during a slide show.

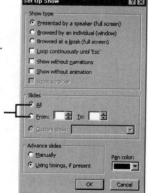

Fig. 16.2
Use the Set Up Show dialog box to control which slides are shown.

Choose the slides you want to show from here

TIP   **I run Slide Show view quite often as I'm creating my presentation.** Seeing the slide show gives me a sense of continuity and gauges my progress. When I view even one or two sequential slides in Slide Show view, I can really see my presentation coming together, and I can tell if I'm on the right track or not.

The PowerPoint Viewer is a great friend

The PowerPoint Viewer is a small utility program used to run slide shows on computers that don't have Microsoft Office 97 or PowerPoint installed. You can add the Viewer to the same disk as a presentation by using the Pack and Go Wizard. (We'll learn more about the Pack and Go Wizard later in this chapter.) When you get where you're going, you can be sure that you'll be able to run the slide show on another computer, as long as it's running Windows 95. If you're running more than one presentation, you can create a play list to use with the Viewer. The Play list lets you run multiple presentations, one after another.

If you didn't install the Viewer when you installed PowerPoint 97, there are a few ways you can get a copy of this utility:

- The Viewer is located on the Office 97 CD-ROM, in the ValuPack folder.

- Microsoft allows the Viewer to be freely distributed with no additional license. If you didn't install PowerPoint from a CD-ROM but you have access to the World Wide Web, open the Help menu, choose Microsoft on the Web on the Help menu, and then click Free Stuff. (Remember, your modem must be connected to your service provider before you can connect to the Microsoft site.) See the section that follows for download and installation instructions.

- The PowerPoint Web site is another great place to download the Viewer; you can also get updates and loads of great information about PowerPoint. Once your modem is connected to your provider, open the Help menu, choose Microsoft on the Web, and then click Product News.

The Viewer that comes with PowerPoint 97 supports all PowerPoint 97 and 95 features. However, if you're using a Macintosh computer, you'll need a special Macintosh version of the viewer. Installing the PowerPoint viewer takes only a few minutes. Because the PowerPoint Viewer is a program, you only need to install it one time—just like PowerPoint. After it's installed, you can use it over and over again.

Downloading and installing the PowerPoint Viewer from the Web

After you're connected to your Internet Service Provider and have opened the Free Stuff or Product News from Help, Microsoft on the Web, Free Stuff or Product News, follow the on-screen prompts to begin downloading the file. When you're prompted from the Internet Explorer dialog box, choose the Open It option. Once the download is complete, the file will be installed to your computer's hard disk—ready for your use.

Installing the Viewer from the CD-ROM

If you're installing the Viewer from the Office 97 CD-ROM point to the Start menu and choose Find, Files and Folders. The Find: All Files dialog box appears, as shown in Figure 16.3. Type the file name **pptvw32.exe** in the Named text box. Make sure that the drive letter that accesses the CD-ROM is selected in the Look in text box. (The drive letter that accesses the CD-ROM on my computer is drive D.) When the information has been entered correctly in the boxes, click Find Now. Windows searches through the CD-ROM and displays the file name in the Results box.

Don't assume anything about your equipment

Preshow jitters are the worst! Even if you were giving a presentation to your mother you'd be nervous, so give yourself every possible advantage. Spend as much time as you can working with the hardware you'll use for the presentation before it's time to run the show.

If the equipment you're using for the presentation is not what you normally use (translation: it's on loan), spend 15 minutes or so getting the feel of it. How will you turn on the projector? Will it be on when the audience comes in, or will that ruin the effect of your first slide? Does the computer you'll be using let you load the first

slide and then simply turn the monitor on at the moment you're ready to start?

It's a good idea to put yourself through a dry run before the presentation, particularly if there are some slides you're concerned with. One of the most neglected presentation transitions is how you'll start. Try to avoid starting the show with a clumsy entrance; the show's start is just as important as the middle and end.

Like a great dinner party, every element of a presentation takes planning. Remember, hors d'oeuvres don't grow in cupboards and presentations don't spring out of computers.

Fig. 16.3
Search for the
PowerPoint Viewer
installation file in the
Find: All Files dialog
box.

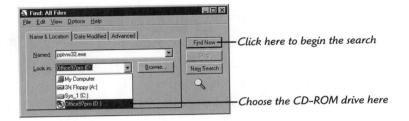

Click here to begin the search

Choose the CD-ROM drive here

Windows searches the CD-ROM and displays the file name in the Results box. Double-click the file name pptvw32.exe to install the PowerPoint viewer to the hard disk of your computer.

Starting your presentation from the PowerPoint Viewer

In addition to showing slides from within PowerPoint, you can use the PowerPoint Viewer to start your presentation. You only use the PowerPoint Viewer to present a slide show—that means no editing!

CAUTION   **Regardless of whether you start your show from PowerPoint or the** PowerPoint Viewer, it may distract from your show if the audience sees you locating the presentation file. The first thing your audience should see is the first slide in the presentation.

After you've installed it on the hard disk of your computer, Windows adds a shortcut to the Programs section of the Start Menu. Follow these steps to show a slide show using the PowerPoint Viewer:

To show a slide show using the PowerPoint Viewer, click the Start button on the Windows taskbar. Point to Programs and choose PowerPoint Viewer 95. The Microsoft PowerPoint Viewer dialog box opens. Locate the presentation you want to show. Notice that when you click a presentation file, a thumbnail of the first slide is displayed in the lower-right corner, as shown in Figure 16.4. Click Show once you've selected the file you want and the presentation will begin.

Fig. 16.4
A thumbnail of the selected presentation is displayed in the Microsoft PowerPoint Viewer dialog box.

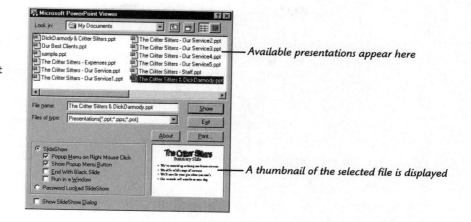

Available presentations appear here

A thumbnail of the selected file is displayed

TIP You can also quit a running presentation by pressing Esc.

After I've worked out all the kinks in my presentation, I like to run my show directly from the PowerPoint Viewer. Of course, the audience can't tell how you started the show, but you'll know. Starting the show from the PowerPoint Viewer lets me know that the presentation is really finished. The Viewer is the icing on the cake!

It sure would be helpful if I could write on a slide!

Many times, when you're giving a presentation, you'll feel the need to write on a slide—just as you would on an overhead acetate. PowerPoint lets you do this, and the great part is that you never have the messy clean-up you have with an acetate!

66 *Plain English, please!*

In PowerPoint, writing comments on a slide, or **annotating**, is done using the mouse—right on the slide—during the slide show. You'll know you can write on a slide by the appearance of the mouse pointer: when it looks like a pen, you can write! 99

To annotate (write on) a slide, make sure a slide show is running, starting it with either Slide Show viewer or the PowerPoint Viewer. Turn on the annotation pen while you're on any slide by pressing Ctrl+P. When you do this, the arrow pointer changes into a pen. Change back to the arrow pointer by pressing Ctrl+A.

You can also change back and forth between the pen and arrow pointer using the Slide Show shortcut menu. Click the right mouse button anywhere on the slide. The shortcut menu opens, as shown in Figure 16.5. (Even though the pointer looks like an arrow, the shortcut menu indicates the pen is active. When the Slide Show shortcut menu is open, the pointer always looks like an arrow.)

Fig. 16.5
Turn the annotation pen on and off using the Slide Show shortcut menu.

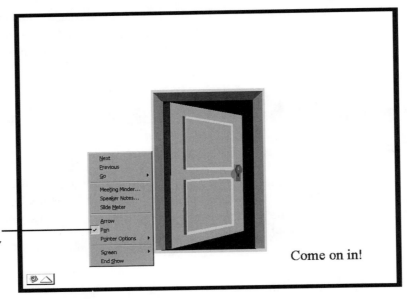

Click anywhere with the right mouse button to open the Slide Show shortcut menu

Come on in!

After the pointer changes to the pen, you can use the mouse to "write" on the slide by holding the left mouse button and dragging the mouse as if it were a pencil. An example of writing on a slide is shown in Figure 16.6. You can return to the mouse pointer by pressing Ctrl+A.

Fig. 16.6
Writing on a slide adds emphasis to your presentation.

The pen tool

You can draw a line by holding down the Shift key and dragging the pointer

 CAUTION **The pen is not an artistic tool—by any stretch of imagination.**
Be careful when you use the pen. It's easy to turn your carefully designed slide into something that looks like a child's scribble!

 **Q&A** ***Will any annotations that I add remain on my slides permanently?***

No. Your annotations will disappear as soon as you go to the next slide. Also, you can erase your annotations by pressing the E key or right-click to bring up the shortcut menu and choose S̲creen, E̲rase Pen.

Can I see that slide again?

In a perfect world, no one ever interrupts your presentation to ask you something you don't know the answer to. And you're never asked to go back to see the slide from two slides before. But in the real world, we know that's not the case. Rather than having to admit that you can't go back—I actually heard someone say that once—PowerPoint makes it easy to return to previously shown slides.

Fortunately, PowerPoint is prepared for all the imperfections life has to offer. There are different ways to return to a previous slide. If you want to move to the last slide, you can press either the Backspace, P, left arrow, up arrow, or Page Up key. If you need to move more than one slide, the quickest way to get there is to click the right mouse button, Go, then click Slide Navigator. The Slide Navigator dialog box, shown in Figure 16.7, lets you choose to which slide you want to go. Click the slide in the list you want, then click Go To.

Fig. 16.7
Move to any slide using the Slide Navigator.

Presentation showmanship

You want to deliver the right kind of presentation to the right kind of audience. Naturally, the type of people you're speaking to will influence your presentation. A presentation to a group of AIDS activists is likely to be quite different than a presentation to Disney World vacationers. The type of people you'll be speaking to—as well as the subject matter itself—dictates how much humor, graphics, and text you should use.

As you do more presentations, you'll get a feel for what works and what doesn't. Although you have a lot to think about while you're making the presentation, try to pay attention to the reactions of members of the audience. Watch viewer responses to slides, their body language, and whether they appear to be enjoying the show or just enduring it.

If possible, it would be great if you could observe someone else's presentation, or have a rehearsal in front of colleagues who can give you both positive and negative feedback. Watching another person's presentation gives you the opportunity to critique another slide show. Watch the show with an open mind and see what is effective and what isn't.

Each audience is unique, but there are factors you should consider that can ensure your success. Some of the information you want to know about your audience might include:

- Their average age and education level, so you know how to phrase the text

- How much they already know about the subject, so you know how much detail you need to include

- Whether they're willingly attending the presentation or have been asked to attend. Then you will know whether they are interested in the subject when they come in, or if you have to get them interested.

In addition to information about your audience, you should know when and where you are going to give the presentation. For example, is the presentation scheduled

- Just before or just after lunch? Just before lunch might mean your viewers are hungry and uncomfortable—after lunch they might be drowsy and inattentive.

- First thing in the morning or at the end of the day? Either of these times might mean that you're not catching viewers when they're most attentive.

- In a small or large room? A small room is more intimate, while a large room can be impersonal and makes it harder to make contact with the audience.

- In a dark or light room? A dark room can seem oppressive and impersonal, while a light room seems friendlier and more personal.

- In a cold or hot room? Either extreme can make your audience (and you) uncomfortable. I prefer the room a little chilly; if the room is too warm, your audience might fall asleep.

- In a room with comfortable seating? Let's face it—uncomfortable seats will make your audience squirm. And that means they won't enjoy your presentation.

While many of these items may seem trivial to you, they can have a big impact on you and your audience. Giving a presentation is part show biz, and the conditions in the theater are as important as the script.

TIP   **Whenever possible, try to see the room where you'll be giving the** presentation beforehand. This gives you a chance to know how comfortable your viewers might be, and how easy or difficult it may be for them to see and hear you.

When designing a presentation, always imagine yourself as a member of the audience. Pretend that you're sitting in the last seat in the room, where the sound and lighting is at its worst. Tailor your presentation to this location.

Take your presentation on the road with the Pack and Go Wizard

Not every computer has PowerPoint. Does that mean that you can't run your presentation on it? Well, yes and no. If a computer doesn't have PowerPoint installed on it, you won't be able to run your presentation even though you might have your work on a disk. However, PowerPoint has a utility called the Pack and Go Wizard that puts your presentation and the information necessary to run it on as many disks as necessary.

The Pack and Go Wizard is a series of six dialog boxes that leads you through the process of putting one or more presentations on disks. Open this Wizard by choosing File, Pack and Go. The first dialog box welcomes you to the Pack and Go Wizard and tells you what the wizard does. Click the Next button to advance to the second dialog box. In this dialog box, shown in Figure 16.8, you indicate the file or files you'd like to pack. If you want to package more than one presentation file, instructions appear in the dialog box telling you how. Click the Next button to continue.

Fig. 16.8
Choose the presentation you want to pack.

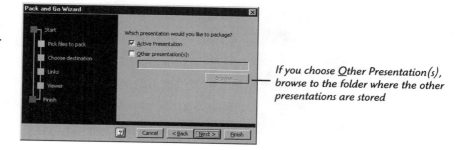

If you choose Other Presentation(s), browse to the folder where the other presentations are stored

The third dialog box, shown in Figure 16.9, lets you choose where you'd like the Pack and Go Wizard to put your packaged file. In most cases, the Wizard assumes you want your files on a floppy disk, which is usually Drive A. Click the Next button to continue.

Fig. 16.9
Decide where you want your file packed.

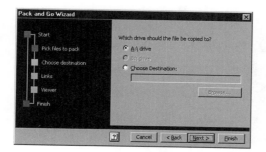

The fourth Pack and Go Wizard dialog box, shown in Figure 16.10, lets you include linked files in your presentation and embed any TrueType fonts. If your presentation contains linked files, click the check box next to Include Linked Files. (See Chapter 12 for information about linking files.) Click the check box next to Embed TrueType Fonts if you've used fonts in your presentaion that may not be installed on the computer that will be running the slide show. If the computer can't find the same font, different fonts will be substituted—giving your slides a new, unwanted look.

Including linked files, the default option, takes up less disk space than including the actual files, or embedding. Embedding always results in larger files than linking. However, embedding means you'll always have the information you need. With linking, any missing or broken link can result in data missing in your presentation. Once you've made your selection, click Next to continue.

Fig. 16.10
Choose whether you
want to embed or link
files.

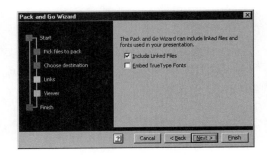

The fifth dialog box, shown in Figure 16.11, lets you include the PowerPoint
Viewer in the package. If you're not sure if PowerPoint is installed on the
computer you'll be using, it's a good idea to have the PowerPoint Viewer
along. Make sure the Include PowerPoint Viewer check box is checked, then
click Next to continue.

Fig. 16.11
If you need the
PowerPoint Viewer,
indicate it here.

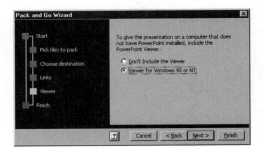

The sixth and final dialog box, shown in Figure 16.12, lists where your files
will be packed and whether you've chosen to include the PowerPoint Viewer.
It also lets you know you'll be prompted if more disks are needed to pack all
the information. Click the Finish button and you're done!

 **CAUTION**   **Your PowerPoint file—saved using the default file format—won't**
work on a computer that runs a previous version of PowerPoint. Find out
before packing your presentation what version of PowerPoint is available
and save your presentation in that format using File, Save As.

Fig. 16.12
That's it: you're
finished!

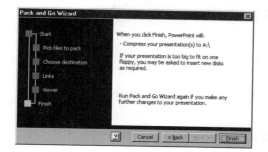

Running the show in a continuous loop

You've probably been to a store where you've seen a computer running a slide presentation and no one is baby-sitting it. Wouldn't it be wonderful to be able to do that?

Self-running presentations seem more difficult than they actually are. It seems to me that once I'd learned about how to set up unattended presentations, I started noticing them everywhere—at the make-up counter in a department store, at the grocery store, even at the office of my son's pediatrician! Look around. I'll bet you'll start noticing them, too.

> ❝❝ *Plain English, please!*
>
> Running a presentation unattended is called running it in a **continuous loop**. In an attended show, you cycle through all the slides, from the first to the last. In a continuous-loop show, all the slides are shown over and over again until you stop the show. ❞❞

Running a show unattended has its own rewards. You've already put a lot of work into your presentation, now you can run it and forget it. Get some coffee…go shopping!

To run a PowerPoint presentation in a continuous loop, open the presentation, click Set Up Show on the Slide Show menu, and then click the option next to Browsed at a kiosk (Full screen). See Figure 16.13. When you click this option, the presentation will loop continuously until Esc is selected.

Fig. 16.13
You can run a show
continuously just by
clicking a check box.

TIP **The text you use in a continuous-loop show may differ from what** you'd put in a "regular" show. Your slides have to contain all the information you want to express, since there's no room for explanation or ad-libbing. You also need to make sure slide transitions and text builds are timed so that all the text can be read.

Will different versions of PowerPoint affect my presentation?

File formats are frequently changed when a new version of a program is released. On the surface, a new file format will be invisible to you. A new file format can determine what special effects are available or the size of the file, to name a couple of features. The file format that's being used affects you when you're planning on taking your show "on the road." You should know what version of PowerPoint awaits you at your destination.

With all the planning and preparation you've been doing, wouldn't it be a shame—not to

mention an embarrassment—to be unable to give your presentation because the available computer couldn't read your file?

Here's a rule of thumb: A new version of a software program can generally read files saved in a previous version. Older software versions may not be able to read a new version. To play it safe, save your file in a previous format, or better yet, save your work using both an older and the current file format. That way, you'll be prepared for anything.

Q&A ***How can I prevent observers from pressing Esc and stopping my presentation when it runs unattended?***

The best way to prevent people from disrupting your presentation is to remove the problem: take the keyboard away. Once the presentation is up and running, I always hide the keyboard and mouse underneath the computer (if it's on a cart) or else I just disconnect them.

Part IV: PowerPoint at the Office and on the Internet/Intranet

Chapter 17: **Customizing PowerPoint**

Chapter 18: **Sharing Your Presentation with Colleagues**

Chapter 19: **Share Your Presentation with the World**

17

Customizing PowerPoint

● **In this chapter:**

- **Can I create a PowerPoint shortcut for my desktop?**

- **I'd like PowerPoint to open the last presentation I used**

- **What settings can I change in PowerPoint?**

- **I want to customize my toolbars**

Customizing PowerPoint means you can have the features you want, and toolbar buttons the way you want them—all right at your fingertips! . . . . ●>

PowerPoint is a pretty spectacular program right out of the box, but in this chapter you'll find out just how much you can do to change its appearance to make it even more efficient for the way you work. In addition to opening a recently used file right from the Windows 95 Start menu, you can create a shortcut on your desktop that you can use to start PowerPoint.

Why would you want to customize the program? Well, everyone has their own ideas about what works best for them. Some like working with a lot of toolbars on their screen; others prefer a more spartan look. You can customize your program to fit your working style.

Creating a shortcut on your desktop

You know those beautiful icons you see on your desktop? The icons with the white arrows in the lower-left corner are called **shortcuts**. Double-click the mouse, and a shortcut opens a program or document. With the PowerPoint shortcut icon, all you do to start the program is double-click the icon.

Creating a PowerPoint shortcut is easy. Before you can put the shortcut icon on your desktop, you have to locate the file that starts PowerPoint. Point to the Start menu and then choose F̲ind, F̲iles or Folders. The Find: All Files dialog box appears. Type **powerpnt.exe** in the N̲amed text box, as shown in Figure 17.1. Click the F̲ind Now button to begin the search.

Fig. 17.1
Find the file that starts
PowerPoint.

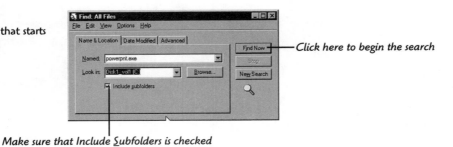

— *Click here to begin the search*

Make sure that Include S̲ubfolders is checked

Windows looks through all of the folders on your C drive and shows you the location of powerpnt.exe (the file that starts PowerPoint). Click the file name to select it and drag it onto the desktop. Release the mouse button and the PowerPoint shortcut appears on your desktop.

That's it! To open PowerPoint using the shortcut, just double-click the shortcut icon. To get rid of the shortcut, drag the icon to the Recycle Bin.

 TIP **After you've created lots of shortcuts, the icons often become** scrambled and cluttered. To rearrange the icons on your desktop, right-click the mouse anywhere on the desktop and choose Arrange Icons and then click Auto Arrange. The desktop will look neat and tidy. (Bet you wish you could do this to your desktop in the office!)

I'd like to open the PowerPoint file I used yesterday

There are several ways you can open a previously used PowerPoint file. One of them comes to you courtesy of Windows 95, the other through PowerPoint.

 One of the easiest ways of opening a recently used PowerPoint file is to click the Start button on the taskbar. Point to Documents to see a list of recently used files created in various programs, as shown in Figure 17.2.

When you click the name of the file you'd like to open, the file you selected opens in its program. If PowerPoint is already open, you can open a recently used file by clicking the File menu and selecting the file from the bottom of the menu, as shown in Figure 17.3.

Fig. 17.2
Open a program and
file using the Start
menu.

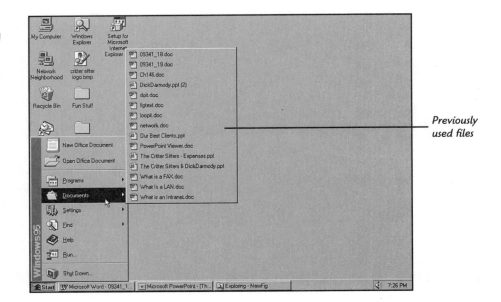

Previously
used files

Why should you customize PowerPoint?

You may wonder why you should customize PowerPoint. Don't the programmers know the best way of working with it? After all, they wrote it. But only you know how you work best. If you don't need all 20 Undo levels, why should you have to live with them? If you'd rather see the last 10 files you've used, who's to say you're wrong? And if you regularly use fairly obscure menu commands, aren't you entitled to have them on a toolbar? Absolutely.

Perhaps there are several buttons you use frequently, but they're located on different

toolbars. You could create a new toolbar that contains all the buttons you use, even if they're already in use on other toolbars. If there's a command that doesn't currently have a button, you could assign a button to that command and add the new button to your toolbar, as well.

The point of customizing the PowerPoint program is to make your working environment as efficient and comfortable as possible. If PowerPoint is set up the way you like it, you'll be more productive!

Fig. 17.3
Four recently used files
are listed in the File
menu.

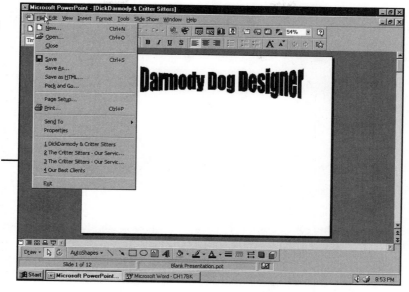

*Most recently used
PowerPoint files*

Change PowerPoint's printer settings

Any printer installed in Windows can be used to print your presentation. If
you've got more than one printer attached to your computer or you're on a
network with several different printers from which to choose, you can switch
to another printer at any time.

Q&A **Why would I want to switch printers?**

If you've got more than one printer from which to choose, there are many
reasons why you might want to switch. If you want to print your slides in
color, you'd route your print job to the color printer. Black–and–white
acetates, on the other hand, would print best on a laser printer. On my
network, I'm lucky to be able to choose from nine different printers. If your
computer is part of a network, you might want to ask your Network
Administrator about sending your print jobs to other printers on the
network.

You can change the default settings on the printer that's currently selected.

To view the current print settings, open the File menu and choose Print. The
Print dialog box opens, as shown in Figure 17.4.

Fig. 17.4
The Print dialog box
shows the printer that's
currently selected.

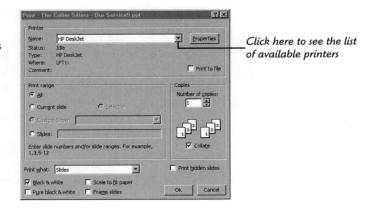

*Click here to see the list
of available printers*

Change the default printer by clicking the down arrow next to the printer
name to view the list of available printers. If you click one of the listed
choices, the new printer name immediately appears in the box.

To view current printer settings, including page size, orientation, and how
graphics are handled, click the Properties button. The Properties dialog box,
which displays the name of the printer currently selected, opens, as shown in
Figure 17.5. You can reverse any changes and revert to the original settings
by clicking Restore Defaults.

Fig. 17.5
The Print Properties
dialog box shows
current default print
settings.

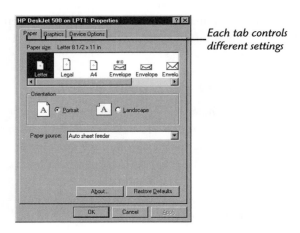

*Each tab controls
different settings*

Depending on the current printer, the Print Properties dialog box offers different groups of settings that you can change, including:

- **Paper.** The size, orientation (the way the paper is turned) and paper source for your printer are determined from this tab.

- **Graphics.** This tab determines how the printer handles graphics. Resolution is represented by dots per inch—the higher the number, the cleaner the image. Dithering relates to how colors will be handled, especially on black-and-white printers. A finer resolution will result in cleaner printed images, but requires longer print times and uses more printer memory.

- **Fonts.** This tab determines how the printer handles the TrueType fonts installed on your computer—as bitmapped, soft fonts or as graphics images.

- **Device Options.** Specifies the text quality that appears in the printed document. Depending on the printer that's selected, this tab may display different options.

 *CAUTION* **Changes you make to the tabs in the Properties section of the** Print dialog box affect the printing of both the on-screen presentation and future print jobs. If you want to change the orientation for one presentation, use Page Setup under the File menu instead of altering the Printer defaults.

Change PowerPoint's behavior to suit your style!

You can change the way PowerPoint behaves by clicking a few check boxes. For example, you can change the number of recently used files that appear in the File menu, the appearance of the Startup dialog box that's displayed when PowerPoint first opens, or whether you have straight quotes or Smart Quotes. (Smart Quotes are the "curly" quotation marks that curve around the words they surround.) All the changes you can make affect your efficiency, not the way in which the program functions.

Changes are made in PowerPoint's behavior by clicking Tools, Options. The Options dialog box contains seven tabs, each of which is explained briefly here. I won't cover each item in each tab—only the ones that I think you might need to change!

Use the View tab, shown in Figure 17.6, to change the amount of information shown on your screen, as well as the appearance of that information. Some of the changes you can make from the View tab include:

- Make sure the Status bar is displayed by clicking its check box.

- A check mark in the Startup dialog box option causes the dialog box in which you can select an existing or new presentation to open.

- The New Slide dialog box automatically opens when the New Slide button is clicked if the New Slide Dialog option is checked.

- During a slide show, the popup menu is available using the right-mouse button if the Popup Menu On Right Mouse Click check box is selected.

- The popup menu button is displayed during a slide show if the Show Popup Menu Button option is checked.

- End a slide show with a black slide by checking the End With Black Slide check box.

Fig. 17.6
Change screen displays using the View tab.

The General tab of the Options dialog box is shown in Figure 17.7. The following functions can be controlled by clicking the check boxes for these options:

- Change the number of displayed recently used files that appear at the bottom of the File menu by clicking the Recently Used File List check box. After this check box is selected, change the number of displayed file names by clicking the up or down arrows next to the Entries text box.

- The Macro virus protection check box displays a warning whenever you open a file that might contain a macro virus which could be potentially damaging to PowerPoint.

- The User information and user initials are displayed.

Fig. 17.7
Modify the Recently Used File List using the General tab.

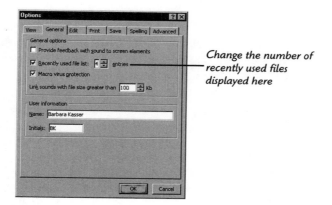

Change the number of recently used files displayed here

 TIP **As you experiment with options, try changing one at a time unless** you're familiar with their effects. That way, if your computer's performance is adversely affected, you'll know which option to return to its original setting.

Options in the Edit tab affect the way information is presented and edited on a slide. The following options can be controlled using the Edit tab, which is shown in Figure 17.8:

- If checked, the Replace Straight Quotes With Smart Quotes check box automatically turns straight quotation marks into curved quotation marks that curve around the text they enclose.

- Selecting the Automatic Word Selection option means that whenever you drag the mouse over part of a word, the entire word is selected.

- The Use Smart Cut And Paste option lets you include trailing spaces between words and sentences in the cut-and-paste operation. (A trailing space is the space that follows a word; that way, when you cut and paste text, the new text is separated from the existing text by a space.)

- Specify the maximum number of actions you can reverse by clicking the up or down arrows next to the Maximum Number of Undos option.

Fig. 17.8
Use the Edit tab to
change text operations.

CAUTION **Many options, such as increasing the Undo levels, can decrease** the level of your computer's performance. Depending on the amount of RAM installed and your computer's processor chip, you might notice degraded system performance when you change options.

The Print tab, shown in Figure 17.9, is used to control some of the following features:

- The Print In Background check box allows you to continue your work while jobs are being printed.

- The Print TrueType Fonts as Graphics check box prints TrueType fonts as graphics images instead of taking more time to down the fonts to the printer.

Fig. 17.9
The Print tab lets you
set several options.

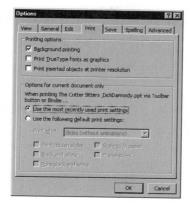

The Save tab, shown in Figure 17.10, is used to control some of the following
features when you save your presentation:

- The Allow Fast Saves only the changes you've made to the presentation.
  When you're done with the presentation, uncheck this box and let
  PowerPoint save the complete file. (The total file size may decrease.)
- If the Prompt For File Properties box is checked, you're asked to supply
  information for the File Properties dialog box.
- Checking the Full Text Search Information option lets you find the file
  easily at a later date.

Fig. 17.10
The Save tab lets you
define the way your
presentation is saved
to disk.

TIP **Any time you want to see an explanation of any of the items on**
the tabs in Options, use the What's This help feature. Click the question
mark on the title bar of the tab so that a question mark attaches to your
mouse pointer and then click the question mark on the item you want to
learn about. An information box pops up on the screen. When you're done
reading the information in the box, click anywhere outside the box to close
it and turn off the What's This feature.

The Spelling tab, shown in Figure 17.11, is used to track spelling errors in your presentation:

- If the check box next to Spelling is on, you'll be notified of spelling errors as you type text.

- The default Spelling option, to Always Suggest alternative words when misspellings are found, is on. That means that the spelling checker will always try to make alternative suggestions when a misspelled word is found.

Fig. 17.11
The Spelling tab tracks spelling errors.

The Advanced tab controls some of the less obvious features in PowerPoint, as shown in Figure 17.12.

Fig. 17.12
The Advanced tab tracks many features.

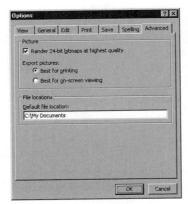

- Click the Render 24-Bit Bitmaps At Highest Quality option to make sure your graphic images appear in the best quality.

- Click the option that's most appropriate for the action you're about to perform: Best For Printing gives you the highest print quality; Best For On-Screen Viewing gives you sharp on-screen images.

- Define the folder where you'd like your presentations automatically saved by typing the folder name and location in the Default File Location text box.

When you're finished making your selections, click OK to close the Options dialog box.

Have it your way—customize the toolbars

The ability to customize your toolbars means you can create an efficient workplace for yourself. After all, why should your toolbars be cluttered with buttons you may never use?

You can add or remove buttons from existing toolbars by clicking Tools, Customize. The Customize dialog box opens to the Toolbars tab, as shown in Figure 17.13.

Fig. 17.13
Modify toolbars using the Customize Toolbars dialog box.

Make sure that the toolbar you want to modify has a check mark in the box next to its name

The names of the toolbars that are currently displayed appear with check marks next to them. If the toolbar you want to modify is not checked, click the box next to its name to display it on the PowerPoint screen.

After the toolbar you want to customize is visible, click the Commands tab. The Commands are organized according to menu categories. As you can see, the categories are the same as the commands on the menu bar. Click any category containing a button you'd like to add, then click the actual button you want to add. Drag the button to any position on one of the toolbars, then release the button. You'll see the outline of the new button on the toolbar, as shown in Figure 17.14.

Fig. 17.14
Drag a button to a toolbar.

Outline of dragged button in its new location

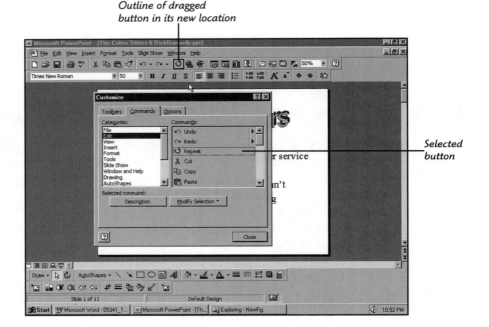

Selected button

After the Customize Toolbars dialog box is open, you can delete a button from a toolbar by clicking the button on the toolbar and dragging it off the toolbar. When you're finished adding and deleting buttons, click Close.

TIP **With the Customize box open on the screen, you can drag a** button from one toolbar to another.

Can I create my own toolbar?

You can create your own toolbars to meet your specific needs. For example, there are some buttons I use over and over again, so I've created a toolbar just for me.

Create your own toolbar from the Customize dialog box. Open the box by clicking Tools, Customize. When the Customize dialog box appears with the Toolbars tab in front, click the New button. In the New Toolbar dialog box, type a unique name for the new toolbar you're creating, as shown in Figure 17.15. The new toolbar appears as a floating toolbar.

Fig. 17.15
Name the new toolbar in this dialog box.

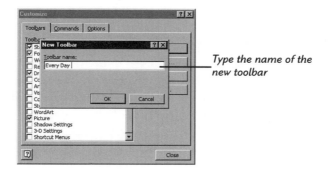

Type the name of the new toolbar

Click the Commands tab. Click any category containing a button you'd like to add, then click the actual button. Drag the button onto the toolbar. When you release the mouse button, the new button will appear on the toolbar, as shown in Figure 17.16.

Fig. 17.16
Add buttons to the new toolbar.

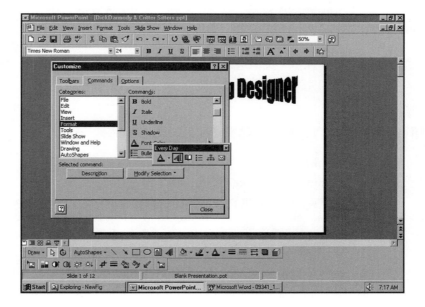

When you're finished adding buttons, click Close. You're returned to whatever view was active when you began, and your toolbar is floating.

TIP **To delete a customized toolbar, select it from the Toolbars dialog** box, click Delete, then click Yes. (The Delete command doesn't appear in the dialog box until you select an existing toolbar.)

 Plain English, please!

Toolbars can be either **docked** or **floating**. A docked toolbar, such as the Standard toolbar or Formatting toolbar, is vertically or horizontally located against a perimeter of the PowerPoint screen. A floating toolbar is not on the perimeter and has a title bar. A floating toolbar can be docked by dragging its title bar to the vertical or horizontal edge of the screen; a docked toolbar can float by clicking an area within it (not a button, however), and dragging it away from the edge into the screen.

 Q&A **Can I rearrange the order of the buttons on a PowerPoint toolbar, like the Standard toolbar, for example?**

Of course you can. Open the Tools menu and choose Customize to open the Customize dialog box. (Although you're not going to use the Customize box, it has to be open to modify toolbars.) Click and drag the button you want to move to its new location. In fact, you can even drag a button from one toolbar onto another. Click Close to close the Customize box when you're done.

Changing menu animations

Menu animations change the way a menu displays when you click on a menu command. Although it probably won't affect your work, changing menu animations is just plain fun! To change menu animations, open the Tools menu, choose Customize and then select the Options tab on the Customize dialog box. Click the down arrow next to Menu animations and choose an effect from the drop-down list, as shown in Figure 17.17. Click Close to return to whatever view was open on the PowerPoint screen. The next time you click the PowerPoint menu, you'll see the animation effect.

Fig. 17.17
Change the way menus
display when you click
a command.

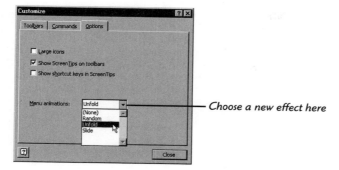

Choose a new effect here

 TIP **If you have the Office Assistant open, many of the options you'd**
see in dialog boxes appear in ballons from the Office Assistant. When the
balloon appears, click the option you want—as if it was in a regular dialog
box.

18

Sharing Your Presentation with Colleagues

● **In this chapter:**

- **I'd like to learn more about networks**

- **How do I fax my slides from my computer?**

- **Can I send my presentation through e-mail?**

- **Can I run my presentation over a network?**

PowerPoint provides you with some advanced editing techniques to make your slides extraordinary . . . . ➤

A brief introduction to networks

A computer network, or LAN for Local Area Network, is two or more computers connected in a way that lets them share data and devices such as printers. LANs are usually located in corporate, business and educational environments where the users share a common interest (for example, they all work for the same company). A LAN can be as simple as two or more PCs sharing a printer, or as complex as several hundred computers sharing multiple printers and other resources.

Many different kinds of services can be provided on a LAN. Network users usually have e-mail, shared printers and files, and automated backups of their important files. A LAN allows users to share files with colleagues.

Q&A ***My office doesn't have a LAN. Would a network help us?***

Yes, a lot! Just think of how much time you'd save if you could access all your data from any computer in your office. Also, instead of paying for multiple copies of software, your company could get network versions for quite a bit less. Plus, instead of buying a printer for each computer, all of the computers in your office could share centrally located printers.

TIP **A WAN is a Wide Area Network. Instead of being confined to** small geographical sites, like a building or a college campus, a WAN can cover the world.

Faxing your presentation

The easiest way to send a slide show to co-workers at another location is to give them a copy of the presentation file on a disk. This method, nicknamed "sneakernet," has some major drawbacks. First, before you send the disk, you've got to make sure that the group you're sending the file to has a computer running the same version of PowerPoint that you used to create the file. Then you've got to copy the file onto a blank disk, label it and send it off, preferably by overnight mail.

After the disk gets to its destination, the group needs to open the file on their computer. (Although it doesn't happen often, disks can get damaged in the mail. While I was writing this book, one of the disks Que sent to me arrived in several pieces!) If you've used a font that isn't installed on your co-worker's system or linked a movie or sound clip that's located only in your files, the presentation may not work correctly.

If your co-workers need to look at just the hard copy of your slides, a better solution may be to fax them the presentation. If your computer is equipped with a **fax modem** you can fax it directly from your computer.

 Plain English, please!

A **fax modem** is a combination fax machine and data modem that enables users to send a fax without leaving their desks. A fax modem can transmit a fax to another computer that's also equipped with a fax modem or a fax machine. A fax modem is installed into your computer exactly the same way as a standard modem. If your computer or modem has been purchased in the last three years, it's probably a fax modem.

If your computer has a fax modem installed, you can fax your presentation right from your computer. When you fax from your computer, you print to the fax instead of your regular printer. Rather than route the document to the printer, the fax modem dials the telephone number of the receiving computer or fax machine and prints the document on the other end.

Sending your presentation by fax

When you installed Windows, you probably installed the Microsoft Fax print driver. If you send or receive a lot of faxes, you may have installed a program like WinFaxPro, or you might be using the fax capabilities from Microsoft Outlook. It doesn't matter which one you use, because they all work the same way.

Follow these steps to fax a presentation from your computer:

1 Open the presentation you want to fax.

2 Choose File, Print. The Print dialog box opens, as shown in Figure 18.1.

Fig. 18.1
Fax directly from your computer.

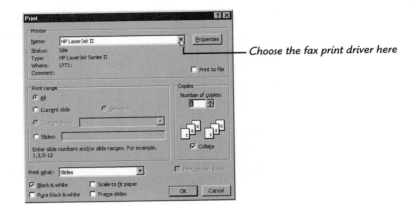

Choose the fax print driver here

3 In the <u>N</u>ame box, select the fax driver.

4 Select any print options you want, from the <u>P</u>rint Range and Print <u>W</u>hat sections of the dialog box and then click OK.

5 Follow the on-screen prompts to fill in the receiving fax phone number and other requested information.

That's all it takes. In a few seconds, your modem will dial the receiving number and your presentation will be on its way.

TIP **Remember to change the print driver back to the regular printer** after you've sent a fax. Otherwise, the next time you print, your computer will try to fax the new print job.

E-mail speeds your presentation to its destination

One of the most commonly used services on any network is e-mail. With e-mail, you can be in contact with everyone in the company, no matter where they work. You can attach files to e-mail messages or just send text. If you're not on a corporate network, but have an account with an Internet service provider or online service, like the Microsoft Network, you have Internet e-mail capabilities.

Office 97 includes an e-mail and scheduling program called Microsoft Outlook. You can use the settings you installed in Outlook or Microsoft Exchange to send your presentation or you can send it through your Internet mail account.

Sending the presentation

Send a presentation through e-mail when you want all of the recipients to receive their copies at the same time.

Open the presentation you want to e-mail to others. Choose File, Send To, and then Mail Recipient. The New Message dialog box opens, as shown in Figure 18.2, with your presentation as a mail attachment. Type the e-mail address of the recipient or click the To button to open your personal address book to choose a recipient. If you wish, you can type a message to accompany the attachment. When you're ready, click the picture of the envelope to send the e-mail and attached presentation.

Fig. 18.2
Send an e-mail
message with your
presentation attached.

The presentation is attached here

Type a brief message here

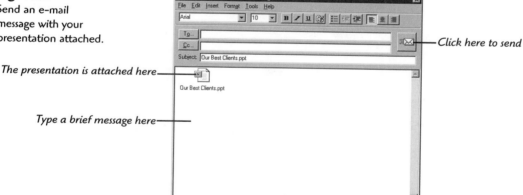

Click here to send

TIP **If you're using an e-mail program other than Microsoft Outlook,** your screen may look different from the one shown in Figure 18.2. Don't worry, you'll be able to send your message. Look for a Send button somewhere on the screen. After you click the Send button, follow the on-screen instructions (if any) and your e-mail will be on its way.

Routing the presentation

Route your presentation if you want your co-workers to review your presentation, one after another. When a presentation file is routed, it is sent sequentially to each user on a list. Routing your presentation enables each recipient to see the comments made by others. You can track the status of a routed presentation as it travels to each person. After all the recipients have reviewed it, the presentation is automatically returned to you.

Follow these steps to create a routing slip:

1 Make sure the presentation you want to route is displayed on your screen.

2 Choose File, Send To, Routing Recipient. The Add Routing Slip dialog box appears, as shown in Figure 18.3.

Fig. 18.3
Route your presentation to recipients, one at a time.

Click here to select the names from your address book

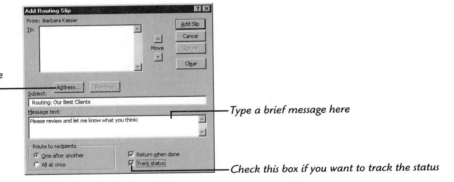

Type a brief message here

Check this box if you want to track the status

3 Click Address to select recipients from your Personal Address book. (You would have previously set up your address book.) Figure 18.4 shows the Address Book dialog box.

4 Click the name of the person you want to send the routing slip and then click To:->. After you've entered the last name, click OK.

Fig. 18.4
Choose the Recipients
from the Personal
Address Book.

*Click a name you want
to add, then click To:*

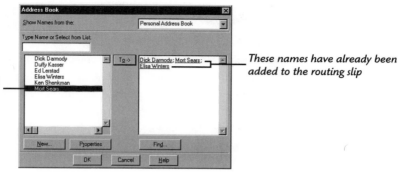

*These names have already been
added to the routing slip*

5 Click <u>R</u>oute to route the presentation.

To route a presentation to the next recipient on the list, choose <u>F</u>ile, Sen<u>d</u> To, Next Routing Recipient.

 TIP **Change the order that recipients receive a routed presentation by** changing the order of the names in the To list. Select the name you want to move up or down in the list, and then click the appropriate up or down arrow.

 CAUTION **Some corporate networks do not allow e-mail attachments to go** through gateways to other companies or the Internet. To be on the safe side, check with your Network Administrator before you send an attachment.

Saving comments from your presentation

No matter how well you've thought out your presentation, chances are someone will make a point or ask you a question you have not considered. With this in mind, PowerPoint created the Meeting Minder. This feature, accessed from Slide or Notes Page view, lets you take notes during a presentation that can later be incorporated into a Word document. The Meeting Minder also lets you record **action items**. While the Meeting Minder is open, you can read any notes you've added to the active slide.

Plain English, please!

An **action item** is a point or reference made during a presentation that requires some action (by yourself or someone else) once the presentation is over. For example, during the presentation, an attendee might ask you when the next proposed merger will be announced. You could create an action item such as "Write and distribute a press release on the Dick Darmody/Critter Sitters merger. Send a copy to all department heads before the release is given to the press." **"**

 CAUTION **You can only create action items, minutes, and notes for the slide** that's currently active. Make sure you know which slide you're in before opening the Meeting Minder, or you could enter information for the wrong slide.

Here's how to use the Meeting Minder:

1 In Slide view, activate the slide to which you want to add comments.

2 Choose <u>T</u>ools, Mee<u>t</u>ing Minder. The Meeting Minder dialog box opens (see Figure 18.5). There are two tabs in this dialog box; here, the Meeting Minutes tab is selected. Each tab in this dialog box contains a text box in which you can type any comments you'd like to record regarding a slide.

Fig. 18.5
Use the Meeting Minder dialog box to create notes for later use.

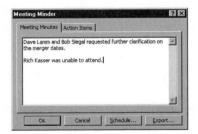

3 Click the Action Items tab. Record any items in this text box that you'd like to address later. A sample of an action item entry is shown in Figure 18.6.

Fig. 18.6
Create an action item as a reminder to yourself and others.

—*Click here to add the information you've typed*

4 If Microsoft Outlook is installed on your computer, you can click the Schedule button to activate the Outlook Appointment feature.

5 Click OK when you're finished recording any information. The information will be saved with each slide when the presentation is saved. To reread any comments, click Tools, Meeting Minder.

6 If you want to see all the Meeting Minder comments in one document, click Export in the Meeting Minder dialog box. The Meeting Minder Export Options dialog box appears, as shown in Figure 18.7. To compile all the information in the Meeting Minder in a Word document, click Send Meeting Minutes and Actions Items to Microsoft Word, then click Export Now.

Fig. 18.7
Export text created in the Meeting Minder to Microsoft Word.

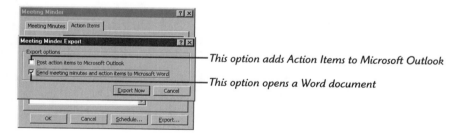

—*This option adds Action Items to Microsoft Outlook*

—*This option opens a Word document*

7 If you choose the first option, Post Action Items to Microsoft Outlook, PowerPoint sends the items to the Outlook Schedule feature. (If Outlook is not installed on your computer, this option will not be available.)

8 If you choose the second option, Send Meeting Minutes and Action Items to Microsoft Word, PowerPoint opens a Word document, which lists all the slides in your presentation, and any notes and action items you've created. Figure 18.8 shows a sample Word document created with the Meeting Minder.

Fig. 18.8
PowerPoint recaps your meeting minutes in Word.

This text was entered in Meeting Minutes

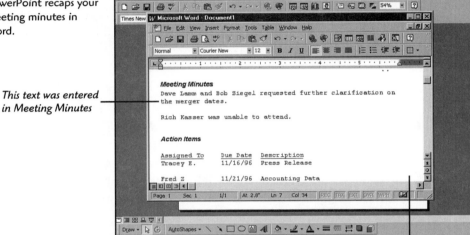

A Word document appears on top of PowerPoint

TIP **Because exporting the Meeting Minutes and Action Items to Word** includes all your comments for all the slides, you should wait until the end of the presentation before you use this feature.

Can I run my presentation over a network?

Using PowerPoint's Presentation Conference feature, you can run your presentation over a network, the Internet, or through a modem and make a presentation to people in the next room or the next state! While you're delivering the presentation, others can view the slide show (as if they were all in an auditorium together), and you can take notes using the tabs in the Meeting Minder. To make the slide show truly interactive, those watching the show can write and draw on the slides during the show.

To make conferencing easy, PowerPoint includes a Presentation Conference Wizard. However, before you try to run the Wizard for the first time, here are a few things you should check:

1 Click the Start button on the taskbar and choose Settings and Control Panel. In the Control Panel, double-click the Network icon to open the Network dialog box. There are three tabs (see Figure 18.9). Click the Configuration tab and look in the list box for Client for Microsoft Networks. If this isn't installed, click the Add button and select Client, Add, Microsoft Client. You'll be asked for the Windows 95 CD. Insert the CD and follow the installation prompts.

Fig. 18.9
Make sure your computer is configured correctly using the Network dialog box.

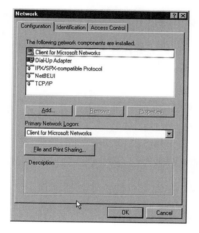

2 Click the File and Print Sharing button. In the dialog box, choose the option called I Want to Be Able to Give Others Access to My Files (see Figure 18.10). Click OK.

Fig. 18.10
Enable other people to access your files.

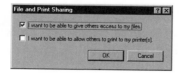

3 Click the Identification tab to find your computer name (see Figure 18.11). Audience members need to know their own computer name; the presenter needs this information for all participants in the conference.

Fig. 18.11
Identify your computer
in the Network dialog
box.

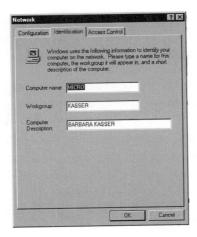

4 Click the Access Control tab (see Figure 18.12). Make sure that <u>U</u>ser-
Level Access Control is selected. Click OK.

Fig. 18.12
Control the access to
your presentation file.

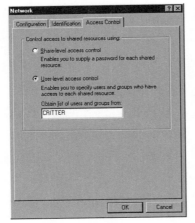

 TIP **If you have problems connecting, contact your Network**
Administrator for help.

After your settings are correct, you're ready to begin your conference session. All participants in the conference sign on using the Presentation Conference Wizard. The presenter must also have the presentation file open. To start the conference:

1 Choose Tools, Presentation Conference. The first dialog box in the Presentation Conference Wizard, which tells you about the feature, opens (see Figure 18.13). After you've read it, click Next.

Fig. 18.13
The opening dialog box in Presentation Conference Wizard provides information about the feature.

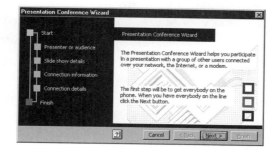

2 The second dialog box, shown in Figure 18.14, appears. Choose either Presenter or Audience, then click Next. If you choose Audience, you can jump to step 5, as the Wizard will take you to the last dialog box (see Figure 18.15).

Fig. 18.14
The second dialog box in Presentation Conference Wizard lets you choose whether you're the presenter or an audience member.

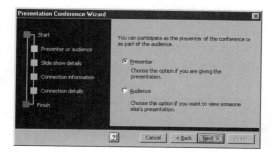

3 In the third dialog box, read the details of how PowerPoint will show the presentation. If you agree, click Next.

4 In the fourth dialog box, choose whether you're connecting to anyone over the Internet or a network. If you're connecting via the Internet, make sure your modem is connected to your Internet service provider before you proceed.

5 Type the Computer Name for each conference participant in the Computer Name text box (see Figure 18.15). After each entry, click Add.

If you think you may want to give a presentation to the same group at some other time, choose Save List and give the group a name. Next time, you won't have to type in everyone's name—you can simply click Open List and choose the group.

When all participants have been added, click Next.

Fig. 18.15
Type the Computer Name for each conference participant.

6 In the final screen of the Presentation Conference Wizard (see Figure 18.16), audience members click Finish. When all audience members have selected Finish, the presenter clicks Finish.

Fig. 18.16
The final dialog box for audience members.

7 The Trying to Connect dialog box opens on the presenter's screen (see Figure 18.17).

Fig. 18.17
The Trying to Connect
dialog box.

After the connection is made, the presenter's first slide appears, full-screen, on all participants' screens. At the bottom left of each participant's screen is a button. Clicking this button opens a menu that lets members of the audience move among slides, select a pen and pen color to draw on the slide, or end the show.

 **CAUTION**   It's a good idea to check with your network administrator before you attempt to run a Presentation Conference over the network. Your administrator will be able to tell you if there are any special network rules you might need to know or if this feature is supported by your network configuration.

19

Share Your Presentation with the World

● **In this chapter:**

- **Tell me about the Internet**

- **How can I search the Web?**

- **I'd like to create and save a presentation for the world to view**

- **How can I add a hyperlink to the Web to a slide?**

PowerPoint and the Internet team up to send your presentation to the world. . . . .●

T he Internet is a giant computer network that connects millions of computers together. By connecting to the Internet, government agencies, corporations, universities, special interest groups, and people like you and me can communicate with one another. Once you're connected to the Internet, you can access all types of resources stored on other computers. For example, you can copy files, send and receive e-mail, go shopping, or read from thousands of publications. As you move from site to site, you'll visit a lot of **home pages**. More and more home pages appear daily.

❝❝ *Plain English, please!*

The Web is made up of millions of "pages," which are nothing more than small collections of text, pictures, and graphics, and usually contain references to other pages with related material. A Web site can have many of these pages. A **home page** is the page at each site that serves as a kind of book cover or table of contents for organizing and introducing the other pages and material at that site. Even if a site consists of just one single page, it's still called a home page. ❞❞

The World Wide Web, or the Web, for short, is the part of the Internet that's made up of a collection of networks that allows you to browse through on-screen documents. These documents can be placed on the Web by anyone—small businesses, large corporations like Microsoft, individuals, and clubs can all create Web sites. The Microsoft Office site is shown in Figure 19.1.

When you're are viewing one Web site, you can click a hyperlink to move quickly to another site. Hyperlinks usually appear highlighted or underlined on the screen. When you click the link, you are whisked to a different page. By moving around with hyperlinks, you can find many related documents that are filled with information.

In order to place a document on the Web, you must have a modem and an Internet Service Provider. The Internet provider grants you access to the Web and stores and maintains your Web site. Because Internet providers generally charge a fee, you should shop around a bit before you sign up with one.

 TIP   **For more information on the Internet and how to connect to it,** consult *Using the Internet* or *The Complete Idiot's Guide to the Internet,* available from Que.

Fig. 19.1
The Microsoft Office
home page.

The Web toolbar

The URL (Web
address) is
shown here

Use the
scroll box
to move
down
through
the page

Hyperlinks
jump you
to a new
page

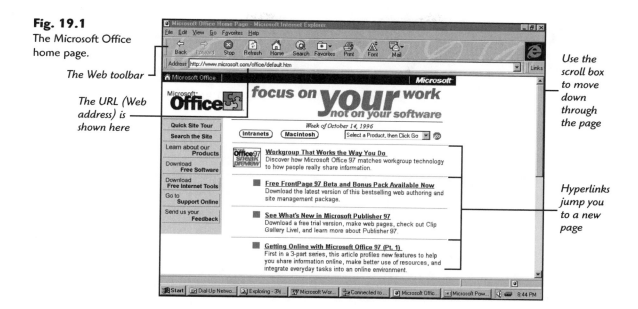

An uncharted wilderness

Because I teach people how to use many software programs, I'm accustomed to overcoming students' fears in my classes. At least one student in every class I teach is concerned that he won't be able to master the program, won't be able to finish the exercises, or won't be able to accomplish a task he really wants to do. In my Internet classes, the majority of students are scared.

Let's face facts, it's new, it's exciting, and it's intimidating. No matter where you go, people are talking about the Internet or telling you to visit their home page. (My local fruit market now has a page on the Web!) The Internet and all of its related terms are enough to make anyone feel small. When you first begin your Internet journey, it's so easy to get lost.

First, what is the Internet? Second, what does it do? Third and most important, what will the Internet do for you? If you're asking those three questions, you're in good company! Almost everyone who ventures out onto the Internet wonders the same thing.

Well, sit back and relax. You didn't learn how to create your PowerPoint presentation overnight, but I'll bet you're putting together slides that you never thought you'd be able to create. Traveling the Internet is similar—you start off slowly and before you know it you're an expert.

PowerPoint makes working on the Internet easy. Because Microsoft has integrated its Web browser right into Office 97, you'll be a pro before too long. Enjoy the ride!

Exploring the Web from PowerPoint's Help menu

The Web has a language all its own. Table 19.1 shows you some common Internet terms and what they mean.

Table 19.1   Common Internet Terms

Internet term	What it means
Browser	A computer program that enables a user to search throughout the Internet easily. The browser retrieves and interprets documents on the World Wide Web. Microsoft Internet Explorer is an example of a popular browser.
IP	Internet Protocol—the packets of data that are transported across the Internet
IP Address	The 32-bit number that identifies a location on the Internet. It is usually broken down into four groups, such as 123.456.7.891
Domain Name	A text version of the IP address. An example of a domain name is **www.mcp.com**
HTTP	HyperText Transport Protocol—starts most Web addresses, followed by a ://, as in **http://www.mcp.com/que** (Que's address on the World Wide Web)
FTP	File Transfer Protocol—a protocol that describes file transfer between a host and remote computer
HTML	Hypertext Markup Language—the coding language in which Internet Web pages are written
TCP/IP	Transmission Control Protocol/Internet Protocol—the basic building blocks of the Internet. TCP is a connection-oriented (network) protocol; IP is a lower-level packet-handling (transport) protocol. Together they make sure that data gets from one point to another on the Internet, enabling all computers to speak the same "Internet language".
URL	Uniform Resource Locator—the address of a document on the World Wide Web, as in **http://www.mcp.com/que** (Que's address on the World Wide Web)

PowerPoint has many links to the Web, available directly from the Help menu. After you're attached to your Internet Service Provider, open the Help menu and choose Microsoft on the Web. Figure 19.2 shows you the available choices.

Fig. 19.2
Click a menu choice
to visit one of the
PowerPoint sites.

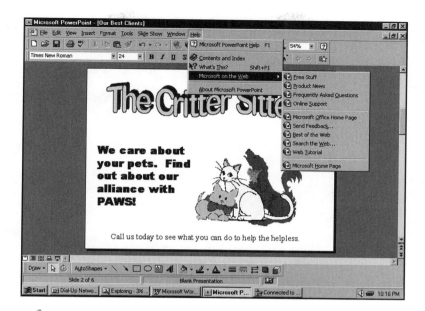

TIP **Visit the Frequently Asked Questions site every few weeks. It's a**
great place to learn about PowerPoint; Microsoft adds the answers to new
questions every few weeks. Figure 19.3 shows the Microsoft PowerPoint
FAQ (Frequently Asked Questions) list.

You can launch the Microsoft Internet Explorer directly from PowerPoint to
search for information for your presentation. Follow these steps:

1 Choose Help, Microsoft on the Web.

2 Select Search the Web. The Find Fast page opens in the Microsoft
Internet Explorer browser, as shown in Figure 19.4.

66 *Plain English, please!*

A **search engine** is a giant index of Web pages. The search engines shown
on the Find Fast page each send out electronic spiders that roam the Web
looking for new pages. When a spider finds a page it hasn't seen before, it
adds it to the index of pages. 99

Fig. 19.3
The PowerPoint FAQ contains hyperlinked answers to questions about PowerPoint.

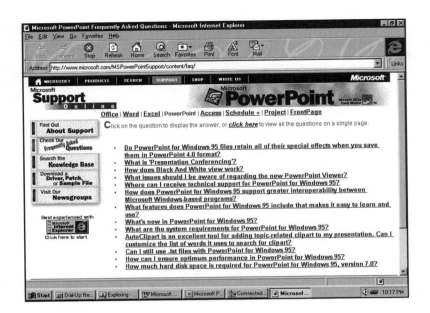

Fig. 19.4
Search for a topic that interests you.

Type the search topic here

Choose a search engine here

Click here to begin the search

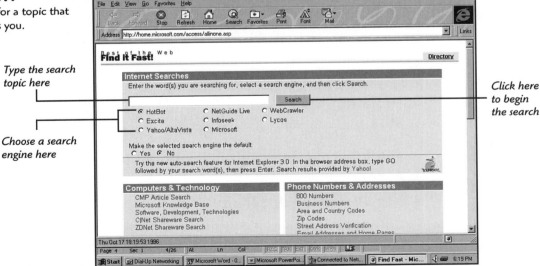

3 Type some keywords of the topic you want to find. If you want to find the words in phrase, like Dick Darmody Dog Designer or poodle groomer, put quotes around all the words in a phrase, (see Figure 19.5).

4 Click the option next to the search engine you want to use. (I've chosen HotBot.)

Fig. 19.5
Ready to search the Web.

The search topic is typed here

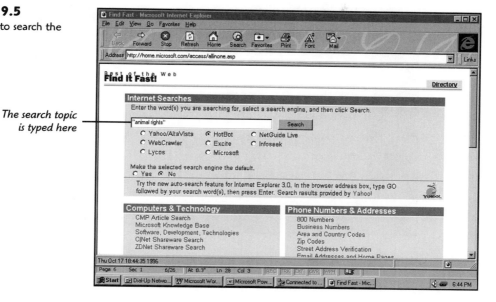

5 Click Search. The search engine you chose looks through the Web to find the keywords or phrase you typed.

6 When the search is completed, the number of Web pages that matched your search criteria is displayed at the top of the search engine page. Each page that the search engine found is shown, with both the page title and the Web address set as hyperlinks, as shown in Figure 19.6. Also shown is a brief description of the first few lines of each page. Generally, 20 "hits" appear on each page; its not uncommon for a general search to produce 20 pages—each containing 20 hits.

TIP **If your search did not find any pages, click the Search** button on the Web toolbar to return to the Find Fast page. Try entering different or more specific criteria and run the search again.

7 To view a particular page, position the pointer over the page's title or address so that it turns into the shape of a hand and click. After a few seconds, the page appears on your screen.

Fig. 19.6
The search engine found many pages that match the search criteria.

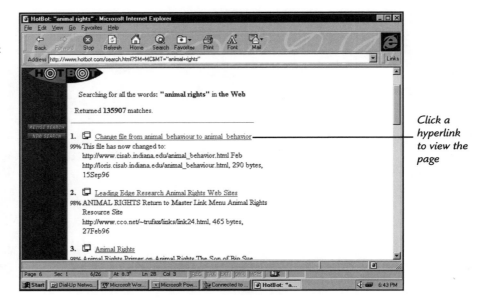

Click a hyperlink to view the page

8 The page you've moved to may contain additional hyperlinks to pages with related information. (Your pointer will take the shape of a hand when it passes over a hyperlink.) Click a hyperlink to jump to the new page.

 TIP Favorites ▾ **When you find an interesting presentation or** a site you'd like to visit again on the Web, click the Favorites button on the Web toolbar. Then click Add to Favorites to post the address to your Favorites folder so you can quickly find it at another time.

 9 Click the Back and Forward buttons on the toolbar to move between pages you've visited.

 10 If you want to close the Internet Explorer, click the Close button on the Title Bar.

 **CAUTION** **You can leave the Internet Explorer open and return to** PowerPoint by clicking the PowerPoint icon on the taskbar. Be careful, though, if you're connected to the Internet through an Internet Service Provider, minimizing the Internet Explorer could result in extra charges for empty connect time. If you're not going to use the Internet Explorer for a while, disconnect from your provider.

TIP **Give yourself lots of time when you're searching the Web. There** are so many interesting pages to view that you'll find yourself "surfing" longer than you originally planned.

Using the Web toolbar

The Web toolbar is available in your PowerPoint and makes it simple to browse through presentations and other Office documents that contain hyperlinks. You can use the Web toolbar to open a start page or a search page in Microsoft Internet Explorer. The Web toolbar should be visible whenever you're working on slides that may appear on the Internet or your company's intranet. (You'll learn more about intranets later in this chapter.) Table 19.2 shows the Web toolbar buttons.

Table 19.2　Web toolbar buttons

Button	Name	What it does
⇦	Back	Returns you to the previous location
⇨	Forward	Returns you to the previous location after you've moved back
⊗	Stop Current Jump	Cancels current jump and returns to previous location
⟳	Refresh Current Page	Repaints the current page on the screen
⌂	Start Page	Jumps to Microsoft home page or a page you've specified whenever you connect to the Web
◉	Search the Web	Opens the Internet Explorer Find Fast page
Favorites ▾	Favorites	Displays a list of pages you've marked to revisit

continues

Table 19.2 Continued

Button	Name	What It Does
	Go	Displays a Web shortcut menu
	Show Only Web Toolbar	Toggles between displaying all selected toolbars and only the Web toolbar
Document1 ▼	Address	Displays the page address or the file and folder path of the current page or document

Q&A *Can you tell me how a Web hyperlink works?*

Sure. Think of a hyperlink as a special hot spot marked on the Web page. When you click it with your mouse, you jump to an entirely different page— possibly to a whole different Web site in another state or country— that has material related to the link.

Q&A *What exactly is a URL?*

It's an acronym for "uniform resource locator," or "universal resource locator"—the complex address that directs your computer to the location on the Internet of any Web page.

A URL address looks like this: **http://www.mcp.com/que**, which is the location of Que's home page. The **http** refers to a protocol, or communications method. The **www** stands for World Wide Web and **mcp.com** refers to a big computer at Macmillan. The Que portion directs you to the Que site at Macmillan. The suffix **com** means the site is commercial. Colleges use the suffix **edu** and government agencies use **gov**.

If a URL points to a page located outside the United States, it also includes a two-letter country code, like **uk** for the United Kingdom. The Web gives you access to sites in virtually every country in the world.

What's an intranet?

Many corporations now have local Internets, called intranets, that only their employees can access. Intranets share the look and feel of the World Wide Web. Most intranets use their own search engines, rather than the commercial ones used on the Web.

Intranets are a great way for all the employees in a large corporation to share information. Policy manuals, company announcements, and corporate forms can all be placed on a company's intranet. If you need to share a PowerPoint presentation with your co-workers in a different location, saving it in HTML and then placing it on the corporate intranet is an easy way to let everyone in the company see it.

Because intranet technology is fairly new, your company may not have one yet. In the next few years, more and more companies will turn to intranets as a solution for providing information to their employees.

Because intranets and the Internet share so many common features, the directions you'll see in the following sections can be applied to both.

Designing a presentation for the Web

You don't need any special skills or talents to design a presentation for the Web. Create a Web presentation exactly as you'd create any other slide show. With a Web presentation, instead of just select audience members, your work has the potential to be viewed by everyone in your company or even the world. When you design a presentation for the Web, you need to consider how your slides will look as Web pages.

If you're not sure what works best on the Web, PowerPoint comes with several Web templates that make Web presentation design a snap. If you want to use a PowerPoint Web template, open the File menu, choose New and then click the Web Pages tab. Choose a template from the available templates (see Figure 19.7).

Fig. 19.7
Choose a template for a Web presentation.

Click a template to preview it

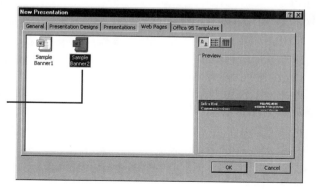

Create your presentation in the normal way. You can add colors, WordArt, graphics objects like pictures and clip art, and sound and video clips.

CAUTION   **Because you don't know what kind of computer equipment the** people who might be viewing your slides are using, use multimedia, like sound and video clips, sparingly. That way, your global audience will be sure to get the most out of your presentation.

Adding a hyperlink to a slide

One of the most dynamic new features in PowerPoint is the ability to jump to a Web site directly from your presentation. Jumping to the Web shows your audience additional information about your presentation. For example, The Critter Sitters is very active in animal rights issues. From within one of the slides, the audience can be transported to the home page of a large national animal rights group.

Because you're linking a presentation to the Web, it's a good idea to do your homework before you start the linking process. Make a list of the URLs or addresses of the pages you want to add hyperlinks to.

Follow these steps to add a hyperlink to a slide:

1 Make sure that your presentation is saved with a unique name. You can't create a relative link to an unsaved presentation.

2 From Slide view, select the text or object you want to add the hyperlink to, as shown in Figure 19.8.

3 Choose Slide Show, Action Settings. The Action Settings dialog box opens, as shown in Figure 19.9.

4 Click the Mouse Click tab if you want the jump to occur when the selected object is clicked.

Click the Mouse Over tab if you want the jump to occur when the mouse moves over the selected object.

5 Click the option next to Hyperlink To, and then click the down arrow next to Next Slide to open the drop-down list of possible hyperlinks. Select URL to open the Hyperlink to URL dialog box, as shown in Figure 19.10. Type the URL and click OK.

Fig. 19.8
The slide is ready for a hyperlink to be added.

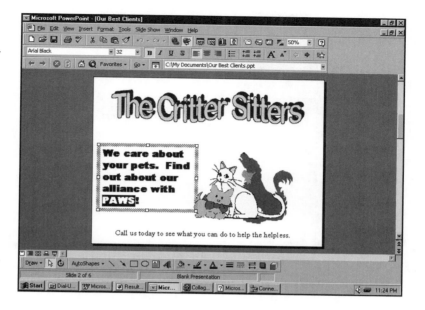

Fig. 19.9
Use the Action Settings dialog box to add a hyperlink.

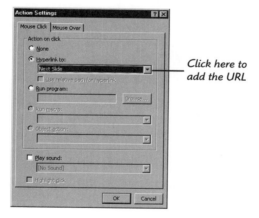

Click here to add the URL

6 If you want to add a sound, click the Play Sound option and choose a sound from the drop-down list.

7 Click OK to close the Action Settings dialog box and return to the slide. The selected text appears underlined and in a different color.

8 To preview how a hyperlink will appear in the slide show, click Slide Show at the lower left of the PowerPoint window. Click the hyperlink to jump to the Web page you specified. Figure 19.11 shows the slide in Slide Show view with the hyperlink in place.

Fig. 19.10
Type the URL of the
hyperlink.

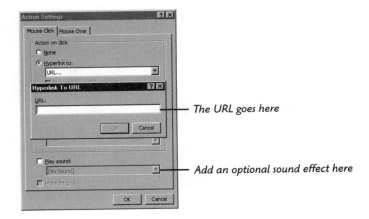

The URL goes here

Add an optional sound effect here

Fig. 19.11
The hyperlink appears
in Slide Show view.

Click to open
the link

CAUTION **Always test your Web hyperlinks before your presentation.**
Because Web pages come and go, you wouldn't want to be embarrassed
if you received an error message that the site does not exist during your
slide show. If a hyperlink doesn't work, or you decide to remove it, highlight the hyperlink and press Delete.

Saving your presentation for the world

Even though you may not be aware of any special coding when you look at a Web page, all documents on the Web must be created in a special programming code called HTML (HyperText Markup Language). Think of HTML as the language of the Web. HTML provides a common standard that all computers—PCs, Macs, and UNIX computers can read. Fortunately, you don't need to take any special classes to learn HTML code—PowerPoint does it for you!

It's easy to save a presentation in HTML. When you're all done with the presentation, choose File, Save as HTML. Follow the on-screen prompts and you're done!

 TIP After you've saved your presentation in HTML format, contact your Network Administrator about placing it on your company's intranet. If you're planning to save it on the Web, contact your Internet Service Provider about how you should proceed.

Follow these steps to save a presentation to the Web:

1 Open the presentation you want to save to the Web.

2 Choose File, Save as HTML.

3 The Save as HTML Wizard appears, as shown in Figure 19.12. Click Next to continue.

4 In the second dialog box, which deals with Layout selection, you're asked to choose an existing layout or create a new one. Unless you've created presentations on the Web before and you have existing page layouts to choose from, choose New Layout and click Next.

Your link to the world

It's really exciting to think that something you do at home or in the office has the potential to be viewed by millions of people! Whenever you save a presentation to the Web, you never know exactly how many people will see it and be affected by your work. Even if you're saving your presentation to your company's intranet, your work might be viewed by many of your co-workers.

Fig. 19.12
The Save as HTML
Wizard helps you save
your presentation for
the world to view.

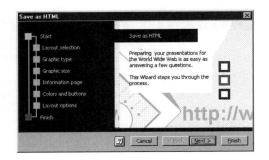

5 In the third dialog box, which also deals with Layout selection, you're asked to choose a page style. Choose the Standard option and click Next.

6 In the fourth dialog box dealing with Graphic types, you're asked to choose the type of graphics you want to appear on your Web pages. Unless you've added animation to your slides, choose the GIF option. If your slides contain animation, choose the PowerPoint Animation option. When viewers look at your site, they'll be prompted to download the PowerPoint Animation player (if their computer doesn't already have one) to view the animation effects on your slides. Click Next to continue.

7 In the fifth dialog box, which deals with the Graphics size, make sure that the option of 640×480 is selected and click Next to continue.

8 In the sixth dialog box, you're asked to customize your Web presentation with your e-mail address, the URL of your home page and other information, as shown in Figure 19.13. The information in this dialog box customizes your presentation and is not necessary for your presentation to appear on the Web. Click Next to continue.

Fig. 19.13
The information typed
here customizes your
Web presentation.

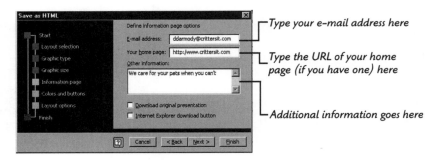

Type your e-mail address here

Type the URL of your home
page (if you have one) here

Additional information goes here

9 In the seventh dialog box, select the presentation page colors and how the buttons will look. If you're not sure, choose Use Browser Colors, the default. Click Next to continue.

10 In the eighth dialog box, select a button style for your presentation. You can choose a graphical style or choose a text hyperlink. Once you've chosen a button style, click Next to continue.

11 In the ninth dialog box, select the position of the navigational buttons your viewers will use. If you want any presentation notes to appear, check the box next to Include slide notes in pages. Click Next to continue.

12 In the tenth dialog box, select a location on the hard disk of your computer or the network drive where the folder to store your HTML presentation will be created, as displayed in Figure 19.14. By default, the folder will have the name of your presentation, although you can change this later.

13 In the eleventh dialog box, you're ready to save your slides as an HTML presentation. Click Finish.

14 In the twelfth dialog box, you're prompted to name the settings you've used in this HTML presentation so you can use them for future presentations you create for the Web. If you want to save these settings, type a name in the text box and then click Save. If you don't want to save the settings, click Don't Save. (If you don't save your settings, your slides will still be converted to HTML.)

Briefly, a box appears, showing that the slides are being processed to HTML. Your slides are now converted to a Web presentation. To view your slides as others will see them, open Microsoft Internet Explorer and choose File, Open. In the Open dialog box, click Browse to switch to the drive and folder where the HTML presentation is located. (The location you chose in Step 12.)

Notice that your each slide in the folder has its own file. If your Windows configuration is set up to view file extensions, you'll also notice that each file has an .HTM file extension. Select the file named index and click Open, then click OK. The Web presentation opens, as shown in Figure 19.14.

Fig. 19.14
The index file starts
your Web presentation.

*Click here to start
the slide show*

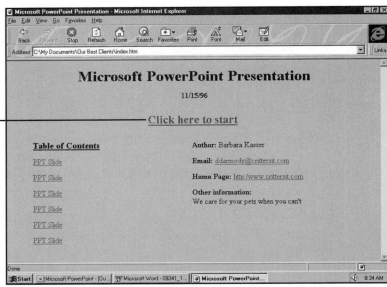

The slide show begins, as shown in Figure 19.15. Click the navigation buttons
to view each slide. If you want to edit the slide, click the Edit button. (Editing
changes you make to the HTML presentation will not be reflected in the
original PowerPoint slides.) When you're through viewing the Web presentation, choose File, Close to close Microsoft Internet Explorer.

Fig. 19.15
The first slide appears
in Microsoft Internet
Explorer.

*Click here to
edit the slide*

*Click these navigational
buttons to move through
the presentation*

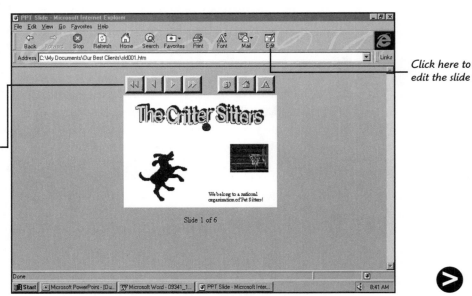

Part V: Appendix

Appendix A: **Installing PowerPoint**

Installing PowerPoint

In this appendix:

- **Does my computer have what it takes to run PowerPoint?**

- **How do I install PowerPoint?**

- **I'd like to add or remove some PowerPoint components**

It's simple to set PowerPoint up on your computer—you can even pick and choose the components you want. . . . .

Not so many years ago, installing software was a complicated and humbling experience. The instructions were confusing and misleading and assumed that you knew a lot more about your computer than you probably did. Worse, you were forced to play "disk jockey" as the computer prompted you to `Insert next disk`. By the time the new software was up and running, you were exhausted. In contrast, installing Microsoft Office 97 programs is a fairly easy procedure. In this appendix, you'll find out just how simple it is to install and remove PowerPoint.

In this explanation, I'm assuming that most of you will be installing PowerPoint as part of the Microsoft Office 97 suite. I'm also assuming that you'll be installing this software using one CD-ROM, rather than a lot of disks.

Make sure this software will work on your computer

Before you tear off the plastic shrink-wrap, and definitely before you open any sealed packages needed for the installation, make sure this software will work on your computer. Take a look at the box the software came in and it'll tell you what type of computer is required.

 *CAUTION* **It's important that you know that your computer meets the** minimum requirements for this software *before* you open any sealed packages. See all the fine print on that envelope? What it says is that once you've broken any seals, you own the software and, among other things, you can't return it even *if* it won't run on your computer.

The minimum requirements for running any Microsoft Office 97 components are listed on the side of the software box. To run PowerPoint 97, your computer must have a minimum of these features:

- Microsoft Windows 95 or Windows NT 3.51 or newer installed on your computer.

  This fact is not negotiable—your computer must be running either Windows 95 or Windows NT before you can install any Office 97 programs.

- Personal computer having an 80486 or higher microprocessor.

  An 80486 processor is the very minimum I'd recommend. PowerPoint runs best on a computer with a Pentium processor.

- Minimum 8M of memory (RAM).

  If you're planning to run Microsoft Access, you'll need a minimum of 12M. In my experience, 16M is advisable. Of course, if you're running Windows NT, you'll need a minimum of 16M.

- Hard disk with at least 200M of available disk space.

  According to Microsoft, 121M is required for a Typical installation, 121 to 191M is required for a Custom installation, and 60M is required to run Office 97 from the CD.

- 3.5-inch high-density (1.44) disk drive or CD-ROM player.

  It's becoming more and more common for programs to ship on CD-ROM. Installing software from a CD is much easier than from disks; you don't have to keep feeding the disks in the disk drive.

- VGA, SVGA, XGA, or any video adapter supported by Microsoft Windows 95.

  These video requirements let you take advantage of PowerPoint's graphics capabilities.

- Microsoft mouse or compatible pointing device.

  The mouse lets you make menu and button selections, as well as select and manipulate data with ease.

These are only minimum requirements. More RAM, a powerful processor, and more room on your hard disk means you'll get better performance from your computer, and that means a whole lot more efficiency and enjoyment for you.

Before you install PowerPoint...

When you open the box containing your software, you'll find that it's filled with lots of information. Nearly all software comes with a booklet called "Read Me First" or "Getting Started," as well as a sealed package of disks or a CD-ROM.

Q&A ***What if I already have an earlier version of PowerPoint on my computer?***

The PowerPoint installation program is smart! If you have a previous version of the program, as soon as the installation process begins, you'll see a message saying that a previous version of PowerPoint has been found. You'll be offered the choice of either installing the new version over the existing one or keeping both versions (assuming your computer has enough room).

Installing the software

Make sure you've cleared an area on your desk; you'll have a lot of information to read, and you won't want to misplace any items. The installation process is fairly straightforward, so there's no need to be nervous.

TIP **Always allow ample time to complete an installation. Although** I'm not terribly superstitious, I'm willing to bet that if you try to fit in time for an installation, you'll probably not have enough of it. So relax and give yourself more time than you could possibly need.

The following steps explain how to install PowerPoint:

1 Start your computer. Windows 95 or Windows NT opens automatically.

2 Close any open programs.

3 Insert the CD-ROM into the CD-ROM drive. If AutoRun is active on your computer, the CD-ROM will automatically open and you can skip steps 5 and 6. If AutoRun is not active, continue with steps 5 and 6 as shown.

4 Click the Start button.

5 Click <u>R</u>un; the Run dialog box opens.

6 Type **D:\SETUP.EXE** (assuming that D is your CD-ROM drive) in the <u>O</u>pen text box, as shown in Figure A.1, then click OK. Follow the on-screen instructions and respond to the screens and dialog boxes that appear. The installation program starts, and you're asked to choose the type of installation you want.

Fig. A.1
Type the file name of
the file you want to
run in the Run dialog
box.

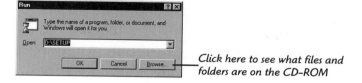

*Click here to see what files and
folders are on the CD-ROM*

7 Click the type of installation you want: Typical, Custom, or Run from
CD-ROM.

8 Supply your name and your company name, if required, and any other
information the program needs.

Q&A *How do I know what type of installation to choose?*

For most of us, a Typical installation is just fine. The Custom installation lets
you pick and choose to install whatever features are available. If you're fairly
new to installing software, choose Typical and let Microsoft handle the
major decisions about what to install on your hard disk. If you're really short
on disk space, or if you're using a laptop computer with a CD-ROM drive,
you might decide to choose Run from CD-ROM. Of course, if you choose
this type of installation, the Office 97 CD must always be inserted in the
CD-ROM drive before you open PowerPoint or any other Office 97
program.

Why use the Custom installation?

Some features you'll probably want to use, such as the Web Page Authoring
(HTML), are not installed during a Typical installation. Of course, you can
always install additional features at any time, but I'd rather you know this
up front.

If you decide to do a Custom installation, you'll see the Microsoft Office 97–
Custom dialog box shown in Figure A.2.

For example, if you want to install the Equation Editor feature, click the line
for the Office Tools Option, then click Change Option. A dialog box appears
similar to the one shown in Figure A.2. Find the Equation Editor option and
click its check box, then click Continue. Select all the features you want to
install, then click Continue and the installation process will be underway.
As you add components, you'll see an increase in the number of kilobytes
required next to the Space Required on C: toward the bottom of the dialog
box.

Fig. A.2
Components to be
installed are indicated
with a check mark.

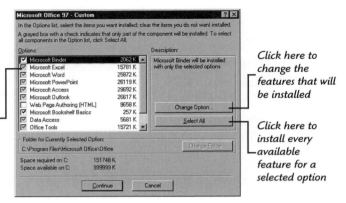

*A grayed check mark
means not all features
have been selected to
be installed*

*Click here to
change the
features that will
be installed*

*Click here to
install every
available
feature for a
selected option*

Can I add or remove PowerPoint components?

The day may come when you're pressed for disk space and you no longer want certain program features on your hard disk. If so, PowerPoint has an easy way to remove components of the program, or add any components you neglected to install.

Here's how to add or remove PowerPoint components:

1 Start your computer. Windows 95 or Windows NT opens automatically.

2 Close any open programs.

3 Insert the CD-ROM into the CD-ROM drive.

4 Click the Start button.

5 Click Run; the Run dialog box opens.

6 Type **D:\SETUP.EXE** in the Open text box, then click OK. You also can click the Browse button, click the command you want to run (in this case, D:\SETUP.EXE), click Open, and then click OK from the Run dialog box.

The installation program starts and you're shown the Microsoft Office 97 Setup dialog box (see Figure A.3).

7 Click Add/Remove.

Fig. A.3
Use the Microsoft
Office 97 Setup dialog
box to add or remove
components.

The Microsoft Office 97–Maintenance dialog box appears.

8 Select Microsoft PowerPoint and then click Change Option. The
Microsoft Ofice 97–Microsoft PowerPoint dialog box appears.

You can pick and choose options and features just as if you were
preparing for a Custom installation.

As you click components, the amount of space you gain or lose is
displayed just above the Continue and Cancel buttons in the dialog box.
A feature that's unchecked is added if you click it, making the check
mark appear. A feature that's already checked is deleted if you click it
again, making the check mark disappear.

9 After you've made your selections, click Continue. The components you
checked or unchecked are added or deleted.

Q&A *Why do I have to uninstall components? Can't I just
delete program files using the Explorer?*

Software is so complicated now. When you install a new program, not
only are files copied to the program's folder on your hard drive, but files
are copied to other folders such as Windows, Microsoft Shared, etc. The
program is registered into Windows 95 as well. The removal of one inno-
cent-looking file can have disastrous side effects, such as causing another
feature to quit working. That's why Microsoft lets you uninstall components
using the same Setup dialog box you used to install the program. The Setup
dialog box removes any components you no longer want without affecting
any other part of the PowerPoint program. Setup also tells you if removing a
component will affect other parts of the program.

Action Index

Creating a presentation

When you need to...	Turn to...
Start PowerPoint	p. 11–13
Get help	p. 21–25
Create or open a presentation	p. 42–43
Save a presentation	p. 40–42
Quit PowerPoint	p. 44–45
Print slides, notes, outlines, or handouts	p. 232–238
Add a slide	p. 36–37
Delete a slide	p. 37–38
Select a design template	p. 38–40
Create a summary slide	p. 221
Work in Outline view	p. 26, 28
Change the look of the text	p. 56–57
Check your spelling	p. 134–136
Add headers and footers	p. 84–86
Find and replace text	p. 140–143
Conduct on-screen research	p. 143–146
Create audience handouts	p. 253

Working with the Slide Master

When you need to...	Turn to...
View the Slide Master	p. 75–77
Edit the Slide Master	p. 74–77
Place a logo on a slide	p. 81–83
Change the background color	p. 83–84

Adding clip art or imported graphics

When you need to...	Turn to...
Add clip art	p. 61–63
Change the size of the image	p. 71–72
Change the color	p. 188–189
Arrange several pieces of clip art	p .186–190
Use only part of the image	p. 180–181

Adding tables

When you need to...	Turn to...
Add a table	p. 119–121
Edit the text	p. 122–125
Add a row	p. 122–123
Delete a row	p. 122–123
Change the width of a column	p. 123–124
Add a border	p. 126–127

Adding a chart

When you need to...	Turn to...
Create a chart	p. 90–94
Select a chart type	p. 90
Edit the data in a chart	p. 93
Change the color or pattern	p. 96–97
Add legends or grid lines	p. 97–98
Add text	p. 98–99
Add an arrow	p. 98
Use data from a spreadsheet	p. 100–101

Adding an organizational chart

When you need to...	Turn to...
Create an organizational chart	p. 106–108
Edit the organizational chart	p. 108–113
Change relationships	p. 108–110
Change the style	p. 113–114
Add circles and arrows	p. 114–115

Adding information from other files

When you need to...	Turn to...
Add a hyperlink to another presentation	p. 202–203
Link data so it updates	p. 195–197

Using special effects

When you need to...	Turn to...
Add WordArt	p. 148–154
Make bulleted text appear one bullet at a time	p. 161–162
Create transition effects between slides	p. 222–225
Add sounds	p. 167–172
Add movie clips	p. 174–176
Record a comment	p. 172–174

Running the presentation

When you need to...	Turn to...
View the presentation	p. 313
Write on the slides during a presentation	p. 249–251
Run a slide show in a continuous loop	p. 257–259
Skip a slide during a presentation	p. 226
Run a presentation conference	p. 293–295

Customizing PowerPoint

When you need to...	Turn to...
Change the number of most recently used files in the File menu	p. 271
Change the printer settings	p. 267–269

When you need to...	Turn to...
Add or delete toolbar buttons	p. 275–276
Add a menu command to the toolbar	p. 278

Sharing a presentation with colleagues

When you need to...	Turn to...
Fax a presentation	p. 283–284
E-mail a presentation	p. 284–287
Create a routing slip	p. 286–287
Add Action Items	p. 288–290

PowerPoint and the Internet

When you need to...	Turn to...
Visit PowerPoint Central	p. 176–177
Get Help from Microsoft on the Web	p. 300
Visit Microsoft's Home Page	p. 298
Search the Web	p. 301
Create a presentation for the Web	p. 307–308
Add a hyperlink to the Web	p. 308–310
Save a presentation for the Web	p. 311–314

Index

Symbols

(...) ellipsis commands, 19
200% Of Actual command
(View menu), 112
50% Of Actual command
(View menu), 112

A

action
 buttons, 212-214
 items, 288
action settings, 171-172
 command
 (Slide Show menu), 171
 dialog box, 171, 214, 308
active cells (charts), 91
Add option (Spelling
 dialog box), 136
Address Book dialog
 box, 286
Advanced tab (Options
 dialog box), 274-275
alignment
 text, 159
 table columns, 124-125
animation, 206-207
 custom animation,
 209-212
 Preview command (Slide
 Show menu), 208
 present, 207-212
annotating on slides,
 249-251
Apply button (Background
 dialog box), 84
Apply Design
 dialog box, 39, 78
 Template, 38
Apply to All button
 (Background dialog
 box), 84
applying
 attributes, 55, 79
 color schemes, 155-156
arranging, *see* sorting

B

arrows
 adding to org charts,
 114-115
 button (Graph toolbar), 99
 charts, inserting, 98-99
articles (Bookshelf
 Basics), 146
attributes
 applying, 55, 79
 copying, 56-57
 editing within placeholders, Slide Master, 78-79
 formatting
 tables, 126
 text, 54-56
audience
 considerations, 253
AutoClipArt
 command
 (Tools menu), 63-64
 dialog box, 63
AutoContent
 dialog box, 34
 Wizard, 32-36
AutoCorrect, 138
 command
 (Tools menu), 138
 dialog box, 138
AutoFit button (Cell
 Height and Width dialog
 box), 123
AutoLayouts, 38-40, 106

Back button (Web
 toolbar), 305
Background
 command
 (Format menu), 83
 dialog box, 83
 items (Slide Master), 75
backgrounds, slides
 (color), 83-84
bar charts, 89

Black Screen command
 (Screen menu), 230
blackening screens, 230
Bold button (Formatting
 toolbar), 55
Bookshelf Basics, 143-146
borders, 126-127
Borders and Shading
 command
 (Format menu), 127
 dialog box, 127
Bring Forward button, 190
browsers, 300
Bullet
 button (Formatting
 toolbar), 160
 command
 (Format menu), 163
 dialog box, 163
bulleted lists, 160-163
buttons
 action, 212-214
 Apply (Background dialog
 box), 84
 Apply to All (Background
 dialog box), 84
 Arrow (Graph toolbar), 99
 AutoFit (Cell Height and
 Width dialog box), 123
 Bold (Formatting
 toolbar), 55
 Bring Forward, 190
 Bullet (Formatting
 toolbar), 160
 Center Alignment
 (Formatting
 toolbar), 159
 Collapse (Outline
 toolbar), 59
 Collapse All (Outline
 toolbar), 60
 commands, 20
 Cut, 64

Decrease Paragraph
  Spacing (Formatting
  tool, 160
Demote (Outline
  toolbar), 59
Draw (Drawing
  toolbar), 183
Expand (Outline
  toolbar), 60
Expand All
  (Outline toolbar), 60
Font Color
  (Drawing toolbar), 157
Format Painter
  (Formatting toolbar), 56
Format WordArt
  (WordArt toolbar), 152
Formatting toolbar, 55
Free Rotate (WordArt
  toolbar), 152
Hide Slide (Slide Sorter
  toolbar), 220, 226
Horizontal Gridlines
  (Graph toolbar), 97
Import File
  (Graph toolbar), 100
Increase Paragraph
  Spacing
  (Formatting tool, 159
Insert
    Clip Art, 65, 67
    Graph (Standard
      toolbar), 91
    Microsoft Word
      Table, 119
    New Slide (Standard
      toolbar), 49, 50
    WordArt, 150, 152
Italic (Formatting
  toolbar), 55
Left Alignment (Format-
  ting toolbar), 159
Microsoft
    Graph, 95
    Organization Chart
      toolbar, 108-110
Move
    Down (Outline
      toolbar), 59
    Up
      (Outline toolbar), 59
New Slide (Standard
  toolbar), 36
Open (Standard
  toolbar), 42
option, 20

Outline toolbar, 59-60
Pause (Rehearsal
  dialog box), 228
Presentation Elapsed
  Time (Rehearsal dialog,
  box), 229
Print
  (Standard toolbar), 44
Promote
  (Outline toolbar), 59
Recolor Picture (Picture
  toolbar), 188
Record (Rehearsal dialog
  box), 228
Rehearse Timing (Slide
  Sorter toolbar), 220
Repeat (Rehearsal dialog
  box), 228
Replace
  (AutoCorrect), 140
Right Alignment (Format-
  ting toolbar), 159
Save (Standard
  toolbar), 41
Send to Back, 190
Shape (WordArt
  toolbar), 153
Show Formatting (Slide
  Sorter toolbar), 221
Shows Formatting
  (Outline toolbar), 60
Slide
    Elapsed Time
      (Rehearsal dialog
      box), 229
    Sorter toolbar, 220-221
    Transition (Slide
      Sorter toolbar), 220,
      223, 227
Spelling (Standard
  toolbar), 135
Start, 11
Subordinate (Microsoft
  Organization Chart
  toolbar), 110
Summary Slide, 60, 221
Text
    Preset Animation
      (Slide Sorter
      toolbar), 220
    Shadow (Formatting
      toolbar), 55
    Tool (Drawing
      toolbar), 115

toolbars, 275-276
Underline (Formatting
  toolbar), 55
Undo (Standard
  toolbar), 51
view, 15
View Datasheet (Graph
  toolbar), 93, 101
WordArt, 152-153

C

**CD-ROMs, installing
  PowerPoint Viewer,
  247-248**
**Cell Height and Width
  dialog box, 123**
cells, charts, 91
**Center Alignment button
  (Formatting
  toolbar), 159**
changing
    files, recently used
      number, 271
    menu animations, 278-279
    preferences, 269-275
    printing features, 272-273
    printing settings, 267-269
    quality preferences,
      274-275
    saving preferences, 273
    screen displays, 270
    text operations, 271
    see also editing
charts, 88-90
    bar, 89
    cells, 91
    column, 89
    commands, 92
    creating with Microsoft
      Graph, 90-94
    customizing, 94-99
    data, editing, 93
    defined, 88
    doughnut, 89
    grid lines, 91
    importing data from
      spreadsheets, 100-101
    legends, 91
    line, 89
    menu commands
      (Microsoft Graph), 92
    org
        adding charts to
          slides, 115-116
        adding relationships,
          110-112

AutoLayout, 106
creating with
    Organization Chart
    (Microsoft), 104-108
defined, 104
deleting relationships,
    110-112
drawing with Drawing
    toolbar, 114-115
editing, 108-113
placeholders, 107
relationships, 108-110
styles, 113-114
views, 112-113
pie, 89
titles, 92
types, 90, 94
check boxes, 20
circles, adding to org
charts, 114-115
clicking (mouse
operation), 11
clip art
AutoClipArt, 63-64
colors, editing, 188-189
converting into
    objects, 182-184
cropping, 180-181
defined, 60
deleting, 64
handles, 62-63
inserting into Clip
    Gallery, 61-63
moving, 70-72
rearranging, 189
sizing, 71-72
WWW (World Wide Web),
    downloading to Clip
    Gallery, 67-69
see also graphics; pictures
Clip Gallery, 60-64
adding to slides
    sound clips, 168-169
    video clips, 174-176
clip art, 61-64, 70-72
downloading WWW
    (World Wide Web),
    67-69
inserting pictures into,
    65-69
Clip Properties
dialog box, 66
Close command
(File menu), 44
closing
PowerPoint, 44-45

tables, 120
toolbars, 17
Collapse All button
(Outline toolbar), 60
Collapse button (Outline
toolbar), 59
Color dialog box, 156
colors
bullets, 163
charts, editing, 96-97
clip art, 188-190
schemes, 155-157
slide backgrounds, 83-84
text, 157-158
columns
charts, 89
tables, 122-125
commands
buttons, 20
Chart menu
    (Microsoft Graph), 92
Data menu
    (Microsoft Graph), 93
Edit menu
    Copy, 146
    Delete, 101
    Delete Slide, 38
    Find, 141
    Find Next, 141
    Links, 198
    Paste Special, 195-197
    Replace, 141
    Select All, 184, 221
ellipsis (...), 19
File menu
    Close, 44
    Exit, 44, 114
    Files and Folders, 247
    Mail Recipient, 285
    New, 307-308
    Open, 313
    Pack and Go, 254
    Print, 43
    Print Article, 146
    Routing Recipient, 286
    Save, 19, 41
    Save As, 41, 256
    Save as HTML, 311
    Update, 107
Format menu
    Background, 83
    Borders and
        Shading, 127
    Bullet, 163
    Slide Color
        Scheme, 155-156

Go menu
    Hidden Slide, 226
    Slide Navigator, 252
Help menu
    Contents and Index, 21
    Microsoft on the
        Web, 25,
Insert menu
    Movies and
        Sounds, 168
    Object, 115
    Picture, 65
Programs menu,
    PowerPoint Viewer,
    95, 248
Screen menu
    Black Screen, 230
    Erase Pen, 251
selecting from menus, 18
Slide Show menu
    Action Settings, 171
    Animation Preview,
        208
    Custom Animation,
        209, 211
    Hide Slide, 226
    Preset Animation, 207
    Record Narration, 215
    Rehearse Timings, 229
    Set Up Show, 215, 244
Start menu, Find, 247
Table menu, 121, 123, 128
Tools menu
    AutoClipArt, 63
    AutoCorrect, 138
    Customize, 19, 275
    Language, 138
    Look Up Reference,
        144
    Meeting Minder,
        288-289
    Options, 136
    PowerPoint
        Central, 177
    Presentation
        Conference, 293
    Style Checker, 142
View menu
    200% Of Actual, 112
    50% Of Actual, 112
    Handout Master, 235
    Header, 85
    Master, 76
    Options, 39
    Ruler, 161
    Size to Window, 112

Toolbars, 17, 150
Zoom, 30
comments
slides, 172-174
recording, 172-174
writing on, 249-251
**company logos, adding to
slides with Slide
Master, 81-83**
**conferences, presenta-
tions, 290-295**
**connecting to PowerPoint
Central, 176-177**
**Contents and Index
command (Help
menu), 21**
**converting pictures into
objects, 182-184**
**Copy command
(Edit menu), 146**
copying
articles (Bookshelf
Basics), 146
attributes, 56-57
fonts, 56-57
text or graphics,
Clipboard, 193-194
correcting
mispelled words, 134-136
AutoCorrect
feature, 138-140
creating
hyperlinks in presenta-
tions, 201-203
shortcuts on desktop,
264-265
Speaker Notes, 239-241
toolbars, 276-278
cropping clip art, 180-181
custom animation, 209-212
Custom Animation
command (Slide Show
menu), 209, 211
dialog box, 209
Custom dialog box, 321
**custom installation,
321-322**
Customize
command (Tools
menu), 19, 275
dialog box, 275, 277-278
customizing
charts, 94-99
PowerPoint, 266-267

presentations
adding company logos
with Slide
Master, 81-83
Slide Master, 77-81
tables, 125-129
toolbars, 275-278
see also formatting
Cut button, 64
**cutting text or graphics,
Clipboard, 193-194**

D

data
charts, editing, 93
linking, 195, 195-197
spreadsheets, importing
into charts, 100-101
tables, sorting, 121
**Data menu commands
(Microsoft Graph), 93**
**dates, inserting into
slides, 84-86**
**Decrease Paragraph
Spacing button
(Formatting tool, 160**
**defaults, design of
slides, 78**
**Delete Cells command
(Table menu), 123**
**Delete command
(Edit menu), 101**
**Delete Entire Column
command
(Table menu), 123**
**Delete Entire Row
command
(Table menu), 123**
**Delete Slide command
(Edit menu), 38**
deleting
buttons from
toolbars, 275-276
clip art, 64
columns in tables, 122-123
placeholders, 51
Slide Master, 79-81
relationships from org
charts, 110-112
rows in tables, 122-123
slides, 37-38
worksheets, 102
**Demote button
(Outline toolbar), 59**
deselecting
attributes, 56
grouped objects, 187

text boxes, 81
see also selecting
**design templates,
selecting, 38-40**
**designing presentations
for the Web, 307-308**
desktop, 10, 264-265
**destination
documents, 195**
dialog boxes
Action Settings, 171,
214, 308
Address Book, 286
Apply Design, 39, 78
AutoClipArt, 63
AutoContent Wizard, 34
AutoCorrect, 138
Background, 83
Borders and Shading, 127
Bullet, 163
Cell Height and Width, 123
Clip Art Gallery, 169
Clip Properties, 66
Color, 156
Color Scheme, 155-156
Custom, 321
Custom Animation, 209
Customize, 275, 277-278
Edit WordArt Text, 150
elements, 20
File Download, 69
File Save, 41
Find, 140
Find: All Files, 247
Header and Footer, 85
Hyperlink to URL, 308
Import
Data Options, 101
File, 100
Insert Hyperlink, 202
Insert
Object, 116, 200
Picture, 82
Internet Explorer, 69
Language, 138
Links, 198
Look Up Reference, 144
Maintenance, 323
Meeting Minder, 288-289
Microsoft
Clip Gallery, 61, 65, 67
PowerPoint
Viewer, 248
Network, 291
New Message, 285
New Slide, 36, 50, 106
Open, 313

opening, 19
Options, tabs, 270-275
Paste Special, 196
PowerPoint, 13
Print, 43, 234
Print Properties, 268
Record
  Narration, 215
  Sound, 173
  Rehearsal, 228-229
  Replace, 141
  Routing Slip, 286
  Run, 320, 322
  Save As, 41
  Setup, 323
  Slide
    Navigator, 252
    Show, 244
    Transition, 223
  Spelling, 135-136
  startup PowerPoint, 33
  Style Checker, 142
  Table AutoFormat, 128
  Toolbars, 278
  WordArt Gallery, 150
dictionary (spell checker), 136-138
displaying toobars, 17
Distribute Columns Evenly command (Table menu), 123
Distribute Rows Evenly command (Table menu), 123
docked toolbars, *see* **floating toolbars**
documents, 195, 199
domain names, 300
double-clicking (mouse operation), 11
doughnut charts, 89
downloading
  PowerPoint Viewer from Web, 247
  WWW (World Wide Web) clip art to Clip Gallery, 67-69
drag and drop method, 194
Draw button (Drawing toolbar), 183
drawing toolbar, charts, 16, 114-115
drop-down lists, 20

E

Edit menu commands
  Copy, 146
  Delete, 101
  Delete Slide, 38
  Find, 141
  Find Next, 141
  Links, 198
  Paste Special, 195-197
  Replace, 141
  Select All, 184, 221
Edit WordArt Text dialog box, 150
editing
  chart data, 93
  clip art, 188-189
  color schemes, 156-157
  files, 271
  menu animations, 278-279
  org charts, 108-113
  preferences, 269-275
  printing
    features, 272-273
    settings, 267-269
  screen displays, 270
  tables, 122-125
  text operations, 271
  WordArt, 152-154
  worksheets, 102
  see also changing
ellipsis (...) commands, 19
embedding objects, 199-201
Erase Pen command (Screen menu), 251
erasing annotations, 251
errors, spelling, 274
  see also troubleshooting
Excel worksheets, 101-102
Exclude Row/Column command (Data menu, Microsoft Graph), 93
Exit command (File menu), 44, 114
exiting
  Internet Explorer (Microsoft), 314
  PowerPoint, 44-45
Expand All button (Outline toolbar), 60
Expand button (Outline toolbar), 60

F

Favorites button (Web toolbar), 304-305
fax modems, 283
faxing presentations, 282-284
File Download dialog box, 69
file extensions, viewing, 39
File menu commands
  Close, 44, 107, 314
  Exit, 44, 114
  Files and Folders, 247
  Mail Recipient, 285
  New, 307-308
  Open, 313
  Pack and Go, 254
  Print, 43
  Print Article, 146
  Routing Recipient, 286
  Save, 19, 41
  Save As, 41, 256
  Save as HTML, 311
  Update, 107, 110
File Save dialog box, 41
files
  opening, 265-266
  saving, 19
Files and Folders command (File menu), 247
Find command
  dialog box, 140
  Edit menu, 141
  Start menu, 247
Find Next command (Edit menu), 141
Find: All Files dialog box, 247
finding words in slides, 140-141
flipping objects, 185
floating toolbars, 17, 278
floppy disks, saving presentations, 40
folioing slides, 84-86
Font Color button (Drawing toolbar), 157
fonts
  bullets, 163
  copying, 56-57
  formatting text, 52-54
footers, 75, 84-86
foreign languages, spell checking, 138

Format menu commands
Background, 83
Borders and Shading, 127
Bullet, 163
Slide Color Scheme, 155-156
Format buttons
Painter (Formatting toolbar), 56
WordArt (WordArt toolbar), 152
formatting
bullets, 162-163
defined, 52
text, 51-57
toolbar, 16, 53-54
see also customizing
Forward button (Web toolbar), 305
Free Rotate
button (WordArt toolbar), 152
tool (Drawing toolbar), 184
FTP (File Transfer Protocol), 300

G

Go button (Web toolbar), 306
Go menu commands
Hidden Slide, 226
Slide Navigator, 252
graphs
buttons, 95
charts, 93-101
worksheets, 101-102
graphics
clip art, *see* clip art
cropping, 180-181
grouping into one, 186-188
pictures, *see* pictures
see also clip art; pictures
graphs, *see* charts
grid lines (charts), 91, 97-98
grouping objects, 182-183, 186-188

H

handles, clip art, 62-63
Handout Master, 234-238
handouts, 232-238
hard disks, saving presentations, 40

hardware, requirements for installing PowerPoint, 318-319
Header and Footer dialog box, 85
Header command (View menu), 85
headers, 84-86
height, columns in tables, 123-124
help, 21-25
features, What's This, 273
menu commands
Contents and Index, 21
Microsoft on the Web, 25, 246, 301
ScreenTips, 11, 15
wizards, *see* wizards
Hidden Slide command (Go menu), 226
Hide Slide
button (Slide Sorter toolbar), 220, 226
command (Slide Show menu), 226
hiding
Office Assistant, 23
slides, 226
home pages (Web pages), 298
Horizontal Gridlines button (Graph toolbar), 97
HTML (HyperText Markup Language), 300, 311
HTTP (HyperText Transport Protocol), 300
Hyperlink to URL dialog box, 308
hyperlinks, 201-203, 298
adding to slides for the Web, 308-310

I

icons, desktop, 265
Import Data Options dialog box, 101
Import File
button (Graph toolbar), 100
dialog box, 100
importing data from spreadsheets into charts, 100-101
Include Row/Col command (Data menu, Microsoft Graph), 93

Increase Paragraph Spacing button (Formatting toolbar), 159
Insert Clip Art button, 65, 67
Insert Columns command (Table menu), 123
Insert Graph button (Standard toolbar), 91
Insert Hyperlink dialog box, 202
Insert menu commands
Movies and Sounds, 168, 175
Object, 115, 200
Picture, 65
Insert Microsoft Word Table button (Standard toolbar, 119
Insert New Slide button (Standard toolbar), 49-50
Insert Object dialog box, 116, 200
Insert Picture dialog box, 82
Insert Rows command (Table menu), 123
Insert WordArt buttons, 150, 152
inserting
action buttons on slides, 213
arrows into charts, 98-99
bullets into lists, 160
buttons on toolbars, 275-276
clip art into Clip Gallery, 61-63
columns into tables, 122-123
company logos into slides, 81-83
custom animation into charts, 211-212
dates into slides, 84-86
misspelled words into spell checker dictionary, 136
page numbers into slides, 84-86
pictures into
Clip Gallery, 65-69
slides, 64-65
relationships into org charts, 110-112
rows into tables, 122-123

slides into
  presentations, 36-37
text into
  charts, 98-99
  outlines, 58-59
  slides, 50-51
times into slides, 84-86
video clips into
  slides, 174-176
words into spell checker
  dictionary, 137
installing
  PowerPoint, 318-323
  Viewer from
    CD-ROM, 247-248
IntelliMouse, 23-24
Internet
  PowerPoint Central,
    176-177
  service providers
    (ISP), 298, 304
Internet Explorer, 301, 314
  dialog box, 69
intranets, 306-307
IP (Internet Protocol), 300
**Italic button (Formatting
  toolbar), 55**

K-L
keyboard, 10
keys, Delete, 64
**keywords (searching the
  Web), 302**

**LAN (Local Area
  Network), 282**
Language
  command (Tools
    menu), 138
  dialog box, 138
**languages, spell checking
  foreign languages, 138**
lauching, *see* starting
layout (slides)
  AutoLayout, 38-40
  editing, 37
leading, 159-160
**Left Alignment button
  (Formatting
  toolbar), 159**
legends (charts), 91, 97-98
levels (outlines), 58-60
line charts, 89
line spacing, 159-160
linking
  data, 195-197
  files, presentations, 255

Links, 198
  command (Edit
    menu), 198
  dialog box, 198
lists
  boxes, 20
  bulleted, 160-163
**logos, adding to slides with
  Slide Master, 81-83**
Look Up Reference
  command (Tools
    menu), 144
  dialog box, 144
**loops, running
  presentations, 257-259**

M
**magazines (online),
  PowerPoint Central,
  176-177**
**Mail Recipient command
  (File menu), 285**
**Maintenance dialog
  box, 323**
**Master command (View
  menu), 76**
**Master text
  (Slide Master), 75**
Meeting Minder
  command (Tools menu),
    288-289
  dialog box, 288
  saving comments, 287-290
menus
  animations, editing,
    278-279
  commands, 18-19
**Microsoft Office 97,
  192-193**
**Microsoft Bookshelf
  Basics, *see* Bookshelf
  Basics**
Microsoft Clip Gallery 3.0
  adding to slides
    sound clips, 168-169
    video clips, 174-176
  dialog box, 61
  downloading Clip Gallery
    Live Web site sound
    clips, 169-170
Microsoft Clip Gallery
  dialog box, 65, 67
  Live Web site, 68-69
  see also Clip Gallery
Microsoft Graph
  buttons, 95
  charts, 90-99

  worksheets, 101-102
**Microsoft Internet
  Explorer, launching, 301**
**Microsoft on the Web,
  24-25**
  command (Help
    menu), 25, 246, 301
**Microsoft Organization
  Chart**
  org charts
    adding charts to
      slides, 115-116
    adding relation-
      ships, 110-112
    AutoLayouts, 106
    creating, 104-108
    deleting relation-
      ships, 110-112
    drawing with Drawing
      toolbar, 114-115
    editing, 108-113
    relationships, 108-110
    styles, 113-114
    views, 112-113
  toolbar buttons, 108-110
  troubleshooting, 108
Microsoft Outlook, 285
**Microsoft PowerPoint, *see*
  PowerPoint**
**Microsoft PowerPoint
  Viewer dialog box, 248**
misspelled words
  adding to spell
    checker, 136
  AutoCorrect feature,
    138-140
  correcting, 134-136
modifying, *see* editing
**monitoring presentations
  with Slide Meter,
  229-230**
mouse, 10-11, 23-24
**Move Down button
  (Outline toolbar), 59**
**Move Up button
  (Outline toolbar), 59**
**Movies and Sounds
  command (Insert
  menu), 168, 175**
movies, *see* video clips
moving
  clip art, 70-72
  placeholders, Slide
    Master, 79-81
  text, drag and drop, 194
  WordArt objects, 152

N

narrations (presenta-
tions), recording,
215-216
navigating among
slides, 252
Network dialog box, 291
networks, 282
  presentations, running
    conferences, 290-295
New command
  (File menu), 307-308
New Message dialog
  box, 285
New Slide
  button (Standard
    toolbar), 36
  dialog box, 36, 50, 106
Notes Page view, 26, 29-30
nudging objects, 185
numbering slides, 84-86

O

Object command
  (Insert menu), 115, 200
objects
  converting pictures,
    182-184
  defined, 60
  embedding, 199-201
  flipping, 185
  grouping, 182-183, 186-188
  nudging, 185
  rearranging, 189
  rotating, 184-186
  ungrouping, 188
  WordArt, *see* WordArt
Office 97 (Microsoft),
  192-193, 285
Office Assistant, 22-23
OLE (Object Linking and
  Embedding) objects,
  199-201
online magazines,
  PowerPoint Central,
  176-177
online research, Bookshelf
  Basics, 143-146
Open
  button (Standard
    toolbar), 42
  command (File
    menu), 313
  dialog box, 313

opening
  dialog boxes, 19
  files, 265-266
  Microsoft Organization
    Chart, 108
  presentations, 42-43
Options
  commands
    Tools menu, 136
    View menu, 39
  dialog box, tabs, 270-275
org charts
  adding existing charts to
    slides, 115-116
  arrows, 114-115
  circles, 114-115
  creating with Organization
    Chart, 104-108
  defined, 104
  drawing with Drawing
    toolbar, 114-115
  editing, 108-113
  placeholders, 107
  relationships, 108-113
  styles, 113-114
  views, 112-113
Organization Chart
  org charts
    adding charts to
      slides, 115-116
    adding relation-
      ships, 110-112
    AutoLayouts, 106
    creating, 104-108
    deleting relation-
      ships, 110-112
    drawing with Drawing
      toolbar, 114-115
    editing, 108-113
    relationships, 108-110
    styles, 113-114
    views, 112-113
  toolbar buttons, 108-110
  troubleshooting, 108
organizing information in
  tables, 121
outlines, 57-60
  levels, 58-60
  text, inserting, 58-59
  toolbar buttons, 59-60
  view, 26, 28

P

Pack and Go
  command (File
    menu), 254

  Wizard, 254-257
page
  home, 298
  numbers, inserting into
    slides, 84-86
paragraphs, line
  spacing, 159-160
Paste Special
  command (Edit
    menu), 195-197
  dialog box, 196
pasting graphics/text,
  193-194
Pause button (Rehearsal
  dialog box), 228
pictures
  command (Insert
    menu), 65
  converting into
    objects, 182-184
  grouping, 186-188
  inserting into
    Clip Gallery, 65-69
    slides, 64-65
  toolbar, 16
  see also clip art; graphics
pie charts, 89
placeholders, 48-49
  deleting, 51
  Handout Master,
    editing, 237
  org charts, 107
  Slide Master, 77-81
pointer (cell), 91
PowerPoint
  Central, 176-177
  dialog box, 13
  exiting, 44-45
  installing, 320-323
  screens, 13-15
  starting, 11-13
    presentations, 244-245
  uninstalling
    components, 323
  Viewer, 246-249
predefined color
  schemes, 155-157
preferences, editing,
  269-275
present animation,
  207-212
Presentation Conference
  command (Tools
    menu), 293
  Wizard, 293-295
Presentation Elapsed Time
  button, 229

presentations
audience
considerations, 253
comments, saving with
Meeting Minder, 287-290
conferences, running over
networks, 290-295
creating AutoContent
Wizard, 33-36
faxing, 282-284
hyperlinks, creating,
201-203
linked files, 255
opening, 42-43
outlines, 57-60
printing handouts, 232-238
proofreading, 142-146
recording narration,
215-216
routing, 286-287
running
in continuous loop,
257-259
quitting, 249
saving, 40-42, 256
schedules, 253
setting, 253
showmanship, 252-254
slides
adding, 36-37
background colors,
83-84
dates, 84-86
deleting, 37-38
finding text, 140-141
footers, 84-86
formatting text, 51-57
headers, 84-86
hiding, 226
inserting company
logos into, 81-83
navigating among, 252
org charts, 106-116
page numbers, 84-86
placeholders, 48-51
printing, 43-44
replacing text, 141-143
Slide Master, 74-81
summary, 221
tables, 119-121
text, adding, 50-51
thumbnails, 29
times, 84-86
transition effects,
222-225
views, 15

WordArt, 148-154
worksheets (Microsoft
Graph), 101-102
writing on, 249-251
see also slides
sound clips, 166, 171-172
spell checking, 134-140
starting, 244-245
timing, 227-230
troubleshooting, running
in continuous loops, 259
video clips, 174-176
WWW (World Wide Web)
designing, 307-308
saving, 311-314
**Preset Animation
command (Slide Show
menu), 207**
previewing animation, 208
Print
button (Standard
toolbar), 44, 234
command (File menu),
43, 234
dialog box, 43, 234
tab (Options dialog
box), 272-273
**Print Article command
(File menu), 146**
**Print Properties dialog
box, 268**
printing
articles (Bookshelf
Basics), 146
handouts (steps), 237-238
preferences, changing,
272-273
presentations, handouts,
232-238
settings, editing, 267-269
slides, 43-44
problems, *see*
troubleshooting
**Programs menu commands,
PowerPoint
Viewer 95, 248**
**Promote button
(Outline toolbar), 59**
**proofreading
presentations, 137-146**

Q-R

**quality preferences,
editing, 274-275**
quitting presentations, 249

rearranging objects, 189
**Recolor Picture button
(Picture toolbar), 188**
recoloring clip art, 188-189
**Record button (Rehearsal
dialog box), 228**
Record Narration
command
(Slide Show menu), 215
dialog box, 215
**Record Sound dialog
box, 173**
recording
comments on slides,
172-174
narrations, 215-216
**Refresh Current Page
button (Web
toolbar), 305**
**Rehearsal dialog box,
228-229**
**Rehearse Timings (Slide
Sorter View)**
button, 220
command, 229
**rehearsing for
presentations, 228-229**
**relationships (org
charts), 108-113**
**Repeat button (Rehearsal
dialog box), 228**
**Replace All option
(Replace dialog
box), 141**
Replace
button (AutoCorrect), 140
command (Edit
menu), 141
dialog box, 141
**replacing text in
slides, 141-143**
**restoring text
deletions, 51**
**Right Alignment button
(Formatting
toolbar), 159**
rotating
objects, 184-186
presentations, 286-287
Recipient command
(File menu), 286
rows, tables, 122-124
**Ruler command
(View menu), 161**

Run dialog box, 320
running presentations,
 continuous loop, 257-259

S

Save As (File menu)
 commands, 41, 256
  HTML (HyperText
   Markup
   Language), 311
 dialog box, 41
Save
 button (Standard
  toolbar), 41
 command (File
  menu), 19, 41
saving
 comments with Meeting
  Minder, 287-290
 files, 19
 preferences, editing, 273
 presentations, 40-42, 256
  WWW (World Wide
   Web), 311-314
screens, 13-15
 blackening, 230
 displays, editing, 270
 menu commands
  Black Screen, 230
  Erase Pen, 251
  ScreenTips, 11, 15
scrolling with
 IntelliMouse, 24
Search button
 (Web toolbar), 303
Search the Web button
 (Web toolbar), 305
Select All command
 (Edit menu), 184, 221
selecting
 charts, 90
 commands from
  menus, 18
 design templates, 38-40
 PowerPoint installation
  type, 321
 see also deselecting
Send Backward
 button, 190
Send to Back button, 190
service providers
 (Internet; ISP), 298, 304
Set Up Show command
 (Slide Show
  menu),
  215, 244

Setup dialog box, 323
Shape button
 (WordArt toolbar), 153
shortcuts, creating on
 desktop, 264-265
Show Formatting button
 (Slide Sorter view), 221
Show Only Web Toolbar
 button (Web
 toolbar), 306
Shows Formatting button
 (Outline toolbar), 60
shutting down
 PowerPoint, 44-45
sites, Web, 68-69
Size to Window command
 (View menu), 112
sizing
 bullets, 163
 clip art, 71-72
 WordArt objects, 152
Slide Color Scheme
 command (Format
 menu), 155-156
Slide Elapsed Time button
 (Rehearsal dialog
 box), 229
Slide Master, 74-77
 adding company logos,
  81-83
 changing default design of
  slides, 78
 creating WordArt, 149-151
 customizing presenta-
  tions, 77-81
 editing WordArt, 153-154
 placeholders, 77-81
 viewing, 75-77
Slide Meter, 229-230
Slide Navigator
 command (Go menu), 252
 dialog box, 252
Slide Show
 dialog box, 244
 menu commands
  Action Settings, 171
  Animation
   Preview, 208
  Custom
   Animation, 209, 211
  Hide Slide, 226
  Preset Animation, 207
  Record Narration, 215
  Rehearse Timings, 229
  Set Up Show, 215, 244
 view, 26-27, 30, 245
 see also presentations

Slide Sorter
 toolbar buttons, 220-221
 view, 26-29, 220-221
Slide Transition
 button (Slide Sorter
  toolbar), 220, 223
 dialog box, 223
slides
 action buttons, 212-214
 adding, 36-37
 animation, 206-212
 backgrounds, color, 83-84
 bulleted lists, 160-163
 charts, 88-90
  adding arrows, 98-99
  colors, 96-97
  creating with
   Microsoft Graph,
   90-94
  customizing, 94-99
  data changes, 93
  defined, 88
  grid lines, 91, 97-98
  importing data from
   spreadsheets,
   100-101
  legends, 97-98
  org charts, 104
  patterns, 96-97
  selecting, 90
  text, 98-99
  titles, 92
 clip art, see clip art
 comments, recording,
  172-174
 dates, 84-86
 deleting, 37-38
 footers/headers, 84-86
 hiding, 226
 hyperlinks for the Web,
  308-310
 layout (AutoLayout),
  37-40
 navigating, 252
 org charts, see org charts
 page numbers,
  inserting, 84-86
 pictures
  converting into
   objects, 182-184
  inserting, 64-69
 placeholders, see
  placeholders
 printing, 43-44
 Slide Master, see Slide
  Master
 special effects, 148-154

tables, 118-125
templates, selecting, 38-40
text
    adding, 50-51
    alignment, 159
    attributes, 54-57
    colors, 157-158
    finding, 140-141
    fonts, 52-57
    formatting, 51-57
    replacing, 141-143
    Style Checker, 142-143
    WordArt, 148
thumbnails, 29
times, inserting, 84-86
transition effects, 222-225
worksheets, Microsoft
    Graph, 101-102
video clips, 174-176
views, 15
writing on, 249-251
software suites, 192
**Sort command (Table
menu), 121**
sorting
    objects, 189
    table data, 121
sound
    cards, 166
    clips, 166, 171-172
    effects, 211
spacing
    between bullets and
        text, 161-162
    lines, 159-160
Speaker Notes, 238-241
special effects
    animation, *see* animation
        troubleshooting, 211
    WordArt, 148-154
spell checker, 134-138
Spelling
    button (Standard
        toolbar), 135
    dialog box, 135-136
spreadsheets, *see*
    worksheets (Excel)
Start
    button, 11
    menu commands,
        Find, 247
**Start Page button
    (Web toolbar), 305**
starting
    Microsoft Internet
        Explorer, 301
    PowerPoint, 11-13

presentations,
    244-245, 248-249
**Stop Current Jump button
    (Web toolbar), 305**
Style Checker
    command (Tools
        menu), 142-143
    dialog box, 142
styles
    org charts, 113-114
    transition effects
        (slides), 222-225
**Subordinate button
    (Microsoft Organization
    Chart toolbar), 110**
**Summary Slide
    buttons, 60, 221**

T

Table AutoFormat
    command (Table
        menu), 128-129
    dialog box, 128
**Table menu
    commands, 121, 123, 128**
tables, 118-119
    closing, 120
    columns, 122-125
    creating, Insert Microsoft
        Word Table button,
        119-121
    customizing, 125-129
    data, 121
    editing, 122-125
    rows, 122-124
    slides, 118-119
    text, 120
    troubleshooting, 119
**TCP/IP (Transmission
    Control Protocol/
    Internet Protocol), 300**
templates
    selecting, 38-40
    Web, 307-308
text
    adding to slides, 50-51
    alignment, 159
    attributes, copying, 56-57
    boxes, 20, 81
    charts, inserting, 98-99
    colors, 157-158
    flipping objects, 185
    fonts, 52-54, 57
    Handout Master, 235
    moving, drag and
        drop, 194

operations, 271
outlines, inserting, 58-59
placeholders, *see*
    placeholders
rotating objects, 185
slides, 141-143
Style Checker, 142-143
tables, 120, 124
WordArt, 148-154
**Text Preset Animation
    button (Slide Sorter
    view), 220**
**Text Shadow button
    (Formatting toolbar), 55**
**Text Tool button
    (Drawing toolbar), 115**
thumbnails, 29, 38
**timing presentations,
    227-230**
tips
    Office Assistant, 22-23
    ScreenTips, *see* screens
toolbars, 15-16
    buttons
        Microsoft Organization
            Chart, 108-110
        Outline, 59-60
        Slide Sorter, 220-221
        WordArt, 152-153
    closing, 17
    command (View
        menu), 17, 150
    Common Tasks, 16
    creating, 276-278
    customizing, 275-278
    dialog box, 278
    Drawing, 16
        charts, 114-115
    floating, 17
    formatting text, 16, 53-55
    Outlining, 16
    Picture, 16
    Standard, 16
Tools menu commands
    AutoClipArt, 63
    AutoCorrect, 138
    Customize, 19, 275-278
    Language, 138
    Look Up Reference, 144
    Meeting Minder, 288-289
    Options, 136
    PowerPoint Central, 177
    Presentation
        Conference, 293
    Style Checker, 142
**transition effects
    (slides), 222-225**

troubleshooting
  action buttons, 214
  Microsoft Organization
    Chart, 108
  PowerPoint
    installation, 320-321
  presentations, running in
    continuous loops, 259
  sound effects, 211
  spell checker, 137
  tables, 119
  WordArt button, 153

U

**Underline button
  (Formatting toolbar), 55**
**Undo button
  (Standard toolbar), 51**
undoing
  border additions to
    tables, 127
  text deletions, 51
ungrouping objects, 188
**uninstalling
  components, 322-323**
**Update command
  (File menu), 107, 110**
**URL (Uniform Resource
  Locator), 300, 306**

V

video clips, 174-176
view buttons, 15
**View Datasheet button
  (Graph toolbar), 93, 101**
View menu commands
  200% Of Actual, 112
  50% Of Actual, 112
  Handout Master, 235

Header, 85
Master, 76
Options, 39
Ruler, 161
Size to Window, 112
Toolbars, 17, 150
Zoom, 30
Viewer, *see* **PowerPoint**
viewing
  bullet characters, 163
  file extensions, 39
  links, 198
  Office Assistant tips, 23
  Slide Master, 75-77
  Web presentations, 313
views
  Notes Page, 26, 29-30
  org charts, 112-113
  Outline, 26, 28
  Slide , 26
    Show, 27, 30, 245
    Sorter, 26, 28-29,
      220-221

W

**WAN (Wide Area Net-
  work), 282**
Web, *see* **WWW
  (World Wide Web)**
**Web sites, Microsoft Clip
  Gallery Live, 68-69**
**What's This help
  feature, 273**
Windows 95, 10
wizards, 32
  AutoContent Wizard,
    32-36
  Pack and Go, 254-257
  Presentation
    Conference, 293-295

Save as HTML, 311
WordArt, 148-154
  buttons, 152-153
**worksheets (Excel),
  101-102**
writing on slides, 249-251
WWW (World Wide Web)
  browsers, 300
  domain names, 300
  downloading (Clip
    Gallery)
      clip art, 67-69
      sound clips, 169-170
  Help menu, 300-306
  FTP (File Transfer
    Protocol), 300
  HTML (HyperText
    Markup Language), 300
  HTTP (HyperText
    Transport Protocol), 300
  hyperlinks, 298, 308-310
  IP (Internet Protocol), 300
  PowerPoint Viewer, 247
  presentations, 307-308,
    311-314
  search engines, 301-305
  TCP/IP (Transmission
    Control Protocol/
    Internet Protocol), 300
  toolbar buttons, 303-306
  URL (Uniform Resource
    Locator), 300, 306

Z

**Zoom command (View
  menu), 30**
zooming
  IntelliMouse, 24
  relationships (org
    charts), 113

Check out Que® Books on the World Wide Web
http://www.mcp.com/que

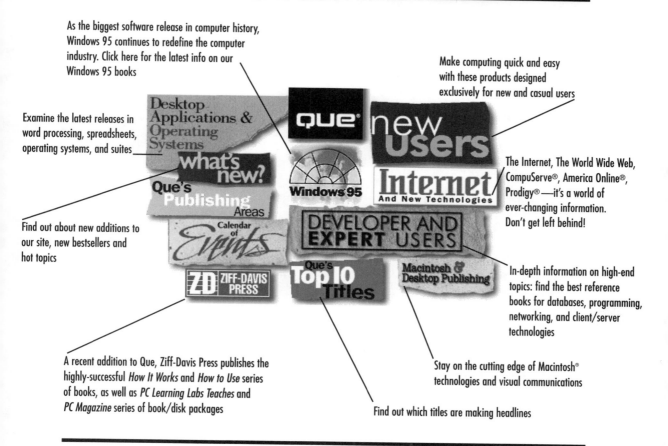

As the biggest software release in computer history, Windows 95 continues to redefine the computer industry. Click here for the latest info on our Windows 95 books

Make computing quick and easy with these products designed exclusively for new and casual users

Examine the latest releases in word processing, spreadsheets, operating systems, and suites

The Internet, The World Wide Web, CompuServe®, America Online®, Prodigy® —it's a world of ever-changing information. Don't get left behind!

Find out about new additions to our site, new bestsellers and hot topics

In-depth information on high-end topics: find the best reference books for databases, programming, networking, and client/server technologies

A recent addition to Que, Ziff-Davis Press publishes the highly-successful *How It Works* and *How to Use* series of books, as well as *PC Learning Labs Teaches* and *PC Magazine* series of book/disk packages

Stay on the cutting edge of Macintosh® technologies and visual communications

Find out which titles are making headlines

With 6 separate publishing groups, Que develops products for many specific market segments and areas of computer technology. Explore our Web Site and you'll find information on best-selling titles, newly published titles, upcoming products, authors, and much more.

- Stay informed on the latest industry trends and products available

- Visit our online bookstore for the latest information and editions

- Download software from Que's library of the best shareware and freeware

Complete and Return this Card
for a *FREE* Computer Book Catalog

Thank you for purchasing this book! You have purchased a superior computer book written expressly for your needs. To continue to provide the kind of up-to-date, pertinent coverage you've come to expect from us, we need to hear from you. Please take a minute to complete and return this self-addressed, postage-paid form. In return, we'll send you a free catalog of all our computer books on topics ranging from word processing to programming and the internet.

Mr. ☐   Mrs. ☐   Ms. ☐   Dr. ☐

Name (first) ☐☐☐☐☐☐☐☐☐☐☐☐   (M.I.) ☐   (last) ☐☐☐☐☐☐☐☐☐☐☐☐☐☐

Address ☐☐☐☐☐☐☐☐☐☐☐☐☐☐☐☐☐☐☐☐☐☐☐☐☐☐☐☐

City ☐☐☐☐☐☐☐☐☐☐☐☐☐☐☐   State ☐☐   Zip ☐☐☐☐☐ ☐☐☐☐

Phone ☐☐☐ ☐☐☐ ☐☐☐☐   Fax ☐☐☐ ☐☐☐ ☐☐☐☐

Company Name ☐☐☐☐☐☐☐☐☐☐☐☐☐☐☐☐☐☐☐☐☐☐☐☐

E-mail address ☐☐☐☐☐☐☐☐☐☐☐☐☐☐☐☐☐☐☐☐☐☐☐☐

1. Please check at least (3) influencing factors for purchasing this book.

Front or back cover information on book .... ☐
Special approach to the content .... ☐
Completeness of content .... ☐
Author's reputation .... ☐
Publisher's reputation .... ☐
Book cover design or layout .... ☐
Index or table of contents of book .... ☐
Price of book .... ☐
Special effects, graphics, illustrations .... ☐
Other (Please specify): _____ ☐

2. How did you first learn about this book?

Saw in Macmillan Computer Publishing catalog .... ☐
Recommended by store personnel .... ☐
Saw the book on bookshelf at store .... ☐
Recommended by a friend .... ☐
Received advertisement in the mail .... ☐
Saw an advertisement in: _____ ☐
Read book review in: _____ ☐
Other (Please specify): _____ ☐

3. How many computer books have you purchased in the last six months?

This book only .... ☐   3 to 5 books .... ☐
books .... ☐   More than 5 .... ☐

4. Where did you purchase this book?

Bookstore .... ☐
Computer Store .... ☐
Consumer Electronics Store .... ☐
Department Store .... ☐
Office Club .... ☐
Warehouse Club .... ☐
Mail Order .... ☐
Direct from Publisher .... ☐
Internet site .... ☐
Other (Please specify): _____ ☐

5. How long have you been using a computer?

☐ Less than 6 months   ☐ 6 months to a year
☐ 1 to 3 years   ☐ More than 3 years

6. What is your level of experience with personal computers and with the subject of this book?

	With PCs	With subject of book
New	☐	☐
Casual	☐	☐
Accomplished	☐	☐
Expert	☐	☐

Source Code ISBN: 0-7897-0915-5

7. Which of the following best describes your job title?

Administrative Assistant .... ☐
Coordinator .... ☐
Manager/Supervisor .... ☐
Director .... ☐
Vice President .... ☐
President/CEO/COO .... ☐
Lawyer/Doctor/Medical Professional .... ☐
Teacher/Educator/Trainer .... ☐
Engineer/Technician .... ☐
Consultant .... ☐
Not employed/Student/Retired .... ☐
Other (Please specify): _____ ☐

8. Which of the following best describes the area of the company your job title falls under?

Accounting .... ☐
Engineering .... ☐
Manufacturing .... ☐
Operations .... ☐
Marketing .... ☐
Sales .... ☐
Other (Please specify): _____ ☐

9. What is your age?

Under 20 .... ☐
21-29 .... ☐
30-39 .... ☐
40-49 .... ☐
50-59 .... ☐
60-over .... ☐

10. Are you:

Male .... ☐
Female .... ☐

11. Which computer publications do you read regularly? (Please list)

_____
_____
_____
_____
_____
_____
_____
_____
_____
_____

Comments: _____
_____
_____

Fold here and scotch-tape to mail